Natural Resources and Environmental Technology

Natural

Resources and

Jasper S. Lee

Agricultural Educator
Demorest, Georgia

AgriScience and Technology Series

Jasper S. Lee, Ph.D.
Series Editor

Environmental Technology

Interstate Publishers, Inc.
Danville, Illinois

**Natural Resources and
Environmental Technology**

Front cover, featuring Research Facility of
The Freshwater Institue of Shepherdstown, West Virginia,
and back cover photos courtesy of Agricultural Research Service, USDA

Library of Congress Catalog No. 99-71695

ISBN 0-8134-3183-2

1 2 3 4 5 6 7 8 9 10   05 04 03 02 01 00

Order from

Interstate Publishers, Inc.

510 North Vermilion Street
P.O. Box 50
Danville, IL 61834-0050

Phone: (800) 843-4774
Fax. (217) 446-9706
Email: info-ipp@IPPINC.com
World Wide Web: http://www.IPPINC.com

PREFACE

People are fortunate in the United States. They have an abundance of material things to meet their needs. They have plenty of food and clothing. They live in housing that is comfortable and climate-controlled to make life easy. People never had it so good!

Some people express grave concern over trends in world population and resource use. They feel that the population is increasing faster than the Earth can support. Resources are being used at a rapid pace. Sometimes resources are used without regard to having any for future generations.

All people live in one world. Nations do not exist in isolation. People who have plenty in one nation should not forget that there are those in other nations who are less fortunate. All nations can take active roles in preventing pollution and supporting a good quality of life. All people have a role in helping sustain life on the Earth. We can do simple things to assure that resources will be available in the future. Where do we begin? That's what this book is about!

We need to know about our natural resources and how to sustain them. In our daily lives, we can make a difference in so many areas. For example, we can use a little less water and produce a little less waste. We can take steps to reuse and recycle many things. We do not want to run out of water, iron, food, or other important resources.

It is exciting to know that we can shape our future. We can influence what we have and how our natural resources are used. This book is the beginning for you. Study the chapter content. Carry out the "exploring" activities. Take steps to get informed and fill an active role. You are important! You can make a difference in our future!

Use this book to help you grow and develop as a responsible user of natural resources. You will be glad you did!

ACKNOWLEDGMENTS

Many people helped make this book possible. Their assistance is gratefully acknowledged. Several individuals are recognized here for their special assistance.

Two individuals recognized for their assistance in reviewing the manuscript for technical accuracy, sequence, and other details are: Clyde Gottschalk, Association of Texas Soil and Water Conservation Districts, Temple, Texas, and Chuck Michel, Agricultural Educator at Marshall High School, North Carolina.

Clay Walker, Mike McHost, and Lora McHost of Forestry Suppliers, Inc., of Jackson, Mississippi, are acknowledged for their assistance with technical information and photographs. Their assistance with state-of-the-art land surveying instruments and other equipment is acknowledged. Jerry Pelley of Forestry Suppliers, Inc., is also acknowledged for his support with this and all areas where technical assistance has been provided.

Tracy Westrom, Dale Payne, and Deone Rosser, students at Piedmont College, Demorest, Georgia, are acknowledged for their assistance with technical photographs.

John Waller and Jimmy Zamora of Kitsap Schools, Poulsbo, Washington, are acknowledged for their assistance with models for photographs in technical areas.

Monte Ladner and students of Leake County Schools, Carthage, Mississippi, are acknowledged for their assistance. Local farms and equipment dealers are also recognized.

Lynn Wagner, Monroe Clark, and students of Newton Career Center, Newton, Mississippi, are acknowledged for their assistance with photographs.

Webb Palmer, teachers, and students at Alvirne High School, Hudson, New Hampshire, show-cased school laboratory facilities and served as models for photographs.

State and university leaders in agricultural education recognized are: Marion Fletcher, Arkansas; Jerry Gibson, North Carolina; Robert Heuvel, California; Ben Shaw, Texas; Delmer Dalton, Kentucky; Van Shelhamer, Montana; and Mike Swan, Washington.

Several individuals with the U.S. Fish and Wildlife Service, the Agricultural Research Service, and the U.S. Department of Agriculture were most helpful in assisting with photographs.

The enthusiastic efforts of several individuals at Interstate Publishers, Inc., are acknowledged. Jane Weller is acknowledged for editing the manuscript. Kim Romine is thanked for designing and laying out the book. Dan Pentony is acknowledged for his support throughout the writing process. Interstate President, Vernie Thomas, is especially recognized for his assistance and support with the book. Thank you Vernie and all of the Interstate group!

CONTENTS

Unit Two—Conservation of Renewable Natural Resources

Unit Three—Conservation of Nonrenewable Natural Resources

1

INTRODUCTION TO NATURAL RESOURCES

What do you need to live well? You may name a number of things. Some of the items you name may be essential, while others may be nice to have. You may also want to assess which are essential and which are nice.

People require certain things to live. These are the essentials for living. Food, clothing, and shelter are included. Each of these comes from the resources that are naturally found on the earth. Without these resources, human life would not be possible.

What about the future? Will we run out of resources? More people require more of the earth's resources. In some cases, the earth's resources are remaining constant. New resources are not being formed or are formed very slowly. Understanding natural resources helps us to be better users.

1-1. Washington students are learning tree identification in an arboretum.

OBJECTIVES

This chapter introduces the meaning and importance of natural resources. It has the following objectives:

1. Define natural resources
2. Name and describe major kinds of natural resources
3. Classify natural resources based on renewability
4. Classify natural resources based on exhaustibility
5. Distinguish between preservation and conservation

TERMS

air
atmosphere
conservation
domestication
environment
environmental technology
exhaustible natural resource
fossil fuels
inexhaustible natural resource
inorganic substance
mineral
natural resources
nonrenewable natural resource
preservation
renewability
renewable natural resource
soil
sustainable resource use
water
wildlife
wind

**Natural Resource
Conservation Service, USDA
http://www.nhq.nrcs.usda.gov/**

OUR NATURAL RESOURCES

Natural resources are resources that are found in nature. They naturally occur. People cannot make more natural resources, but many natural resources can be renewed.

Some natural resources are essential for living, such as oxygen and water. Without the essential resources, people would not be able to live. Other natural resources may not be essential to life, but they are used in ways that are important to us, such as manufacturing automobiles and computers.

Natural resources are closely tied to the environment. **Environment** is the conditions that surround us. All living things must have an environment that meets their needs. If not, they will be unable to live. **Environmental technology** is using science and inventions to understand and improve the environment. This often involves working with natural resources.

Natural resources need to be used wisely. We don't want to run out of the resources that are so important!

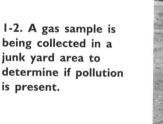

1-2. A gas sample is being collected in a junk yard area to determine if pollution is present.

KINDS OF NATURAL RESOURCES

Natural resources can be classified into eight groups. Each of the groups can be divided into many areas. The groups are wildlife, air and wind, soil, water, minerals, fossil fuels, sunlight, and people. Which of these is most important? As you will see in this book, it is nearly impossible to separate the various natural resources. People depend on all of them for their well-being.

WILDLIFE

Wildlife is all about us. This is true if we live in the city or the open countryside. Sometimes we take wildlife for granted. We fail to consider just how important it is to us.

Wildlife is a plant, an animal, and other living thing that lives in the wild. It has not been domesticated. Many people think only of animals, such as deer and bears, as wildlife. Others think only of game animals–those that are hunted for food and sport. Wildlife includes all species that exist in nature. This includes tiny one-celled organisms, such as fungi, as well as wild flowers, trees in a native forest, fish, insects, and snakes.

Domestication is bringing plants and animals under the control of humans. People may raise or farm them. Domesticated animals are also kept as companion animals. Companion animals are sometimes known as pets. Dogs and cats are common pets. People have learned how to provide for the needs of animals. In most cases, they can provide better conditions than what some species would naturally have if left in the wild. Some people refer to domestication as taming wildlife.

Many animals have been domesticated. These are raised to help meet the needs of people for food and clothing. Examples include cattle, swine, chickens, and sheep. Horses are also kept, but more for recreation than for work or food. Most domesticated animals have been bred to have characteristics that

1-3. A Little Blue Heron wades the water of the Everglades in Florida.

benefit humans. The same is true with crop plants. Common domesticated crop plants include rice, corn, potatoes, cotton, tomatoes, and grapes.

Some wildlife is threatened. This means that conditions are not favorable for its survival. A good example is fish in Monterrey Bay, off the California coast. Overfishing has nearly wiped out some fish from the oceans. Once a lucrative fishing site, taking too many fish has depleted the population of fish in the ocean.

AIR AND WIND

The *atmosphere* is the area that surrounds the earth. It is mostly made of gases that are usually not visible. Water vapor and particulate are visible substances in the atmosphere.

Conditions in the atmosphere cause the weather. Weather is the moisture, temperature, movement, and pressure of the atmosphere. Cold fronts and warm fronts bring changes in the atmosphere.

The climate is the general weather condition in a location. The climate of an area has much to do with the natural resources that are found and how they are used. Air and wind are two important natural resources in the atmosphere.

Air

Air is the mixture of gases that surrounds the earth. We breathe it and live in it. Air is an important natural resource. Like other natural resources, all living things must have air to survive. Oxygen is one of the most important components of the air. It is required by just about all living things.

Air interacts with other natural resources to help sustain life. Polluted air contains substances that may be harmful to people and other

1-4. A cloud forming over dry land in the Southwest may hold the promise of a shower.

resources. Good quality air is essential. We must have good air to be healthy and enjoy life.

Wind

Wind is large-scale air movement across the surface of the earth. The speed and direction of air movement vary. Weather fronts and surface features of the earth influence wind. Some winds are powerful. Those associated with storms can damage property. Wind may move soil, pollen, and other tiny particles hundreds of miles. Some areas have winds that blow almost constantly. There is much power in wind.

Wind power is harnessing air movement. It is free except for the equipment to collect it. Windmills and turbines are used to collect the power. Wind power can be used to pump water, generate electricity, and for other purposes.

Two problems associated with harnessing wind are that its direction may change and the speed varies. Use of wind as power must consider these two problems. That is why windmills are made so they turn to face the wind direction. Ways to store wind power or the products of wind power are needed. For example, using a windmill to pump water does not assure a continuous supply. When the wind stops blowing, the windmill stops pumping water. The solution is to install a water tank. A tank stores water until it is needed. The water is available even if the wind is not blowing!

SOIL

Soil is the outer layer of the earth's surface that supports plant life. Soil is a naturally occurring resource. All living things rely on soil in one way or another.

Soil is the basis of all life. Plants need soil to grow. It provides water and nutrients. Animals eat the plants to live. Without plants, animals cannot survive. Upon completion of their life cycle, animals and their remains decay and become soil again.

Soil is one of the most fragile natural resources. It is damaged and lost by erosion. People use large equipment to move it about. Soil must be protected. It is the source of nutrients for the production of most food crops.

WATER

Water is a tasteless and colorless liquid natural resource. All living things must have it to survive. Water naturally occurs as a compound made of hydrogen and oxygen. Two atoms of hydrogen combine with one atom of oxygen to form a water molecule. The chemical formula for water is written as H_2O. Whether the living organism is a plant or animal, water is essential for life.

Water is the only natural resource found on the surface of the earth in three forms: solid, liquid, and vapor. The solid form is ice. It is formed when water is exposed to temperatures below its freezing point–32° F (0° C). Liquid is the form that we mean when we use the word, water. The gas form is known as water vapor or steam. It results when water molecules become airborne.

1-5. Irrigation is adding water to fertile soil so a good cotton crop will be produced.

Maintaining quality water is essential. Water is easily polluted by daily living and manufacturing activities. The amount of water on the earth is constant. However, its form and condition change in the water cycle. People must try to keep water clean so enough will be available for future needs.

Flowing water is a source of power. Streams move from higher to lower elevations. This elevation difference provides considerable power. People have used different ways of harnessing the power. Large hydroelectric dams have been built to generate electricity. These dams also provide recreation and water supplies for towns and cities.

MINERALS

Another large group of natural resources is the group of minerals. A *mineral* is a natural inorganic substance on or in the earth. An *inorganic substance* does not have the structure of living things. Rocks are not alive! They do not contain the carbon chemical element.

1-6. Stone is being mined and crushed at this Illinois plant.

Minerals are used in many ways. Some are used to make iron; others are used to make brick for our homes. Remember, our coins are made of precious metals, like copper and nickel, and our jewelry may be made of valuable gold or silver. We use minerals in many ways. Just think how important diamonds are to people!

Minerals are mined from the earth. Copper is mined from large open pits. Iron and other minerals are mined in much the same way. Granite is quarried to make monuments. Sand and gravel are mined for road construction and to make concrete for buildings.

FOSSIL FUELS

The fuels we use in our engines began millions of years ago. What we take from the earth is the fossil form of organisms that lived at that time. Hence, the name fossil fuel.

Fossil fuels are materials used to provide energy. The fossil fuels we use today were created long ago by the decomposition of plants and animals that once lived on the earth. Energy in fossil fuels was placed there when plants converted energy from the sun into food energy. The energy is released when the materials are "burned." The three major groups of fossil fuels are petroleum, natural gas, and coal.

Fossil fuels are important in many of our daily activities. Petroleum is a liquid form of fossil fuel used to make gasoline, lubricating oil, and other products, such as plastic. It is sometimes called oil. Natural gas is a form of fossil fuel often used to heat buildings, run factories, and cook food. Coal is a solid form of fossil fuel. Coal is used in factories, electricity-generating plants, and other places to provide energy.

One problem: Fossil fuels are major sources of pollution. Burning gasoline releases exhaust fumes into the air. Oil from engines may pollute our water. We are so dependent on these fuels yet they cause damage to our environment.

SUNLIGHT

Sunlight is the light and warmth of the Sun. The light produces solar energy. This energy is used by plants in photosynthesis. It warms the surface of the earth. The energy creates air movement and weather conditions. Life on Earth depends on sunlight!

I-7. Petroleum is pumped from deep within the earth.

The Sun is a huge mass of glowing gases. It is located in the center of the solar system. The hot gases give off heat and light. People have gotten more

I-8. A solar panel collects energy from the Sun.

Career Profile

CONSERVATION EDUCATOR

A conservation educator provides education about the proper use of natural resources. They develop educational programs, talk to civic groups, help school children, and provide releases to the media. They work with other agencies to identify conservation needs and practices.

Conservation educators need college degrees in agriculture, wildlife management, forestry, or a related area. Some have degrees in agricommunication. Practical experience working with natural resources is needed. An outgoing personality and ability to speak in public are beneficial. Good writing skills are essential.

Jobs for conservation educators are with government agencies, soil and water conservation districts, and large corporations that use resources. This shows a conservation educator demonstrating the effects of rainfall using mist from a sprayer and plastic model of a section of the earth's surface.

interested in finding ways to harness the energy of the Sun. Solar collectors are used to warm water for heating buildings and other uses. These collectors also power equipment and electronic devices, such as calculators and monitoring devices.

The Sun is the source of nearly all energy. The energy in fossil fuels originated long ago with the Sun. The leaves of plants act as solar collectors for the process of photosynthesis. The energy in light is captured and converted to sugar by the plants.

If not collected and used, sunlight is lost from one day to the next. Scientists are studying how to store the energy for use when the Sun is not shining.

PEOPLE

People have many wonderful talents and skills. They can use the earth's resources wisely or abuse and damage the resources. The lives of people are influenced by how they use resources and relate to one another.

Human population is increasing. This places strain on the ability of natural resources to provide people with the needed food, clothing, and shelter. Six billion people now live on the earth. Of these, about 5 percent or 275 million are in the United States. Is there a limit to human population? Should population increases be controlled? Many ethical areas are associated with population control. Some authorities say that responsible use of resources includes population control. Certainly, parents should only have children they can adequately support!

RENEWABILITY

Renewability is whether or not a resource can be restored after it has been used. This has to do with whether the supply can be replenished. Some things can be renewed; others cannot be renewed. This is a basis for classifying natural resources: renewable or nonrenewable.

RENEWABLE NATURAL RESOURCES

A *renewable natural resource* can be replaced when it is used. It may renew itself and be used again. Renewing may take a long time. People can use up a resource before it is renewed if it is carelessly used. Examples of renewable natural resources include air, soil, and wildlife.

Soil, for example, can be renewed. Many years are required for soil to form. Sometimes soil is classified as nonrenewable because of the amount of time required to renew it. People must carefully use soil so it is not damaged or lost. Damaged soil is not as productive. Crop yields are lower.

1-9. Forests can be renewed over time.

Plants are also renewable natural resources. A good example is trees in a natural forest. Under proper conditions, trees will grow on an area that has been harvested, burned, or destroyed. Many plants have seeds that, when provided with the proper conditions, will renew themselves into new plants. People need to remember that many years are needed to grow big trees.

Water is often viewed as a renewable natural resource. The amount of water on the earth is constant. It may change states and need to be cleaned, but the amount never changes. Water goes through a cycle that has a renewing effect. The earth cleans it and prepares it for use again. A problem occurs if the water is polluted. The earth may not be capable of cleaning the pollutant from the water.

NONRENEWABLE NATURAL RESOURCES

A **nonrenewable natural resource** is not replaced when it is used. With careful management, some can be reused. Most minerals are nonrenewable, such as gold. Humans cannot make more gold. This is one reason gold is a valuable metal.

Money systems in many countries are based on gold. Its worth tends to remain constant over the years, with a gradual increase in many instances. Silver and platinum are also valuable metals.

Fossil fuels are nonrenewable natural resources. Neither oil nor coal can be renewed. Of course, over thousands of years it might be possible for some renewing to take place. In terms of our civilization, the fossil fuels are nonrenewable. People know they are nonrenewable and have tried to develop

1-10. Gasoline is so easy to get! What will we do when the supply runs out?

Resource Connection

ENERGY CONSERVATION

Keep down energy use by setting the thermostat properly. A thermostat turns heating and cooling equipment on and off. It measures the temperature in the area and automatically serves as a switch for the equipment.

In the summer, keep air-conditioning temperatures as warm as possible for comfort. Set the thermostat to a higher setting when away from home for a while. Higher settings result in the equipment operating less. Less cooling is needed at 80° F than at 70° F!

In the winter, keep the heating temperatures as cool as possible for comfort. The heating equipment will operate less time than at warmer settings. Some people suggest that the thermostat should be set at 66° F. Some people want it to be slightly warmer.

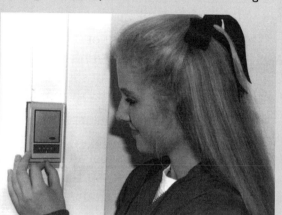

alternative sources of fuel. Wind is sometimes used to power large windmills. Solar energy is sometimes used for heating and other purposes. These alternative sources of energy represent only a very small part of the energy now used. Another approach is to develop engines that make more efficient use of fuel. We tend to think of this as automobiles that get more miles per gallon!

Many scientists warn that resources are being used up too fast. The rate of use is so fast that resources cannot renew themselves. "Renewing" takes time. Most "renewing" processes occur slowly, such as in a forest. Many years are needed for a forest to renew itself. Young trees must grow and become mature before they can produce seed to make additional trees.

EXHAUSTIBILITY

Exhaustibility is whether or not the supply of a resource is replenished as it is used. Some resources can be replenished; others cannot be replenished.

INEXHAUSTIBLE RESOURCES

Inexhaustible natural resources are those that are continually being replenished. The supply will not run out. If not used, they are gone but continue to be available. Three natural resources are inexhaustible: sunlight, air and wind, and water.

Sunlight occurs each day. If not used, it is lost. If used, more will be available tomorrow. Sunlight is available in abundance. Scientists feel that its energy will last for thousands of years.

The air and wind are part of the atmosphere that is present day and night. Much of the energy is due to sunlight creating pressure differences. Wind and gases will continue in the atmosphere. Some care is needed to avoid polluting the air and damaging its ability to support important processes on the earth.

Water is said to be inexhaustible because it is continually being readied for use by the hydrologic cycle. A key with water is quality. People are concerned about the supply of good quality water. Water is used in so many ways. It often gets dirty and must be cleaned. As people use more water, the problem is not if there will be water. The issue is its quality.

EXHAUSTIBLE RESOURCES

Exhaustible natural resources are resources that are available in limited quantity that can be used up. Minerals and fossil fuels are examples. The supply of iron and most other minerals is limited. The supply of coal and petroleum is also limited. Wise use of exhaustible resources is essential.

To help classify exhaustible resources, they may be further placed in two categories: irreplaceable and replaceable.

Irreplaceable natural resources are gone once they are used. Most minerals and fossil fuels are irreplaceable. Using these resources properly can sustain the available supply. Some people classify soil as irreplaceable. This is because it is replaced so slowly. Soil loss to erosion may require far more than the lifetime of an individual to replace. Do you agree that soil is not replaceable? (Most people would say that soil can be replaced.)

Replaceable resources can be replenished once used. Most species of wildlife can be replenished. Trees can be planted to replace lost trees. Wildflowers can be seeded to replace those that have been destroyed. Most animals will replenish their populations if they have suitable habitat.

CONSERVATION AND PRESERVATION

How natural resources are used and protected may be controversial. Some resources must be used for people to live. But, how much does one person need? Major questions focus on the nature of use.

CONSERVATION

Conservation is using resources wisely. The resources are not abused, wasted, nor destroyed. The meaning of the word, wisely, varies. What is wise to one person may not be wise to another!

"Wise" use is using a resource in ways that do not diminish its value and assure that supplies will be available for future generations. In recent years, the focus has been on sustainable use.

Sustainable resource use is using resources so they last a long time. As possible, the resource is renewed, reused, and recycled. Many resources will last a long time if appropriate conservation practices are used.

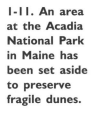

1-11. An area at the Acadia National Park in Maine has been set aside to preserve fragile dunes.

Sustainable agriculture is closely associated with resource use. It involves using soil, water, and other resources so productivity is maintained indefinitely. Practices are used that reduce soil loss, conserve water supplies, and avoid damage to the environment with pesticides.

PRESERVATION

Preservation is maintaining a natural resource without using it up. The resource is protected. It is set aside for the future. People can view the resource but they cannot harvest, mine, or otherwise take it.

Several kinds of preserves are used. Animal wildlife is protected in preserves and refuges. Old-growth forests are protected from cutting. Water in the headwater of a stream that serves large areas downstream is not used. With some preserves people can view the protected resource.

It is hard to know when a resource should be preserved. What do you think? Is it okay to cut the last of the old-growth forests? Is it okay to stop any taking of an endangered species?

REVIEWING

MAIN IDEAS

Natural resources are found in nature. People cannot make them and must use them wisely. Natural resources are essential for life as we know it today.

Many kinds of natural resources are found on the earth. These can be placed in eight groups: wildlife, air and wind, soil, water, minerals, fossil fuels, sunlight, and people. Another group is sometimes used for nuclear energy.

Natural resources are classified in various ways. One way of classifying is based on renewability. This is whether or not a resource can be restored after it is used. There are two classes based on renewability: renewable and nonrenewable. Resources that are renewable can be replaced once they are used. Nonrenewable resources cannot be replaced once they are used.

Natural resources can be classified by exhaustibility. This is whether or not the resource can be replenished. Inexhaustible resources are continually being replaced. Exhaustible resources are available in limited quantity and may or may not be replaceable.

Conservation and preservation are issues with natural resources. Conservation is using the resources wisely. Preservation is protecting resources from use that would deplete or destroy them.

QUESTIONS

Answer the following questions using complete sentences and correct spelling.

1. What are natural resources? Why are they important?
2. Name the eight groups of natural resources.
3. What is domestication?
4. What is the most important component in air? Why?
5. What is wind power?
6. What is the source of nearly all energy used on the earth?
7. Why are people listed as natural resources?
8. What is renewability? What are the two classes of natural resources based on renewability?
9. What is exhaustibility? What are the two classes of natural resources based on exhaustibility?
10. What is sustainable resource use? How does it relate to conservation?

EVALUATING

Match the term with the correct definition. Write the letter by the term in the blank provided.

a. preservation
b. renewable natural resources
c. fossil fuels
d. soil
e. water

f. wildlife
g. atmosphere
h. wind
i. exhaustible natural resources
j. conservation

_____ 1. Using resources wisely.

_____ 2. Maintaining resources without use.

_____ 3. Living organisms that have not been domesticated.

_____ 4. The area of air that surrounds the earth.

_____ 5. A colorless and tasteless liquid.

_____ 6. The outer layer of the earth's surface that supports plant life.

_____ 7. A resource that can be replaced when it is used up.

_____ 8. Materials used to provide energy that were created by the decomposition of dead plants and animals.

_____ 9. Natural resources that are available in limited amounts that can be used up.

_____ 10. The area that surrounds the earth.

EXPLORING

1. Survey your community to determine the natural resources that are available. All communities will have some of the same resources. Other communities will have resources that are unique to that location. Classify the natural resources as to renewability and exhaustibility. Prepare a report on your findings.

2. Take a field trip to a wildlife preserve or refuge. Observe the work that is underway. Interview the manager about the goals and purpose of the facility. Prepare a report on your work.

3. Keep a record of the weather in your area for a week. Use a thermometer, anemometer, barometer or sling psychrometer, and rain gauge for precipitation. Prepare a poster or bulletin board that reports your findings. Use tables and graphs to plot the information. Compare your findings to the normal readings for your area for the time of year in which you made the observations.

4. How we use resources often depends on renewability. People are very dependent on natural resources. If one of them were depleted, such as oil, what would we do? Form a small group and identify ways of dealing with not having oil. Report your discussion to the class.

2

THE USE OF NATURAL RESOURCES

Six billion humans now live on the earth! The number is increasing every day. Can our natural resources support continued population increases? Demands on resources mean we must act to have a good future.

In addition to resource use, human life creates wastes. The average person in the United States creates 4.3 pounds of solid waste trash and about 100 gallons of wastewater each day. In a year, this amounts to 1,570 pounds of trash and 36,000 gallons of water! How much is used by the students at your school in a year? (Multiply the number of students by the gallons of water and pounds of solid waste trash.) You have some very large amounts! Our environment must be able to handle wastes so all people have a good quality life. Nature has processes that convert many wastes into nonwaste materials.

A new term arose a few years ago about the wise use of natural resources. The term was "sustainability." What do you think the term means?

2-1. Transportation is an important use of natural resources.

19

OBJECTIVES

This chapter covers the major uses of natural resources. The following objectives are included:

1. Describe how natural resources meet human needs

2. Explain population trends and demands

3. Assess natural resource supply as related to demand

4. Describe urban and suburban impacts on natural resources

5. Identify ways of recycling and reusing products

6. Explain how to develop personal beliefs about the issues associated with the use of natural resources

TERMS

basic human needs
belief
consumptive use
demography
desertification
greenhouse effect
household waste
hunger
issue
landscape alteration
land-use planning
malnourishment
nonconsumptive use
ozone layer
population
recycling
resource depletion
reusing
sewage
sustainability
undernourishment
waste

**Global Forest Watch
of the World Resources Institute
http://www.wri.org/wri/**

USE OF NATURAL RESOURCES

Life requires natural resources. The resources may be used to make products that people use or to directly support life. Some resources are required for life; others are used to improve the quality of life.

KINDS OF USE

Natural resource use is of two broad kinds: consumptive and nonconsumptive.

Consumptive Use

Consumptive use is using a natural resource so the amount used no longer exists. The supply of the resource is reduced each time it is used.

In some cases, the earth's supply of a natural resource is so large that they could be used indefinitely. An example is crushed stone. The amount of rock available is tremendous. There is little chance that using crushed stone will deplete the supply of rock any time soon.

On the other hand, taking wildlife can lead to the depletion of the species. Hunting has reduced some wildlife numbers. In a few cases the species have become extinct. Of course, most wildlife is renewable. Good management practices may be needed.

2-2. Taking fish from a stream is a consumptive use—but a fun sport to many people.

Consider the consumptive use of nonrenewable natural resources, such as oil and coal. Once used, these materials are gone. Every time you fill the tank of an automobile with gasoline consumptive use has occurred.

Nonconsumptive Use

Some natural resources can be used without reducing the supply that is available for future use. This is *nonconsumptive use*. Any resources that can be "used" without using them up will likely last forever.

2-3. With a well-placed birdhouse, people can enjoy bird watching in their own yard.

Just as hunting game is a consumptive use of wildlife, other uses of wildlife are nonconsumptive. Bird watching (known as birding) is an example. Watching does not kill wildlife. The wildlife is not destroyed and is available for watching on a future day. Other nonconsumptive uses include watching wildflowers, looking at leaves in the fall, viewing waterfalls on streams, and hiking through a forest. (Note: Picking wildflowers, fruit, and seed is a consumptive use. It is illegal in most parks.)

MEETING HUMAN NEEDS

Humans have three **basic human needs** to live: food, clothing, and shelter. These are produced from the earth's resources. As the population increases, more resources are required to meet these basic needs.

Using many natural resources limits the amounts that are available in the future. Steps must be taken to see that they are used wisely and renewed.

An increasing population requires more resources. Here is an example: Suppose the number of students in your school increases so another bus is needed. What impact does this have on fossil fuel resources? How much fuel is needed for a bus that gets 8 miles per gallon and travels 90 miles a day? Project your answer to one year of school. How many gallons would be needed for all 13 school years between kindergarten and high school graduation?

HUMAN POPULATION TRENDS AND DEMANDS

Population is the number of people. Usually, population is given for an area, such as a city, county, state, or a nation. Changes in population occur in each of these.

POPULATION TRENDS

The general worldwide trend in population is rapid growth. Changes in the rate occur as nations become developed. Some nations are having little change, such as France and Japan.

Currently, the population of the earth is more than six billion. Population in the United States is about 275 million. Some authorities predict that the population on the earth will double in the next half century. Is the supply of natural resources great enough to support such a large increase?

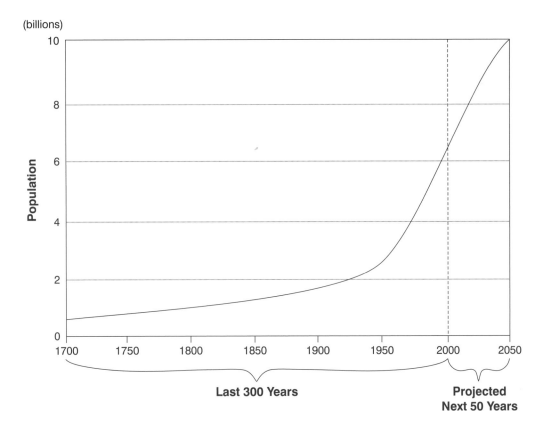

2-4. World population growth.

Social scientists study population changes. They investigate how changes influence the use of resources. The study of human population is known as **demography**. The information that is collected is known as demographics.

2-5. People need a good quality of life.

POPULATION DEMANDS

People make demands on their environment. They use resources and produce wastes. Some impact on natural resources cannot be avoided. That is the nature of human life. All people must have food, breathe air, and produce wastes. The more people we have, the more the environment is impacted.

Resource Depletion

Human life requires natural resources. These resources are used to meet the needs of humans. The seriousness of resource use depends on the nature of the resource and how it is used.

The use of renewable resources is not as critical as nonrenewable resources. Soil fertility is used to produce food. With proper care, soil will remain fertile and capable of producing good crops for many years. With abuse, fertility is lost along with the capacity to be productive.

Human life as it is carried out today requires fossil fuel, minerals, water, air, and other resources. The supply of some resources is being depleted. With others, damage is resulting from human activity.

Waste Creation

Humans create waste! It is created each day through the activities of daily living, as well as by manufacturing, agricultural production, and other activities.

Waste is unused materials or discarded products. Human waste includes household waste and waste from life processes. **Household waste** is garbage and rubbish that originate in the home. **Sewage** is liquid waste containing

2-6. Moving and handling solid waste is a major issue in some communities.

water with solid materials. The solid materials in sewage are human excrement and other materials from the home, such as food particles.

If wastes contaminate the environment, people get sick. Some drinking water can carry diseases, such as diarrhea, typhoid, and cholera. These diseases are problems in countries where good sanitation is not practiced. Water-borne diseases have been largely (but not entirely) eliminated in the industrialized countries. Proper disposal and treatment of wastes are essential.

Landscape Alteration

Landscape alteration is changing the natural features of the earth's surface to get and use resources. Mountains, streams, meadows, and other features of the earth's landscape add beauty and human appeal. How important is it to preserve these natural features?

Natural mountain scenery may be destroyed to build homes. Forests may be cut to get the needed wood. Huge quarries may be made in mining iron, copper, and other minerals. Strips of trees may be cut through the countryside to construct an electric power line. Hills and mountains may be partially removed to construct roads and highways. Wetlands may be drained to build homes, businesses, and highways. Forests have been cut to make land for crops, factories, and golf courses. In many cases, the habitats of wildlife have been destroyed.

Some alterations can be reversed; others cannot be reversed. Most people want to minimize change in the landscape and maintain natural resource areas. Most feel that waste and unnecessary change should be stopped.

Resource Connection

LANDSCAPE ALTERATION

People often change the natural features of the earth. They do this to build homes, roads, factories, and other structures. The surface of the earth may be made quite different from its natural condition.

Opinions differ on landscape alteration. Some people feel that it is okay to cut trees, dig new channels for streams, and remove hills. Other people feel that this is unnecessary or should be kept to a minimum.

What do you believe about landscape alteration? This photograph shows heavy equipment changing features of the earth for a new school building. An area of natural forest was destroyed. Would you want this to happen next to your home? How do we compare the use to be made of the land with the loss of the natural landscape?

Atmospheric Damage

The actions of people release substances into the air creating air pollution. Three areas of concern are unclean air, the greenhouse effect, and destruction of the ozone layer.

People need clean air. If they breathe dirty air, their lungs may be injured by the smoke, harmful gases, or other substances. Long-term health damage can result from breathing dirty air.

The *greenhouse effect* is caused by the buildup of some materials in the air. Fossil fuels release gases and tiny solid materials into the air. Carbon dioxide (CO_2) is a gas produced by burning fossil fuels in automobile engines and electricity-generating plants. The CO_2 collects in the atmosphere and traps infrared radiation near the earth. The radiation would otherwise escape into higher levels of the atmosphere.

The *ozone layer* is about 50 km (30 miles) above the earth. It filters out harmful radiation from the Sun. Scientists have found that the ozone layer is being damaged. Large holes have developed near the polar regions of the

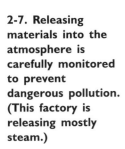

2-7. Releasing materials into the atmosphere is carefully monitored to prevent dangerous pollution. (This factory is releasing mostly steam.)

earth. The damage is greater over the South Pole. Products that humans use contain chemicals that damage the ozone layer. Hair spray, other spray-on materials, and some air-conditioners and refrigerators contain a substance that damages the ozone when it gets into the air. Some materials that damage the atmosphere have been banned in the United States.

RESOURCE SUPPLY AND POPULATION

In the United States, most people are accustomed to having plenty to meet their needs. We are fortunate in this regard. It is difficult to think about not having the things we have. But, how does our consumption affect world supplies?

Population demands may lead to depletion of resources, hunger, and conflict. Population growth in some nations is greater than the ability to provide for needs.

DEPLETION AND SHORTAGES

Resources are being depleted by overpopulation in some nations. This affects human life as well as other living things. Shortages are severe in some places, especially in developing nations.

Resource depletion is using resources faster than they can be renewed. An example is wood, which is a major source of cooking fuel in impoverished

2-8. Trees in this area have been removed and the land left exposed and unprotected.

areas, such as rural India. People may spend most of their time searching for wood. Wood is being used faster than forests grow.

Mineral supplies are dwindling. Without conservation, several minerals will be scarce by 2025. By 2040, 80 percent of the known reserves of 18 minerals will be used up. This includes lead, sulfur, tin, tungsten, and zinc.

Land productivity is being depleted. As this happens, food and other shortages will develop. Some land will revert to desert. **Desertification** is the formation of a desert on land that was once productive. Worldwide, some 15 million acres (six million hectares) become deserts each year. Land must be properly used to stop the loss of productivity.

Shortages of food and other resources result in hunger and threats to human well-being.

HUNGER AND DISEASE

Hunger is a shortage of food. It is not the same as missing a meal. Hunger is failing to have enough food that provides nutrients for growth and health. Infants who do not have enough nutrients may be retarded physically and mentally. Inadequate nutrition for an infant often results in less potential as an adult!

Hunger is in two forms: malnourishment and undernourishment. **Malnourishment** is the lack of proper nutrients. People do not get enough food with the nutrients they need. **Undernourishment** is the lack of calories for energy. Estimates are that 25 percent of the world's population suffers

Career Profile

SOIL SCIENTIST

A soil scientist studies the soil. This includes soil fertility, protection, and use. Soil scientists often specialize in areas of soil, such as preventing erosion, fertilization, pesticide residues, and structure.

Soil scientists need college degrees in agronomy or a closely related area. Most have masters or doctors degrees in specialized areas. Only a few universities in the United States offer advanced study of soil. These are typically in land-grant universities. In addition to education, practical experience in crop production, soil conservation, or other areas is beneficial.

Most jobs for soil scientists are with government agencies, experiment stations, large agricultural corporations, and colleges and universities.

from hunger. It is much higher in Asia, Africa, and Latin America. Hunger weakens people and they are more likely to have diseases. Some of the diseases, such as marasmus, are related to nutrition. Worldwide, some 40 million people die of hunger each year. Many of them are children.

URBAN AND RURAL IMPACTS

All people and their activities impact resources. This is true in large cities, small towns, or rural areas. We all live in one world. What happens in one place has an impact on another.

People in urban areas live close togther. The population is said to be dense. Daily living, factories, and shopping areas use resources. Because of population density, resource use is greater. Release of pollution is also greater.

LAND-USE PLANNING

Land-use planning is deciding how land will be used. It involves careful study of the natural resources and the different ways of use. A land-use plan

2-9. Land is needed for cities, such as Seattle, Washington.

should result from the planning. The plan guides the use of land for agricultural, residential, commercial, and other uses.

Zoning may be used in implementing a land-use plan. Zoning is setting aside certain areas for specified uses. This keeps factories from being next to residential areas. The use of land areas is planned to minimize pollution and maximize quality of life. Before construction begins, a building permit is needed. Detailed construction plans for a site are required before a permit is issued.

Land-use planning must protect land for agriculture and wildlife. Increasingly, urban sprawl is taking fertile land out of agricultural production. How long can this happen before the land is needed for food crop production?

RESOURCE PROTECTION

Resource use is important to both rural and urban areas. Urban areas depend on rural areas to provide quality water and other resources. Rural areas depend on urban areas to promote a good environment. Neither area can act in isolation from the other. A strong interdependence exists.

A good example is the water supply for the city of Atlanta, Georgia. The major source of water for the city is the Chattahoochee River. The headwaters of the river are in the pristine southern edge of the Blue Ridge Mountains in north Georgia. Crystal-clear water is sent southward toward Atlanta. The water is collected in reservoirs and used. After use, the water is treated and released back into the river to flow a few hundred miles toward the Gulf of Mexico. Unfortunately, the treatment process has often failed. Highly polluted wastewater was sometimes released. Poor-quality water flowed in the river south of the city. Steps are being taken to correct the problems.

In the Atlanta example, strong interdependence between rural and urban areas is illustrated. Atlanta wanted rural areas to provide good water and the rural areas wanted Atlanta to release good water!

Urban areas produce large amounts of waste. Disposing of these wastes creates problems. Pollution of the environment and destruction of valuable farmland could result.

AGRICULTURAL LAND USE

Agricultural land use is a concern of both rural and urban areas. Urban areas depend on cropland to produce food, fiber, and other materials. Both areas require the use of these resources to support human life.

Agricultural land is needed for:

- crops, such as corn, wheat, soybeans, lettuce, and oranges
- pasture for cattle, sheep, and horses
- building sites for poultry and hog houses, as well as greenhouses
- ornamental production, such as shrubs and flowers
- ponds and hatcheries for aquatic crops with fish farming
- tree farming to produce paper, lumber, and other wood products

Differences of opinion often develop over the use of land. The interdependence between rural and urban populations is strong. Urban people do not

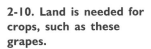

2-10. Land is needed for crops, such as these grapes.

want anything done agriculturally that negatively influences their environment. On the other hand, they want food, clothing, and other things.

Agriculture is a business. Land and resources are used to produce crops and animals. These products are used to meet the needs of people. Most agricultural producers are careful in how they use land. A number of factors influence land management, such as government regulations and weather conditions.

RECYCLING AND REUSING

Recycling and reusing reduce the demand for new natural resources. This saves trees, minerals, and many other resources each year. Most people are willing to buy products made of recycled materials.

RECYCLING

Recycling is using a product or the materials to make a product again. The product produced may be different from the previous use of the material. Recycling can be used with aluminum, iron, and other metals. It is also used with glass, paper, and plastic. Each time a material is recycled resources are saved. For example, recapping tire casings so a worn tire has new tread, saves rubber as well as energy for manufacturing the initial product. This approach to recycling is also known as remanufacturing.

Many communities have recycling programs. Citizens can sort and help ready used materials for recycling. In some cases, curbside pickup is used. In other places, people take their materials to recycling centers. Recycling centers vary. Some pay for the used materials and others do not.

REUSING

Reusing is using a product again without remanufacturing. Cleaning or other forms of conditioning may be needed to safely reuse a product. For example, soft drink bottles must be carefully washed before reusing. Another example is the reuse of boxes used to deliver bread and milk to retail stores. And another example is the reuse of building materials from a demolished building.

There are many ways of reusing products. For example, when you go grocery shopping, save the bags and use them again! Another example is canning food in jars that can be reused.

2-11. Places for collecting materials for recycling are often conveniently located.

PERSONAL BELIEFS

What do you believe about the use of natural resources? Everyone needs to study the issues and develop a sound set of beliefs about our natural resources. Beliefs are important to people as consumers, voters, and citizens.

BELIEFS

A *belief* is a person's conviction or feeling about a topic or issue. Beliefs should be based on factual and truthful information. The information should be trustworthy.

Beliefs are part of a person's value system. Some things are more important than others. These are the things that a person feels are right, worthwhile, and desirable. Think about this: What are your beliefs about our natural resources?

Developing beliefs about natural resources often requires using a problem-solving approach.

DEALING WITH PROBLEMS

Problems sometimes come up that need to be addressed. What is a good approach to use? The answer is to use an approach that is used by scientific researchers. This approach is known as problem solving or the scientific method. It involves getting answers to questions:

1. What is the problem?

    It is very important to know the problem. People sometimes only see symptoms. Study is needed to identify the problem.

2. What information is needed about the problem?

    Information may be available that will help address a problem. Read books, newspapers, and magazines for information. Gather information using the Internet. Go to meetings that deal with the problem.

3. What are the ways of solving the problem?

    This involves listing the solutions to a problem. These will need to be carefully studied.

4. What are the outcomes of solving the problem?

    Collect information on how the possible outcomes will work. Some experimenting may be needed. Talk with authorities on the problem to see how it was approached by others. Get the best possible information.

5. What is the best solution to the problem?

    After going through the first four questions, make a decision about what is best. Be sure to use facts. Avoid letting personal emotions get in the way. Be sure that whatever is proposed is legal, moral, and socially acceptable. In some cases, the solution may be tested on a small-scale basis.

2-12. Talking issues over with friends is a good way to help surface our beliefs.

ISSUES

Issues sometimes arise about the use of natural resources. An *issue* is a problem or question to be solved. Further, an issue has more than one point of view. People will support different sides. Their positions may be based on factual information or emotion.

The best positions on issues are developed by getting good information. It should be free of bias and based on facts. Read scientific-based materials on the subject. Talk with people who have different opinions about the issues. Assess what they are saying. Think clearly and make decisions based on facts.

Issues related to natural resources may involve the following areas:

- maintaining the earth's landscape
- destruction of tropical and old-growth forests
- disposing of wastes
- controlling pollution
- maintaining soil productivity
- taking animal wildlife for food, sport, and other uses
- having a safe place to live and carry out life functions
- maintaining an appropriate level of population
- using fossil fuels
- ownership of natural resources, with wildlife a particular example

Issues emerge in each community every year. How will the issues be solved? They should be solved for the overall benefit of the most people. They should consider approaches in using resources that will sustain the supply for future generations.

BELIEVING IN SUSTAINABILITY

Sustainability is going about life so resources are available for future generations. No individual wastes or damages resources. All people develop the belief that future generations are entitled to a good quality of life.

Sustainability should be a part of our daily living. We can conserve on the use of water, energy, and other resources. It is easy to do. We can do little things that do not change how we live. Using just one gallon less water, when taking a shower, is a small step for one person, but results in huge water savings when all people do it. In daily living, we can use fewer resources and create fewer wastes!

Sustainability should be a part of our work. We can use resources smartly and gain efficiency. How we approach sustainability depends on our occupation. Think about the occupation that you are considering: What resources are used? How can resource use be conserved?

REVIEWING

MAIN IDEAS

People use many kinds of natural resources. The uses vary and can be classified into two broad kinds of uses: consumptive and nonconsumptive. Sustainability is an approach to assuring that sufficient resources will be available for future generations. This includes ways of meeting basic human needs for food, clothing, and shelter.

The earth's population is increasing. Some people feel that there is a limit to the number of people who can be supported by the earth's resources. Overpopulation leads to depletion, wastes, landscape alteration, and pollution, especially of the atmosphere and water. Resources are depleted when they are used faster than they are replaced. Soil and water depletion can result in low agricultural productivity and hunger. As humans and other species compete to meet basic needs, some become endangered. Hunger is an issue in some nations.

Rural and urban uses of natural resources must be based on meeting the needs of people on a sustained basis. Land-use planning, resource protection, and agricultural land use are important to both rural and urban life.

Recycling and reusing help reduce the demand for natural resources. Recycling programs are found in most communities. All citizens have a responsibility to participate. Levels of participation may vary, but all people should realize the benefits of recycling and reusing.

Personal beliefs help guide people in their actions. They help people participate in decision-making. Decisions should be based on the facts and not emotions. Sustainability is an important concept in the beliefs of all people.

QUESTIONS

Answer the following questions using complete sentences and correct spelling.

1. What is the distinction between consumptive and nonconsumptive uses of natural resources?

2. What are the basic needs of humans?

3. What is the trend in the earth's human population?

4. Why is resource depletion a concern in meeting population demands?

5. What is waste? What wastes are created by people?

6. Why is landscape degradation a concern?

7. What are three areas of concern related to the atmosphere?

8. What is hunger? How is it related to malnourishment and undernourishment?

9. What are three areas of urban and rural impact? Why is each important?

10. Why are recycling and reusing important?

EVALUATING

Match the term with the correct definition. Write the letter by the term in the blank provided.

a. belief
b. issue
c. consumptive use
d. demography

e. sustainability
f. landscape alteration
g. greenhouse effect
h. desertification

i. land-use planning
j. hunger

_____ 1. A shortage of food.

_____ 2. A person's conviction about something.

_____ 3. The process of determining how land will be used.

_____ 4. The formation of desert on land that was once productive.

_____ 5. Altering the natural features of the earth.

_____ 6. A problem or question to be solved.

_____ 7. Using a resource so the amount used no longer exists.

_____ 8. The study of human population.

_____ 9. A condition in the atmosphere that traps radiation near the earth.

_____ 10. Using resources so some are available for future generations.

EXPLORING

1. Identify one problem related to natural resources in your community. Investigate how the problem is affecting the welfare of the people individually and collectively as a community. Propose ways to solve the problem. Meet with local government officials to discuss your findings and proposed solutions.

2. Take a field trip to a crop farm. Investigate the sustainable agriculture practices that are being used. Determine how these relate to the conservation of soil, water, fuel, and other resources. Write a report on what you observe.

3. Research population trends in your local community. Relate these to how land is used and the demands on natural resources. For example, determine the water requirements today as compared to years ago. Other areas that you might consider are waste disposal, pollution, and overall quality of life.

3

USING SCIENCE IN NATURAL RESOURCES

Science helps us understand our natural resources. The different areas of science help in answering questions, such as: How were the natural resources formed? Why are they found only in certain places? What happens when we run out of certain natural resources?

People who have a good background in science understand natural resources. They can make informed decisions. They can seek answers to problems based on facts rather than emotions. Of course, the information must be accurate and stand the test of time.

The choices people make are based on their knowledge and experience. Knowing the basic science of natural resources will help people to be better decision-makers. No one wants to make bad decisions about natural resources!

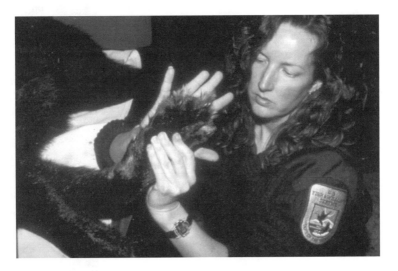

3-1. A wildlife specialist compares the size of the paw of a wolf with her hand. (Note: The wolf has been sedated for this examination.) (Courtesy, U.S. Fish and Wildlife Service)

OBJECTIVES

This chapter introduces and reviews areas of science that are important in understanding natural resources. The chapter has the following objectives:

1. Explain the meaning and importance of science in natural resources

2. Identify and describe areas of science as related to natural resources

3. Describe the three spheres where natural resources are found

4. Describe the role of ecology in natural resources

5. Explain the meaning of succession in natural resource renewal

National Science Foundation
http://www.nsf.gov/

TERMS

aquatic community
atmosphere
biosphere
botany
chemistry
community
crust
earth science
ecology
ecosphere
ecosystem
food chain
food web
groundwater
habitat
hydrosphere
life science
life span
lithosphere
mantle
mathematics
niche
physical science
physics
plate tectonics
protoplasm
revolution
rotation
science
sphere
social science
solar system
succession
surface water
terrestrial community
timberline
topography
water cycle
zoology

SCIENCE IN NATURAL RESOURCES

Natural resources are either living, nonliving, or formerly living. What is the difference? How is the difference related to science?

MEANING OF SCIENCE

Science is knowledge of the world in which we live. The knowledge is based on carefully conducted experiments and research. Many general truths or laws of science have been developed. These laws help guide the study of natural resources.

Science deals with facts. Procedures are used to make and record accurate observations. Principles may be stated that guide future study of natural resources. Of course, science is not limited to natural resources. It is used in all areas of life. Science helps explain events and relationships in our world.

Career Profile

NATURALIST

A naturalist works in parks, forests, or other areas and carries out educational programs for the public. The work may include assisting with habitat for wildlife, doing research, and serving as a tour guide. Naturalists have important roles in preserving the wildlife and beauty of the area where they work.

Naturalists need college degrees in biology, environmental science, wildlife, forestry, or a related area. Some have masters or doctors degrees. A few may work into the job with a high school education and practical experience. Naturalists must enjoy the outdoors and interpreting nature to people.

Most jobs are found in national or state parks. Some are available with refuges, private land holders, and local parks. Many are in areas away from large cities. This shows a naturalist explaining the biology of salmon at the Issaquah Salmon Hatchery in Washington.

IMPORTANCE OF SCIENCE

Science is important in studying natural resources. It helps in several ways:

- ■ Research — Science helps us better understand natural resources. Scientific methods are used in doing research. To investigate problems, we need to know the principles that surround the area being studied. Examples include how smoke damages the atmosphere, the nutritional needs of animal wildlife, methods of promoting forest growth, and new ways of extracting minerals.

- ■ Sustainability — Science helps promote sustainable use of natural resources. It helps get greater efficiency from the resources that we use. Scientific methods provide new ways of recycling natural resources.

- ■ Restoration — Science helps people restore declining populations of organisms. Understanding the needs of wildlife, for example, helps prevent the loss of populations and promotes the growth of new populations.

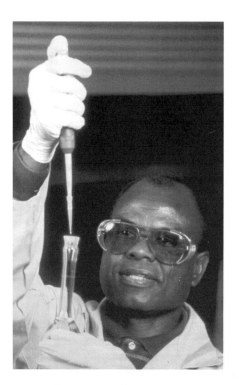

3-2. A physical science technician conducts a laboratory test on a problem in natural resources. (Courtesy, U.S. Fish and Wildlife Service)

- ■ Protection — Science helps protect natural resources. By knowing the nature of natural resources steps can be taken to protect them from loss. This includes all areas where loss might occur, such as preventing soil erosion, providing food plants for animal wildlife, and constructing nesting areas for birds or fish.

AREAS OF SCIENCE

The study of natural resources uses several areas of science. These tend to overlap and create the need for people to be informed in a number of areas.

The four major areas of science are physical science, life science, mathematics, and social science.

Physical Science

Physical science is the study of the nonliving things around us. Many natural resources involve physical science. Minerals, the atmosphere, movement of the planet Earth, and other things are included. Physical science has three major areas: earth science, physics, and chemistry.

Earth science is the area of physical science that deals with the environment in which organisms live and grow. It includes hydrology, geology, and meteorology. Hydrology deals with water and how it moves through a cycle that prepares it for use. Geology deals with the structure and composition of the earth. Soil science is a part of geology. Meteorology is about the earth's atmosphere. This includes weather, air quality, and other factors that influence activities on the earth.

Physics is the area of physical science that deals with the nature of objects. It includes mechanics, heat, light, and electricity. The use of simple machines to gain advantage in doing work is a part of physics.

Chemistry is the study of the makeup of matter. Matter is anything that takes up space and has weight or quantity. Anything that is made of one kind of matter is known as a substance. Combining two or more substances results in a compound.

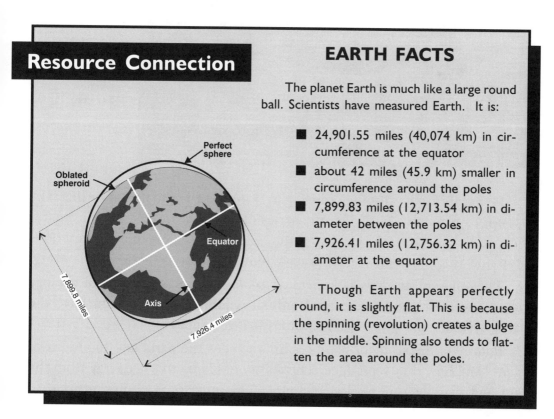

Resource Connection

EARTH FACTS

The planet Earth is much like a large round ball. Scientists have measured Earth. It is:

- 24,901.55 miles (40,074 km) in circumference at the equator
- about 42 miles (45.9 km) smaller in circumference around the poles
- 7,899.83 miles (12,713.54 km) in diameter between the poles
- 7,926.41 miles (12,756.32 km) in diameter at the equator

Though Earth appears perfectly round, it is slightly flat. This is because the spinning (revolution) creates a bulge in the middle. Spinning also tends to flatten the area around the poles.

Perfect sphere

Oblated spheroid

Equator

Axis

7,899.8 miles

7,926.4 miles

Life Science

Life science is the study of living things. This includes plants, animals, and other organisms, such as bacteria and fungi. There is a great deal of overlap. Animals are so dependent on plants! Life science is sometimes known as biology.

Living things are organisms that carry out processes needed to remain in the living condition. This condition involves chemical processes in ***protoplasm***—the only natural substance in which life exists. Protoplasm is found in the cells of an organism. Cells are tiny building blocks that give structure to large animals. One-celled organisms carry out all functions within their single cells.

3-3. A rainbow trout is being tagged as part of a study of fish biology. (Courtesy, U.S. Fish and Wildlife Service)

Living things go through a life span. *Life span* is the period of life. The span goes through a fairly definite series of steps: beginning, growth, maturity, decline, and death. Death results when a living organism's functions stop and the organism can no longer remain alive.

The study of animals is known as ***zoology***. Basic principles of zoology help us relate to and understand animal wildlife. Most of them have the same systems and processes as domesticated animals.

Botany is the study of plants. This includes the parts and functions of plants and how they reproduce. The ability of plants to use energy from the Sun and manufacture food is included. This process is photosynthesis.

Mathematics

Mathematics is the science of numbers. It deals with measuring and us-ing the results of measurement to quantify information. With mathematics, we can make exact statements. Everyone understands the concept of "five" or "sixty." Two systems of measurement are used: metric and standard or Eng-lish. Scientists use the metric system throughout the world. The standard system is used in the United States and a few other places in everyday mea-surements.

Social Science

Social science is the study of human behavior. Many human traits are in-cluded. Studying the behaviors of humans as individuals is known as psy-chology. The study of group behaviors of humans is known as sociology. Hu-man behaviors are important in understanding why people respond as they do to natural resources. This helps develop training in appropriate ways of responding. A good example is the area of forest fires. Unfortunately, some people set forest fires. Social science is used to determine why and develop ways of helping people stop this behavior.

THE EARTH IN ITS SOLAR SYSTEM

Earth is a planet in a solar system. The solar system in which Earth is lo-cated has eight other planets. It also contains other objects, such as aster-oids, meteoroids, and comets.

A **solar system** is a group of objects in space that are held together by a sun. The sun is in the center of the solar system. This system is part of a

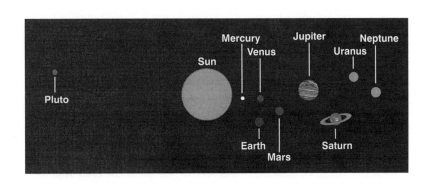

3-4. Earth in its solar system.

larger system known as galaxies. Earth's solar system is in the Milky Way Galaxy.

Within the solar system, Earth moves by turning. It does not go in just any direction, but follows a definite path year after year. Changes in direction create conditions on Earth that are important to natural resources and the environment.

ROTATION

Night and day are due to rotation. Night is the time of darkness. Day is the time of light. Darkness and light create cycles in living organisms. Humans use darkness as a time of rest and light as a time of activity. The reverse is true with some species, such as bats and owls.

Rotation is the turning of Earth on an axis. The axis is invisible but is located at the North and South Poles. One complete rotation is made each day. Light and dark periods are based on the side of the earth that is toward and away from the Sun. The light provides energy and promotes photosynthesis in plants. The darkness provides a time of rest. Processes in living organisms are carried out in both day and night.

REVOLUTION

Each year, the earth makes a revolution. A *revolution* is circling of the earth around the Sun. It takes 365.24 days for a revolution to be completed.

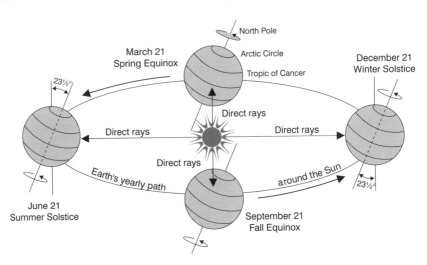

3-5. Seasons of the year as related to the revolution of Earth.

Every fourth year is a leap year in which the month of February has an additional day. This compensates for the fraction of a day required for a revolution.

Seasons of the year are based on the stage of the revolution. The equinox is when the Sun is directly over the equator. Day and night are the same length. This happens twice a year—once when spring arrives and again when fall arrives. As the Sun moves north or south of the equator, the length of day and night change. The distance, the direction, and the tilting of Earth while in revolution determine exposure of the surface to the rays of the Sun. This influences the temperature and the amount of daylight.

SPHERES

Studying natural resources involves overlapping areas of science. Why this happens is easy to understand. A strong interdependence exists between plants, animals, and other organisms and the environment in which they live. Each depends on the other. Further, what happens on the surface of the earth is related to the atmosphere and vice versa.

Spheres are used in studying natural resources. A *sphere* is the environment in which something exists. It is a field or an area that is described by adding "sphere" to another word. Natural resources exist in and are influenced by three spheres: lithosphere, atmosphere, and hydrosphere.

LITHOSPHERE

The *lithosphere* is the solid portion of the planet Earth. It is comprised largely of rock. The lithosphere does not include ice. Minerals, fossil fuels, and other natural resources are found in the lithosphere.

Geology is the study of the physical features of Earth. It reveals the structure of the lithosphere and provides information to help understand events on the earth.

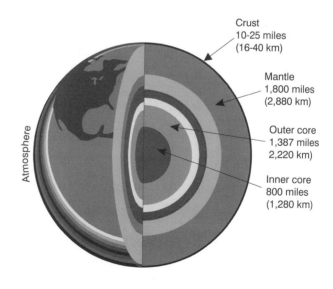

Crust
10-25 miles
(16-40 km)

Mantle
1,800 miles
(2,880 km)

Outer core
1,387 miles
2,220 km)

Inner core
800 miles
(1,280 km)

Atmosphere

3-6. Structure of the lithosphere.

The Earth's Structure

The earth is made up of three layers:

- Crust—The **crust** is the outer portion of the earth. It contains the soil that supports plant life. This area also has many minerals and other resources. The crust is about 10 to 25 miles (16 to 40 km) thick. It is thicker in land areas and thinner in sea areas. The crust provides important minerals, fossil fuels, and other natural resources. About 81 percent of the solid materials in the crust contain silica and oxygen.

  The earth's crust has more area under than above water. Land is the area above water. About 70 percent is covered with water as oceans, ice caps, and lakes. Within the water, large areas of land have been formed. The largest areas of land are known as continents. Smaller areas are islands.

  The crust in many areas is covered with soil. Soil is the part of the crust in which plants grow. It contains the nutrients that are needed by the plants. Soil also helps plants anchor themselves with their roots.

- Mantle—The **mantle** is that part of the earth that is located between the crust and the core. The mantle is made of aluminum, silicon, iron, and other minerals. The upper mantle is just beneath the crust. The lower mantle is beneath the upper mantle and joins the core. The mantle is hot, with temperatures ranging from 1,600° F (870° C) in the upper mantle to 8,000° F (4,400° C) in the lower mantle. Movements in the mantle cause changes in the crust. Crust changes alter the natural resources and landscape.

- Core—The center of the earth is the core. It is divided into the outer core and center. The outer core is next to the mantle. Temperatures in the core range between 8,000 and 13,000° F (4,400 to 7,000°C). Scientists indicate that the core is made of molten iron and nickel. This material and its movement create the electromagnetic field that is found around the earth. This field influences activities on the surface.

Movement

The earth is continually moving deep inside. These movements have and continue to affect the landform. Great pressure causes rocks to move, fold, crack, and bend. Some of these movements cause earthquakes. Other movements merely result in slight changes of the surface or no changes at all.

Plate tectonics is a theory used to explain some movements. This theory holds that there are large plates that float on the mantle. These plates move creating great pressures at the edges of the plates. At times, the pressure becomes so great that the rocks break. Earthquakes may result. Some mountains were formed when huge rocks have broken and pushed upward.

Volcanoes and tsunamis also create movement. Volcanoes are openings in the earth that expel molten rock (lava), ash, and steam. These massive movements from deep within the earth to the surface create surface movement and new landforms.

Tsunamis are large waves on the ocean that result from major movements in the earth. Earthquakes and volcanic action create tsunamis. People and property near coastlines are most affected by the giant waves.

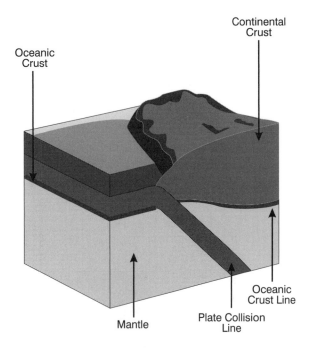

3-7. Plate tectonics is one theory of interior movement of the earth that causes landforms on the surface.

Topography is the study and mapping of the detailed landform features of an area. A topographic map results. The map shows surface characteristics, such as hills, valleys, streams, and lakes.

3-8. The topography of Yosemite Valley reveals the magnificent Half Dome.

ATMOSPHERE

The atmosphere is the air that surrounds the earth. It is made up of gases, water vapor, and particulate. The gases are invisible. Water vapor and particulate may be seen. Water vapor forms clouds and fog. Particulate (tiny pieces of solid material) may create smoky conditions. Particulate makes the atmosphere visible. Air and wind are two major natural resources. They have important roles in our environment.

Layers

The atmosphere has four layers. These layers extend outward from the earth. They provide the weather and support air travel and satellites. The first layer is the troposphere, which extends upward 5 to 11 miles (8 to 18

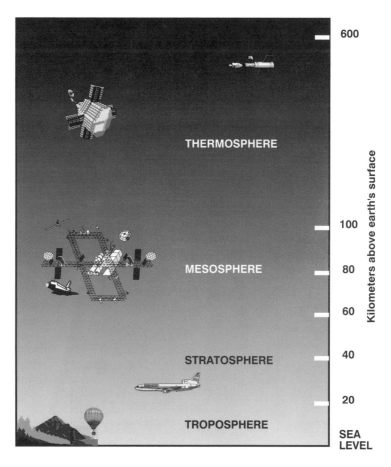

3-9. Layers of the atmosphere.

km). Most of the gases and other materials are in this layer of the atmosphere. The air has low levels of oxygen at the top of the troposphere.

The stratosphere is above the troposphere and extends about 30 miles (50 km) above the earth. The mesosphere is beyond the stratosphere. The thermosphere is the uppermost layer of the atmosphere. It is hot due to the intense heat from the Sun.

Air travel is primarily in the troposphere, with some planes reaching higher altitudes in the stratosphere. Satellites are in the mesosphere.

Gases

Air is a mixture of gases and other materials. Nitrogen is the most prevalent gas, with air being 78 percent nitrogen. The air is 21 percent oxygen. Other gases, such as neon, argon, and carbon dioxide, make up only 1 percent.

The gases in the air are natural resources. They also support the growth of other natural resources. Most living organisms require oxygen. Plants require nitrogen for growth. Good air is needed for plant growth. Polluted air can destroy plants. A good example is the effects of acid rain on some species of trees. (Acid rain is caused by particulate in the air that contains nitrogen. The air moisture and other elements form acid.)

With increased elevation, the air gets "thinner." There is less oxygen and other gases. A good example of how this affects living organisms is to study tall mountains. For example, many plants that grow at low elevations do not grow on the tops of mountains. The air does not contain sufficient oxygen and the temperature may be too cool. The *timberline* (also known as the tree line) is the altitude above sea level at which trees will not grow. The Rocky Mountains have

3-10. Lichens and mosses growing above the timberline in Rocky Mountain National Park form alpine tundra. (Courtesy, Greg N. Freeman, Colorado)

peaks that extend above the timberline. No trees grow there; however, adapted lichens and mosses are found.

HYDROSPHERE

All of the water on Earth forms the **hydrosphere**. This includes all three forms of water: liquid, ice, and vapor. The water may be on the surface or underground.

Surface water is the water that is on the surface of the earth. This includes the water in oceans, ponds, lakes, streams, and other bodies. It also includes the water in the snow and ice on the polar ice caps.

Groundwater is water stored below the surface of the earth. It may be in small amounts held by soil particles or as aquifers.

The earth's water supply is constant. The amount does not increase nor decrease. Its state may change and it may be polluted and not useful. We use water over and over. It is reconditioned by natural processes in the earth that are a part of the water cycle.

The **water cycle** (hydrologic cycle) is the circulation of water through the hydrosphere. It may change states and undergo renewing. If excessively polluted, nature may not be able to renew it for repeated use. (More details on the water cycle are presented later in the book.)

3-11. Waterfalls on the Cullasaja River in North Carolina helps appreciate the beauty of nature.

OVERLAPPING

The lithosphere, atmosphere, and hydrosphere overlap to form environments that support living organisms. These areas of overlap are also known as spheres.

The *ecosphere* is where living things are found on the earth. It includes portions of the three major spheres. For example, animals that live on the land must have air and water to survive.

The part of the ecosphere that supports life is known as the **biosphere**. The biosphere is part of the ecosphere. Some background in ecology will help in understanding the meaning of ecosphere.

ECOLOGY

Living organisms have a certain way of going about life. Species vary in the kind of environment they need. *Ecology* is the study of how living organisms exist in their natural environment. It helps explain how nature is organized and the roles of different organisms.

All of the parts of the environment in which an organism lives form its *ecosystem*. This includes the interactions of organisms with other organisms and with the nonliving parts of the environment. Ecosystems range from large forests to small streams, oceans, swamps, and areas under rocks or logs–any place living organisms are found.

COMMUNITIES

Living organisms form communities. A **community** is the assortment of plants, animals, and other organisms that live together. A kind of harmony between the organisms exists. Some species depend on each other for sur-

3-12. These water lilies, with leaves extending above the surface, are part of an aquatic community. What organisms might be found in the water?

3-13. Life in the desert of Tonto National Forest in Arizona shows terrestrial organisms that are adapted to low moisture.

vival, such as deer that eat plants. Look in the corner of the yard around your home or in a park. What kind of community do you see?

Communities may be aquatic or terrestrial. An *aquatic community* is based in the water. Fish, clams, shrimp, water plants, and alligators are examples of aquatic organisms. Some birds are aquatic, such as ducks and geese.

Terrestrial organisms form terrestrial communities. A *terrestrial community* is one that is based on the land. Examples of organisms in terrestrial communities include rabbits, fox, mice, deer, bear, and birds, such as robins and sparrows.

Certain conditions must be present for organisms to survive in either community. When those conditions fail, the organisms may die and be lost from the community.

HABITATS

Communities form habitats. A *habitat* is the physical, environmental characteristics of a community that allow a particular species to live there. Climate, moisture, soil, and food are needed in a habitat. If these are not present as needed by a species, that species will not be found in it.

Changes in a habitat affect all organisms. Some changes are natural; others may be caused by human activity. Natural changes include drought, cold, heat, and flooding. Human activity may be draining a swamp, cutting trees, or building highways or homes.

3-14. Banded sand snakes fill niche roles in their habitats.

Every organism takes from and contributes to its community. This is known as its niche. A ***niche*** is the unique way a species lives in a community. Certain conditions must be present. For example, deer feed on acorns, twigs, and similar browse. If this disappears due to bad weather, the deer will no longer find food. The niche that supported them is gone.

FOOD RELATIONSHIPS

All living organisms need food to live and go about life. Plants make their food by photosynthesis. To do so, nutrients must be present and available to the plants. Plants are used as food by some species of animals.

A ***food chain*** is the sequence in which organisms obtain their food. Each species has a different food chain. Food chains interlink to form food webs. A ***food web*** is a graphic representation of feeding behavior by the organisms in a community.

3-15. An example of a terrestrial food web.

Animal species can be placed in groups based on what they consume. Knowing the food requirements is needed to promote the growth of a species. The groups are:

■ Herbivore — A herbivore is an animal species that exclusively eats plants for food. This may be any part of a plant–leaves, stems, flowers, roots, fruit, and seed. Herbivores have digestive systems that can use plant products as food. Some herbivores are terrestrial, such as bison; others are aquatic, such as grass carp.

■ Carnivore — A carnivore is an animal species that eats the flesh of other animals. Typically, larger animals feed on smaller animals, such as a hawk that eats a mouse.

■ Omnivore — An omnivore is an animal species that eats both plants and animals. Some omnivores are aquatic; others are terrestrial. An example of an aquatic omnivore is the catfish. Catfish will eat other fish as well as plant sources of food. An example of a terrestrial omnivore is the black bear. Black bears eat berries and other plant parts as well as salmon or other small animals.

3-16. An Alaskan brown bear is an omnivore. (This bear has captured a salmon.)

Animals can be further grouped as feeding on living or nonliving materials. Some eat both living and dead materials. An animal that eats living plants and animals is a biophage. For example, bison prefer living grass. They will, however, eat dead grass in the winter. An animal that eats dead plants and animals is known as a saprophage. Saprophages are sometimes known as scavengers. Crabs, vultures, and gulls eat dead food materials. They help clean the environment and return energy to the food chain.

SUCCESSION

Succession is the replacement of one community by another. A fairly definite sequence is involved. Succession applies to both aquatic and terrestrial communities.

Many years are required for succession to occur. For example, a half century or more may be needed to go from a land area that has been completely cleaned to a mature forest. Succession is often observed on land that has

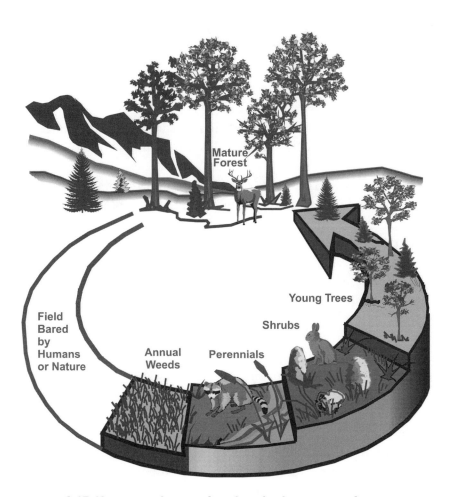

3-17. How succession goes from bare land to a mature forest.

been farmed or burned and left to return to growing native plants. As plants regrow, animals and other organisms return.

The first step in succession is for small grasses and herbs to grow. Insects, birds, and other small animals move in. This is followed by small trees, shrubs, and other plants beginning to grow and replace the grasses and herbs. Later, the trees grow larger and overtake other plants. Larger wildlife animals move in and often feed on or force out the smaller animals.

Succession includes natural selection. Natural selection is the process of organisms that are best adapted to an environment surviving longer and having more offspring. Some species can adapt; others cannot. Adaptation is the adjustment of a species to changes in its community. Those that adapt survive.

REVIEWING

MAIN IDEAS

Science is knowledge of our world. It includes physical science, life science, mathematics, and social science. Each has important roles with natural resources.

Humans use natural resources that are a part of the planet on which they live. Earth is located in a solar system with eight other planets. The source of all energy is from the Sun. The rotation and revolution of the earth create an environment for living and nonliving resources.

The earth has three major spheres: lithosphere, atmosphere, and hydrosphere. These spheres overlap to create the ecosphere, which is the combination of natural resources that support living organisms. Studying the structure, movement, and components of the spheres helps us understand the nature of our natural resources.

Ecology deals with how organisms relate to the nonliving parts of their environment. It includes communities, habitats and niches, and food relationships. Together, these provide an environment that supports a diversity of living organisms.

Communities change through succession. The progressive sequence from immature and young organisms to mature communities is important in the renewing of natural resources. It is also important to understand concepts associated with natural selection and adaptation.

QUESTIONS

Answer the following questions using complete sentences and correct spelling.

1. What is science? Why is it important in studying natural resources?
2. What are the areas of science? Briefly explain each.
3. How does the planet Earth move in its solar system?
4. What is the importance of the rotations and revolutions of the earth?
5. What are the three major spheres associated with the earth?
6. What is the earth's internal structure? How does this structure sometimes cause changes on the surface?
7. What is a community? Distinguish between the two major types of communities.
8. What food relationships exist in the biosphere?
9. Distinguish between herbivores, carnivores, and omnivores.
10. What is succession? Why is it important?

EVALUATING

Match the term with the correct definition. Write the letter by the term in the blank provided.

a. earth science
b. botany
c. solar system
d. revolution

e. sphere
f. lithosphere
g. plate tectonics
h. timberline

i. surface water
j. ecology

_____ 1. The area of physical science that deals with the environment in which organisms live and grow.

_____ 2. Water found on the surface of the earth.

_____ 3. The study of plants.

_____ 4. A group of objects in space that are held together by a sun.

_____ 5. The elevation at which trees stop growing.

_____ 6. Requires approximately 365 days.

_____ 7. The study of how living organisms exist in their natural environment.

_____ 8. The solid portion of the planet Earth.

_____ 9. The environment in which something exists.

_____ 10. A theory of plates deep inside the earth that explains surface movements of the earth.

EXPLORING

1. Tour a natural science museum. Study the physical features of the earth in the area where you live. Investigate the presence and formation of natural resources. Prepare a report on your observations.

2. Study the topography in the area where you live. Obtain an aerial photograph. Sketch a map of the major features of the landscape within a few miles of your home. Prepare the sketch on poster paper or other large sheets. Label the various features, including names of streams, mountains, forests, etc., as may be appropriate. Display your map in the classroom.

3. Hike through a park, refuge, or forest and observe the ecological features of the area. Have a naturalist or other person provide information on the geological features, kinds of wildlife, and other details of the area. Prepare a report on your observations.

4

NATURAL RESOURCE CONSERVATION

Conservation is having and using natural resources wisely! Wise use is essential. Natural resources are too important to be used unwisely. But, people have not always felt that way. Settlers in the United States used, wasted, and abused natural resources. It was the late 1800s before a few people began to realize the importance of conservation.

Soil, water, air, and other resources should be protected to assure long-term use. Damage should be prevented. Wastes should be disposed of properly. Only what is needed should be used. Recycling and reusing as many things as possible promotes conservation. Making wise use is not that hard to do. You can do it!

Conservation is the responsibility of all people. It is not just a matter for factories, mines, and crop producers. It is for everyone!

4-1. Windsurfing in Alaska uses natural resources that are inexhaustible. (Courtesy, Dave Menke, U.S. Fish and Wildlife Service)

OBJECTIVES

This chapter covers important concepts in the conservation of natural resources. The following objectives are included:

1. Explain the importance of natural resource conservation

2. Identify major sources of natural resource damage

3. Distinguish between point and nonpoint sources of pollution

4. Trace major events in the history of natural resource conservation

5. Identify leaders in the natural resource conservation movement

TERMS

aesthetic benefit
Aldo Leopold
Dust Bowl
economic value
exploitation
Franklin D. Roosevelt
Gifford Pinchot
Hugh H. Bennett
interdependent relationship
John Muir
landscape degradation
natural resource conservation
nonpoint source pollution
point source pollution
pollutant
pollution
Rachel Carson
symbiotic relationship
Theodore Roosevelt

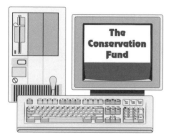

The Conservation Fund
http://www.conservationfund.org/

THE IMPORTANCE OF CONSERVATION

Just think what life would be like without selected resources! A good example is fossil fuel. There would be no petroleum to run engines and do work. Our use of automobiles would change. Of course, an alternative fuel might be used.

NATURAL RESOURCE CONSERVATION

Natural resource conservation is the wise use of natural resources. It is protecting and using them so they will last a long time. We can work and live in ways that use fewer nonrenewable natural resources. If we do not conserve, we might run out of resources. The resources include soil, water, forests, grazing land, wildlife, minerals, and energy.

Reasons for Conservation

Conservation of natural resources is important for two main reasons:

- Meet demand—People need natural resources to live. They also use the products made from resources. Just look at the things around you today that are based on natural resources! You will see cars, pickups, television and stereo sets, and many other things.

- Maintain standard of living—People want certain things in their lives. They want nice homes, electricity, running water, sanitary waste-disposal systems, and all kinds of gadgets. These are part of a standard of living. People also want a good quality of life–one that promotes health and well-being.

Examples of Conservation

A few examples of how to conserve natural resources are:

- Cropping practices—Some resources need to be used carefully to prevent their loss. A good example is soil. Soil that has been plowed is loose. Water and wind can carry it away. Using methods of plowing that do not break the soil into small pieces helps prevent loss. Plowing on-the-contour (across hills) slows the speed of water flow and erosion. Plowing so a cover of mulch and plant materials remains on the soil also reduces loss.

4-2. Proper layout of rice fields conserves both soil and water.

■ Recycling—Many natural resources can be recycled. This saves taking more resources for manufacturing. A good example is iron. Iron is a mineral used in making steel and other products. Iron can be recycled. Recycling prevents mining additional ore. Recycling also reduces energy requirements to extract and transport ore.

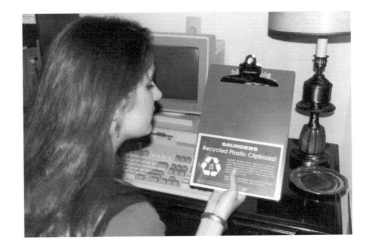

4-3. Plastic has been recycled into a clipboard.

■ Reusing—Some materials can be reused without remanufacturing. This reduces the use of resources and saves energy. Many examples could be named. One is the reuse of pallets. A pallet is a platform on which products are moved. Each time a pallet is reused fewer trees are cut and less energy is used in sawing and assembling new pallets.

■ Preventing damage—Properly disposing of wastes prevents pollution and damage to natural resources. Many things can cause pollution. Disposal methods should reduce pollution. An example is used engine oil. Used oil should never be run onto the ground, drained into storm sewers, or poured down drains. The oil would get into our water supply. Used engine oil should be sent to a place that disposes of used oil.

■ Taking no more than needed—Sometimes people take more than they need. Sport hunting is a good example. Killing more game than is legal or needed is poor wildlife conservation. It is also illegal! Laws vary but people could be arrested, fined, and sentenced for "going over the bag limit."

■ Avoid waste—There are many ways we can make more efficient use of resources. We can begin by using water wisely. Conserving the use of electrical power is another step. Using reusable glasses for drinking rather than disposable paper cups avoids waste. The list of things to do is endless.

4-4. A timer can be used to save electricity by having an appliance operate only when needed.

THE ECOSYSTEM

Life on Earth involves relationships. ***Interdependent relationship*** means that organisms depend on each other. Living things vary in their roles. Some help clean the environment. Others produce useful materials, including food.

Some activities damage how organisms live and may determine whether organisms live. Polluting water, air, soil, and other resources may make these resources unfit to use. Destroying habitats may make it impossible for wildlife to survive. Some organisms no longer exist on the earth. They were not able to adapt to changes in the ecosystem.

Symbiotic Relationships

Animals and plants are symbiotic. A ***symbiotic relationship*** is species living together and benefitting each other. Humans are a part of these relationships. The activities of humans influence symbiotic relationships between wildlife. Destroying a food source can wipe out wildlife.

4-5. Many beneficial relationships are found in old-growth forests, such as Mount Hood National Forest in Oregon.

Human Responsibility

All people should be conservationists. This is responsible living. Continuing to have enough resources depends on the way we use them. We know that natural resources are important to a good quality of life.

Look at the big picture: All human beings affect natural resources and other human beings. The effects may be positive or negative. How do you want to be viewed?

NATURAL RESOURCE DAMAGE

What good is a resource if it cannot be used? Using resources is essential; damaging is not!

Dealing with natural resources is among the greatest issues people face today. Humans have different opinions. How natural resources are used is often a major source of disagreement.

KINDS OF DAMAGE

Damage to natural resources lowers their quality or wastes their usefulness. Harm is caused that reduces the value of the resource. Damage may be due to pollution, loss, and reduced quality.

Pollution

Pollution is releasing hazardous or poisonous substances into the biosphere. The substances are likely from industrial, residential, or agricultural sources. The pollution destroys or lowers the quality of many natural resources.

A substance that causes pollution is a ***pollutant***. Pollutants vary. Some pollutants are natural resources that are out of place. A good example is soil particles suspended in water. No one wants to drink muddy water!

Pollution causes undesirable changes in the biosphere. Some examples of the ways pollution causes damage are:

■ Disease—Some pollutants cause disease. The disease may be in humans, domestic animals, or wildlife. Some pollutants cause cancer and are known as carcinogens. Most carcinogens are chemical substances that accidentally got into the environment (such as a chemical spill) or were applied to help solve a problem (such as a pesticide).

■ Reduced growth—Pollution may reduce growth rate. In some cases, organisms are deformed. Plants may have abnormal leaves, stems, flowers, and other parts. Animals may show defects, such as two tails on fish, calves with two heads, missing parts, and organs that do not function.

■ Reproduction—Some pollutants cause reproductive failures. Organisms may not be able to produce young and maintain an adequate population level. An example was a pesticide known as DDT. It caused birds to lay eggs with little or no shell. The egg would not develop into a living baby bird.

Career Profile

CONSERVATIONIST

People who believe in conservation are known as conservationists. A conservationist is a person who feels that natural resources should be used in ways that assure sustainability. They identify conservation practices and provide technical assistance so that landowners can implement them.

Conservationists need practical knowledge of natural resources. Most have college degrees in agronomy, wildlife, forestry, or a related area. Many have masters and doctors degrees.

Jobs for conservationists are with government agencies, private land companies, and associations with interests in resource use. The work is often outside with wildlife, soil, water, and other resources. This shows a wildlife conservationist working with a bald eagle. (Courtesy, U. S. Fish and Wildlife Service)

4-6. Oil spilled on water has destroyed an otherwise healthy duck. (Courtesy, Brent Esmil, U. S. Fish and Wildlife Service)

■ Death—Organisms can die because of pollution. Death occurs when the pollutant is toxic or when the pollutant is present in high amounts. In other cases, death may result from organisms becoming entangled or having contact with a pollutant. An example is oil spills on water where fowl are present. The fowl become coated with oil and die.

Loss

Loss causes damage to some resources. An example is unprotected soil. Tiny soil particles can be carried away by wind or water. When this happens, the fertility of the soil is lower. The soil is less productive.

Another chapter in this book will explain that many years are required for soil to be renewed. Until renewed, productivity has been reduced. Crops will have lower yields or cannot be grown at all!

Lower Quality

The quality of resources may be reduced. This is known as degradation. The resource that is damaged has less value and appeal. Here are two examples:

■ Landscape degradation—Many human activities degrade the natural landscape of the earth. *Landscape degradation* is doing things that make the natural features of an area less appealing. Ways this happens include:

  - cutting natural trees (not those on tree farms)
  - changing topography by using heavy equipment to move earth around
  - mining minerals, such as copper, sand, and gravel
  - building power lines and roads through forests and over mountains

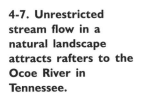

4-7. Unrestricted stream flow in a natural landscape attracts rafters to the Ocoe River in Tennessee.

– other activities that degrade the scenic value of the landscape

Look at how highways have changed where you live. People could not travel without the roads. Are the roads worth the destruction of the landscape?

■ Restricting stream flow—Dams may be built on streams. A dam stores or harnesses the useful energy in water. Dams restrict water flow and create reservoirs. Reservoirs destroy natural habitats that once existed along the stream. Above the dam, the pool of water reaches out over the land. Below the dam, the stream may dry up or be just a trickle. An example is the Tallulah River in Northeast Georgia. Three dams were built to create reservoirs to generate electrical power. The water flow was reduced. White-water canoeing and kayaking ended. Was construction of the dams to produce electricity a worthy change in the river?

CONTROVERSY

People often do not agree on uses of natural resources. Distinguishing use from damage is sometimes difficult. For example, mining degrades the landscape. Is the benefit of what is mined greater than maintaining the natural landscape? This leads to controversy. Disputes may arise. The basis of some disputes may be difficult to understand.

Economic Benefits

The economic value of a natural resource is a factor in all compromises. *Economic value* is the value of a resource and the jobs associated with it. Is the greatest benefit the natural scenery or the human changes that are made?

Aesthetic Benefits

Some natural resources have important aesthetic benefits. An *aesthetic benefit* is a feature that adds beauty and creates psychological benefits. Leaving streams in their natural state is an aesthetic benefit to some people. Others want streams widened, dammed, or changed in ways for economic benefit.

Tourism provides jobs and income in some areas. Aesthetic features attract tourists. Tourists spend money for food, lodging, and other things. Tourists travel to areas that are appealing. If the appeal is lost, tourists will not come! Suppose all of the trees that have colorful leaves in the fall were cut in Maine. Would people still go there to see the leaves?

Maintaining Habitats

Habitats are being lost in small and large ecosystems worldwide. When an area is developed, the food, cover, and water for wildlife are destroyed. Some species can adapt to changes. Songbirds have adapted to urban living. They build nests in shrubs, on the trim of houses, and in other places. Birds get their food from shrubs, trees, and grasses and the insects that live nearby.

Resources help conserve each other. Plant roots help hold soil in place during periods of heavy rain and when the wind blows. When a plant dies, it helps replenish nutrients in the soil. Plants also help clean the air. They can remove some of the carbon dioxide that humans release into the air.

4-8. A trail at Moccasin Creek State Park, Georgia, promotes understanding of habitat succession.

POINT AND NONPOINT POLLUTION

Pollution comes from many sources. Some of the sources are readily identifiable. Other sources are not easy to find.

POINT SOURCE POLLUTION

Have you ever seen a large pipe running polluted water into a stream? If so, you saw point source pollution.

Point source pollution is from sources that are readily identifiable. The pollutant is discharged at places that can be seen or determined by laboratory testing. These sources are easy to locate and pinpoint.

Point sources can be regulated, controlled, and stopped. In some cases, treatment is needed. An example is factories that produce wastewater. Many have lagoons or other water treatment facilities. Once the wastewater has been cleaned it can be released into the stream.

NONPOINT SOURCE POLLUTION

Nonpoint source pollution is from sources that cannot be directly identified. Many places may be involved in producing the pollution. The sources are often scattered over a wide area.

An example is the residential use of pesticides. Many home owners use pesticides on their lawns. Residues may wash into nearby streams. There is no single source of the pollution. It is from all of the lawns where pesticides have been used. Farms are similar in that residues may come from many sources.

4-9. Water flowing from this factory drain is point source pollution—the source of pollution is easy to identify.

4-10. Runoff from this parking lot is nonpoint source pollution—the oil drops that pollute are from many different vehicles.

Nonpoint source pollution is more difficult to stop. Many people have a role in it. This means that every citizen takes steps to end pollution.

HISTORY OF NATURAL RESOURCE CONSERVATION

Early settlers found many natural resources in the United States. These resources helped develop the nation. Fertile soil, large forests, mineral supplies, sources of energy, good water, and other natural resources promoted settlement. People in Europe and other nations viewed the United States as a place to go to have a better life.

EXPLOITATION

With many resources and a small population, people could use all the resources they wanted. This promoted moving to the United States. Many people immigrated in the 1700s and 1800s. They were willing to work hard and pursue their goals. Some people used natural resources for their own personal gain. This resulted in exploitation.

Exploitation is using natural resources for profit. Often the resources were taken without regard to other people. Little thought was given to the fact that the supply of many resources was limited. Some people cut trees and killed game without regard to need!

The industrial revolution was a big factor. Power-driven machines were developed. Large factories sprang up that used natural resources. Energy was required. Pollutants were released. The landscape was altered.

GOVERNMENT POLICIES

In the late 1800s, people began to see that excessive use would deplete natural resource supplies. Attitudes about resource use began to change. Citizens started asking for regulations to prevent waste. Federal, state, and local government agencies got involved.

Wildlife

The federal government enacted laws to conserve wildlife. Many of these related to species that were being threatened. One of the first efforts at preserving wildlife and the natural landscape was the creation of Yellowstone—the first national park. Yellowstone National Park was formed in 1872 when millions of acres in Wyoming, Idaho, and Montana were set aside. Today, this park is among the most popular in the nation. Some 330 protected areas are now part of the National Park Service.

Conservation of wildlife was promoted by federal laws. The Lacey Act (1900) regulated the shipment of illegally killed animals. The Migratory Bird Hunting Stamp Act (1934) required duck and other migratory bird hunters to buy special stamps. Income from the stamps was used to support the well-being of migratory game birds. The Endangered Species Act (1966) protected endangered and threatened wildlife species. In 1966, a Wildlife Refuge System was created to bring all refuges into one unit. There are now more than 400 wildlife refuges in the system.

4-11. This bull elk is protected in Yellowstone National Park.

Forests

Vast areas of forestland were obtained by the federal government starting in the early 1900s. The U.S. Forest Service was set up in 1905 in the U.S. Department of Agriculture. The Service promotes the best use of forestland. Some 191 million acres are now in National Forests. This includes land in trees and rangeland that grows grass and herbs for animal grazing.

Programs of the government and timber companies have promoted forest conservation among private landowners. Funds to help reclaim eroded land and establish forests have been provided. Millions of trees have been planted under these programs.

Soil

Soil loss was a problem from the earliest days of the United States. Jared Eliot carried out experiments on soil erosion in the early 1700s. He recognized the problems that could result if no action was taken to conserve the soil. Most people lacked foresight and only wanted to get all they could out of the soil. Little thought was given to the future.

Farm practices ignored soil fertility and water quality. Steep hillsides were plowed. Rain washed away the topsoil. Gullies developed. The land was no longer productive. New land areas were planted and used until they, too, eroded and were no longer productive. By the 1890s, millions of acres of land had been damaged by bad soil use practices.

In the 1930s, no natural resource received more attention than soil. This was because of droughts that resulted in much topsoil loss caused by wind erosion. The skies were darkened in many areas of the United States with dust-filled winds. Areas of the Great Plains were named the *"Dust Bowl."* Federal agencies were set up with the specific mission of saving fertile soil. Today, the agencies focus on current needs in reclaiming land and promoting conservation.

Water

Water conservation and soil conservation are closely related. Water washes away unprotected soil. The soil particles damage the quality of the water. These particles form silt. Silt settles from water when its flow rate slows. Deposits of silt can clog rivers and create floods over land that is normally above the flood zone. Efforts in the late 1800s focused on improving rivers as waterways for transporting raw materials and products. In the early 1900s, some attention was focused on flood control.

By the mid-1900s, water shortages were beginning to become concerns. Federal programs were set up to promote building terraces, ponds, and other ways of holding water on the land. The water would soak into the soil and gradually restore the groundwater.

Today, federal programs promote the use of water conservation structures. Watershed areas are studied and ponds, terraces, and other structures are used to reduce water runoff. Regulations also restrict access to groundwater. Permits are needed to drill wells into water aquifers. Water use from streams and reservoirs is also controlled. Without controls, some streams would have no flowing water. It would all be used by factories and in agricultural production!

Environmental Conservation

Many factories began during the industrial revolution. The factories often released smoke and wastes into the air and water. These caused pollution. In the air, the materials came to the earth as polluted precipitation. In some cases, the precipitation combined with nitrogen and other elements in the air forming acid rain.

In 1970, the Environmental Protection Agency was established. This Agency sets and enforces guidelines on the release of pollutants. It collaborates with state and local government agencies in an attempt to assure a good environment.

Factories, animal producers, and others cannot release substances that cause damage into the environment. Smoke must be cleaned before release. Water must be cleaned so its release will not alter the natural water in a stream or lake.

New Technologies

New technologies have emerged to promote conservation. These technologies use fewer inputs and allow precise assessment of soil, moisture, and other conditions. Here are a few examples:

■ Global positioning—Global positioning systems were adapted to agricul-

4-12. Using global positioning in Mount Hood National Forest, Oregon.

tural use in 1993. These have now been integrated with controllers and monitors to implement precision farming.

- Genetic engineering—Genetically altered crop plants can be grown that do not require extensive pesticide use.
- Biological pest control—Many approaches are being used to reduce the use of pesticides.
- Minimum/no-tillage cropping—Special equipment is used to plant and grow crops without traditional plowing. This reduces soil loss to erosion. It also helps conserve moisture by not exposing loose soil to the air.
- Wind and solar power—Alternative sources of energy are being used to operate agricultural equipment. This includes using wind to generate electrical power for agricultural facilities.
- Pesticide container reclamation—Pesticide containers can be reclaimed for use by manufacturers. This reduces pesticide residues getting into the water and soil.
- Remote sensing—Remote sensing involves collecting information from a distance away for what is being studied. In some cases, satellites collect information about water, soil, plant diseases, and other conditions. This information helps managers make decisions about what is needed with a crop.

4-13. The Muir Woods National Monument near San Francisco recognizes the work of John Muir. (The area preserves plant and animal life in the area for study.)

LEADERS IN THE CONSERVATION MOVEMENT

Some people began to realize that natural resources were limited in the late 1800s and early 1900s. These individuals were pioneers in the conservation movement. The federal government passed laws and set up agencies to help with conservation. Parks to preserve resources were set up. A few of the leaders in conservation are included here.

JOHN MUIR

John Muir (1838-1914) was an explorer and naturalist. He traveled and studied the forest areas of the United States. He is probably best known for explorations in what is now the Yo-

Table 4-1.
Selected Events in the History of U.S. Conservation

Date	Event/Result
1862	Morrill Act passed — set up a system of colleges to teach agriculture and related areas (Today, these schools teach and research many areas of conservation and environmental technology.)
1872	Yellowstone Park established — to preserve natural features and scenic beauty of the area (first national park in the world)
1900	Lacey Act passed U.S. Congress — made transporting illegally killed wildlife across state lines a federal crime
1903	First wildlife refuge established at Pelican Island, Florida
1911	Weeks Law passed by Congress — provided for multiple use of national forests and other public lands
1917	Smith-Hughes Act passed — provided federal funds for local schools to use in teaching agriculture (Many schools have taught and continue to teach areas related to natural resources and the environment.)
1933	Civilian Conservation Corps established — workers planted trees, built dams to control floods, fought forest fires, and constructed areas for viewing wildlife and nature
1933	Tennessee Valley Authority created — purpose was to conserve the resources of along the Tennessee River and promote hydroelectric power
1935	Soil Conservation Service established — purpose was to work with landowners in designing and promoting plans to conserve soil and water resources (Later changed to the Natural Resource Conservation Service.)
1937	Federal Aid in Wildlife Restoration Act passed — levied a tax on sporting arms and ammunition to support wildlife management
1963	Clean Air Act passed — as initially passed and later amended, the Act set emission standards for automobiles and industry and set standards for air quality
1969	National Environmental Policy Act passed — requires consideration of the environment in construction, including the preparation of impact statements
1970	Environmental Protection Agency created — sets and enforces rules and standards in pollution control
1973	Endangered Species Act passed — provided protection for threatened and endangered species of wildlife
1977	Department of Energy created — purpose was to promote conservation in use of fossil fuels and seek alternative sources of energy

(Continued)

Date	Event/Result
1985	Conservation Reserve Program initiated — provided incentives for landowners to remove marginal land from production and use conservation practices
1993	North American Free Trade Agreement adopted — opened trade with Mexico and Canada; some consumers question conditions under which imported food crops are grown
1998	Federal deadline for replacing underground fuel tanks reached on December 22; new-type tanks that prevent fuel leaks required; thousands of gas stations failed to meet deadline

Table 4-1 (Continued)

semite and Sequoia National Parks in California. Muir wrote about many of the things he saw and how conservation was needed. He was instrumental in encouraging President Theodore Roosevelt to take action to conserve the forest areas. Muir founded the Sierra Club in 1892 to promote conservation.

THEODORE ROOSEVELT

Theodore Roosevelt (1858-1919) made many contributions to conservation. Roosevelt served as U.S. President in 1901-1909. He set up the first wildlife refuge at Pelican Island, Florida, in 1903. Millions of acres of forests were added to the nation's reserves during his presidency. In 1908, Roosevelt promoted widespread conservation by the states. Today, the Theodore Roosevelt National Park in western North Dakota includes one of the land areas that Roosevelt personally owned.

4-14. President Theodore "Teddy" Roosevelt is considered to be the father of the conservation movement in the United States.

ALDO LEOPOLD

Aldo Leopold (1886-1948) pioneered the use of ecology in studying wildlife. He stressed the importance of education in helping people make responsible use of natural resources. He authored a textbook entitled *Game Management* that was widely used in educating wildlife biologists. He is widely known for his efforts to set up professional training in wildlife management.

GIFFORD PINCHOT

Gifford Pinchot (1865-1946) promoted the conservation of forests and other natural resources. From 1898 until 1910, he headed the agency in the federal government that is today known as the Forest Service. Pinchot became president of the National Conservation Committee and wrote *The Fight for Conservation*, a book that described his efforts.

FRANKLIN D. ROOSEVELT

Franklin D. Roosevelt (1882-1945) was instrumental as U.S. President during the 1930s and early 1940s with legislation to protect natural resources. He encouraged all state legislatures to enact conservation laws. His efforts also included setting up an agency in the U.S. Department of Agriculture with the mission of conserving soil and water. The programs involved landowners in planning and implementing conservation practices that were subsidized with federal funds. Roosevelt served longer than any other president. He had some difficult situations to deal with, such as the depression of the 1930s and World War II in the early 1940s.

4-15. President Franklin D. Roosevelt approved numerous programs to protect soil, water, and other natural resources.

HUGH H. BENNETT

Hugh H. Bennett (1881-1960) is known as the "father of soil conservation." He was the first head of the Soil Conservation Service in the U.S. Department of Agriculture. Bennett advocated using scientific methods to determine soil qualities and needed nutrients. He promoted a wide range of soil conservation practices. His birth home in Anson County, North Carolina, is today used as a conservation education center. (Today, the Soil Conservation Service functions are carried out by the Natural Resource Conservation Service of the USDA.)

4-16. Hugh Bennett was the organizer of an agency in the U.S. Department of Agriculture to promote soil conservation.

Resource Connection

RACHEL CARSON NATIONAL WILDLIFE REFUGE

The Rachel Carson National Wildlife Refuge was established in Maine to preserve a place for visitors to observe nature. The Refuge borders the seashore and offers opportunity to observe wetland areas. Changes in plant species are evident as water and land elevation change. Carefully marked trails have signs that explain what is taking place.

The Refuge recognizes the efforts of Carson in promoting environmental responsibility. It is a part of the National Wildlife Refuge System of the U.S. Department of the Interior.

RACHEL CARSON

Rachel Carson (1907-1964) won acclaim for her efforts to inform the public of risks she felt went with the use of pesticides. Her efforts led to government restrictions on using pesticides. Many people tried to discredit her work. Carson was a marine biologist and science writer. As a writer, she stressed the interrelationships of living things. Her best-known book was *Silent Spring*, published in 1962.

REVIEWING

MAIN IDEAS

Natural resource conservation is using resources wisely. The goal is to work and live in ways that use fewer resources. This will help limited resources last much longer.

Humans have a responsibility to conserve natural resources. Complex issues are involved. Symbiotic relationships exist between the species that live on the earth. Living organisms are interdependent.

Natural resources can be damaged in several ways. Pollution releases hazardous materials into natural resources. Some natural resources can be lost, such as soil. The quality of natural resources can be lowered by degrading them.

Pollution sources are of two types: point source and nonpoint source pollution. Point source pollution is from sources that can be readily identified. Nonpoint source pollution is from many sources that cannot be directly identified.

The history of conservation grew out of exploitation. Early settlers used resources for their own personal gain without thinking of the future. Concern began to grow in the late 1800s. Government policies and programs for wildlife, forests, water, soil, and other areas were set up. Today, new technologies are being used to conserve resources.

Several leaders in conservation were John Muir, Theodore Roosevelt, Aldo Leopold, Gifford Pinchot, Franklin D. Roosevelt, and Rachel Carson.

QUESTIONS

Answer the following questions using complete sentences and correct spelling.

1. What is natural resource conservation? Why is it important?
2. What are two reasons for conservation? Briefly explain each.
3. What are two examples of how to conserve natural resources? Briefly explain each.
4. What is the meaning of interdependent relationships?
5. What is pollution?
6. What undesirable changes might be caused by pollution in the biosphere?
7. What are some examples of landscape degradation?
8. What are the two types of pollution sources? Compare and contrast the two.
9. What is exploitation of natural resources? How did it create problems?
10. Why are water and soil conservation closely related?
11. What did the Lacey Act do to protect wildlife?
12. What are the names of two people who were leaders in the conservation movement? Briefly describe what each did.

EVALUATING

Match the term with the correct definition. Write the letter by the term in the blank provided.

a. Dust Bowl
b. symbiotic relationship
c. pollutant
d. landscape degradation
e. economic value

f. aesthetic benefit
g. point source pollution
h. Aldo Leopold
i. Gifford Pinchot
j. Rachel Carson

_____ 1. Occurs when different species live together and benefit from each other.

_____ 2. Area of the Great Plains that suffered severe wind erosion in the 1930s.

_____ 3. Informed the public about environmental risks in using pesticides.

_____ 4. Used ecology in studying wildlife.

_____ 5. A source of pollution that is readily identifiable.

_____ 6. An early leader in the conservation of forests.

_____ 7. A material that causes pollution.

_____ 8. A feature that has human appeal.

_____ 9. The value of a resource in terms of economics.

_____ 10. Changing the features of the earth's surface so natural features are less appealing.

EXPLORING

1. Invite a representative of the local soil and water conservation district to serve as a resource person in class. Have him or her discuss major problems in soil and water conservation and what is being done to solve the problems.

2. Visit a farm where terraces are being laid out and constructed. Study the "lay" of the terrace on the contour of the land. Sketch a map of the area around the terrace. Label features, such as streams, hills, gullies, and ponds.

3. Identify major cropping practices that conserve resources in the local area near your home. Interview a landowner or conservationist about the practices. Prepare a report on your observations.

5

SOIL

Soil is an important natural resource. It provides nutrients that support plant growth. Good plant growth is needed because the products of plants are essential in human life!

Some people fail to appreciate soil. They may call it dirt! Soil is not dirt. Dirt is an unclean material. Soil itself is not dirty. It can sometimes be contaminated. If soil is out of place, such as on the floor of your room, it makes the floor dirty. Give it proper respect—call it soil!

Why is soil so important? It has major roles in most of the things we use. Make a list of all the things you have that in one way or another came from the soil. You will have a long list. Which of these would you be willing to do without? Our future well-being depends on having good soil!

5-1. Corn needs many nutrients from the soil for a high yield.

OBJECTIVES

This chapter is about the nature and importance of soil. The focus is on soil as an important natural resource. The chapter has the following objectives:

1. Explain the importance of soil
2. Identify the components of soil
3. Explain how soil is formed
4. Describe the chemical nature of soil
5. Describe the physical nature of soil
6. Explain soil profiles
7. Explain moisture in soil

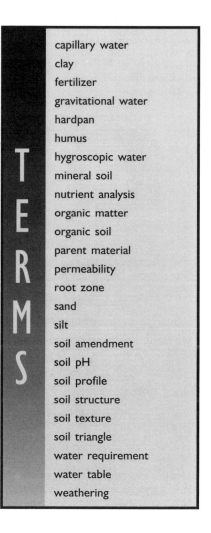

TERMS

capillary water
clay
fertilizer
gravitational water
hardpan
humus
hygroscopic water
mineral soil
nutrient analysis
organic matter
organic soil
parent material
permeability
root zone
sand
silt
soil amendment
soil pH
soil profile
soil structure
soil texture
soil triangle
water requirement
water table
weathering

**Soil Science Education
Home Page
http://ltpwww.gsfc.nasa.gov/globe/index.htm**

THE IMPORTANCE OF SOIL

Every living organism directly or indirectly requires soil. It is the main source of the food supply because it supports and nourishes plants.

Soil is a fragile resource. It can be easily damaged or lost. Many years are needed to renew soil. Because of the time required to renew soil, some people say that soil is a nonrenewable natural resource. Soil is viewed as a renewable natural resource. You may view soil as renewable after learning about soil conservation.

Soil is important for many reasons. A few are listed here:

- Plant growth—Soil provides nutrients for plant growth. Roots of plants grow throughout the area of the soil known as the ***root zone***. Contact by roots with the soil anchors plants. This keeps plants upright so the leaves can gather energy from sunlight.

5-2. Soil promotes attractive landscapes, such as in Butchart Gardens near Victoria, British Columbia.

- Habitat for microbes—The soil is home to many microorganisms. These organisms help renew the soil. They decompose organic matter, such as leaves and stems. This process restores nutrients to the soil and helps clean the environment of wastes.

- Renew water—The movement of water through soil to the layers of the earth below removes impurities from water. This movement is an important part of the water cycle. The soil acts much like a filter.

- Sites for structures—Soil serves as the part of the earth on which homes and other structures are built. In some cases, foundations go well below the surface.

- Reservoirs—Soil can be shaped into lakes and ponds to hold water. These facilities serve cattle and other animals as sources of water. Reservoirs can be used for fish farming. Large ponds with special designs are often used in raising fish.

- Waste disposal—Structures built in the soil are used for waste disposal. Landfills, septic tanks, and other facilities are used. These allow natural decay to occur.

- Aesthetics—Soil allows the surface of the earth to be attractive. Natural landscapes as well as those installed at homes, parks, and other sites provide beauty.

SOIL CONTENT

Soil is made of four major components: minerals, water, air, and organic matter. Minerals and organic matter are solid materials. Water in soil is in liquid or vapor form except when the ground freezes. Air is found in small pockets or spaces between particles not filled with water.

Soil also contains living organisms, such as bacteria, insect larvae, earthworms, and fungi. These have important roles in the usefulness of soil.

MINERALS

A soil that has more minerals than other materials is known as a **mineral soil**. Mineral soils are found throughout the United States. Greater concentration is in the dry areas of the Southwest. The mineral materials in soil are grouped by size. The proportions of the materials vary. The materials by size are:

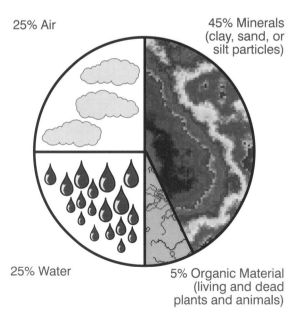

25% Air

45% Minerals (clay, sand, or silt particles)

25% Water

5% Organic Material (living and dead plants and animals)

5-3. Typical soil contents.

- Sand—**Sand** is the component of soil with the largest particle size. Sand is often of quartz origin, but may consist of other minerals. Sand is also known as silicon dioxide (SiO_2). Soil that has a high amount of sand dries out quickly and holds less water than soil high in other mineral materials. Most soils with high sand content have low fertility.

- Silt—*Silt* is the component of soil of medium particle size–smaller than sand and larger than clay. Silt particles fill spaces between sand particles. Silt is often moved by water. Large areas of fertile land near streams are made of silt. It was left behind when the stream overflowed its banks. High-silt soils are fertile and hold more water than soils high in sand.

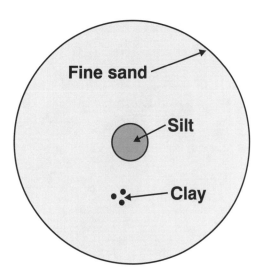

5-4. Proportionate size of mineral soil materials.

- Clay—*Clay* is the smallest-size particle in soil. The particles fill spaces between sand and silt materials. Clay soils hold water better than sand or silt. Clay soils are slow to dry out after a rain. Clay helps hold the nutrients that plants need for growth.

WATER

Water is held between and around soil particles. Some soils hold water better than other soils. The amount held depends on the solid materials that makeup the soil. Soils that both drain adequately and hold water for plant growth are best suited for crops.

AIR

Air is in spaces between soil particles. It shares the space with water. Adding water drives out air. As water dries from the soil, air returns to the spaces between the soil particles.

Most plants need a balance of air and water in the soil. Soil that is wet has little air. Since the roots of terrestrial plants require air, wet soil damages roots and slows plant growth. Plants may die if the soil remains wet too long. The first sign of wet soil is yellowing of the leaves. A good example is corn. Leaves turn yellow on corn plants that have been growing in fields that are too wet. Yellowing can also be due to nutrient deficiencies, such as nitrogen. Check soil moisture before deciding on the cause of yellowing.

5-5. Deep plowing formed rows as one step in preparing a seedbed. (Unfortunately, the surface is unprotected from damage and loss.)

ORGANIC MATTER

Organic matter is decaying plant and animal remains. Dead leaves, stems, fruit, and roots of plants decay to form organic matter. Animal flesh also decays into organic matter. A forest floor is covered with decaying materials. Decay returns nutrients to the soil. These nutrients are used by plants for growth. A soil that is high in organic matter is known as an **organic soil**. Organic matter that is well decomposed is known as **humus**. Soils high in humus have higher fertility and darker colors. Peat and muck are two examples, with dark brown or black colors. These soils tend to hold water for plant growth. Soils with light colors are low in humus and often lack nutrients.

5-6. Plant and animal remains decay under trees in a forest to form organic matter.

Microbes, earthworms, and other organisms living in the soil release nutrients from organic matter. One gram of soil may contain as many as four billion bacteria, one million fungi, and 100,000 algae!

Organic matter is needed for plant growth. Gardeners often collect and return plant clippings to the soil. This adds organic matter and results in the best vegetables and flowers. Some gardeners use composted materials, including manure, to assure fertility. Crop producers chop plant stalks and plow them into the soil or leave them on the surface to protect the soil.

SOIL FORMATION

Soil slowly forms over many years. A number of natural processes are involved in soil formation. Changes are taking place in soil every day. New soil is being formed. Nutrients are being used and lost.

Weathering is the process of materials becoming soil. The process is very slow. Weathering depends on important factors:

■ Parent Material—*Parent material* is the mineral and organic matter from which soil is formed. The mineral parent material is rock, such as shale, limestone, and sandstone. Much weathering is needed for rock to become soil. Natural chemical and breaking processes cause the rock to crack apart. Flowing water, freezing and thawing, acids in water, and other climate factors aid weathering.

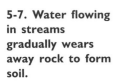
5-7. Water flowing in streams gradually wears away rock to form soil.

5-8. Earthworms live in the soil and improve its aeration.

■ Climate—Climate includes precipitation, temperature, wind, and other factors. These influence weathering. Water in cracks may freeze and force the rocks to move slightly. Movement causes breaking. Rocks in streams bump together and break into smaller rocks.

■ Living Organisms—Soil processes are affected by all organisms that live in it, such as microbes, ants, earthworms, insects, nematodes, spiders, and rodents. Plants affect soil by removing nutrients, sending roots deep below the surface, and covering the surface to protect the soil from damage.

   People have big impacts on the soil. They use machinery to excavate large areas, cut down trees, and drain wetland areas. Using pesticides on plants can kill living organisms in the soil. People sometimes pollute by dumping wastes on the soil.

■ Topography—Topography is the shape of the surface of the earth. It includes hills, valleys, streams, and other features. Weathering occurs faster in some places than others. For example, water moves down a slope faster than it moves on nearly level land. Soil at the bottom of a hill may be rich in organic matter from materials that have decomposed and washed down. Soil on the side of a hill may be drier and have fewer nutrients than soil at the bottom of the hill.

■ Time—Time can neither be replaced, stored, nor increased. Soil can renew itself over time, but humans often interfere with the renewal process. Soil along a creek bottom might be fairly new since it is more recently deposited than soil in an upland region. Soil on a hilltop could be hundreds of years old. This means that extra care is needed to conserve soil on hills.

CHEMICAL NATURE OF SOIL

The chemical nature of soil deals with pH and nutrients. It can be modified using soil amendments. A *soil amendment* is a material added to soil to improve its ability to support plant growth. Soil amendments are used based on the needs of the soil.

pH

Soil pH is the acidity or alkalinity of soil. pH is measured on a scale ranging from 0 to 14, with 7.0 being neutral. pH below 7.0 is increasingly acidic as the number goes down. Above 7.0, soil pH is increasingly alkaline the higher the number. Most soil is in the pH range of 4.0 to 8.0. pH is determined by analyzing a soil sample. The sample can be sent to a laboratory or analyzed using a pH testing kit.

pH can be changed by using soil amendments. With acid soils, amendments that are highly alkaline are used. For example, dolomitic lime is added to acid soil to raise the pH. The amount to add depends on the acidity and pH needed. In alkaline soils, the pH is lowered using amendments that are acidic, such as aluminum sulfate $(Al_2(SO_4)_3)$.

pH influences the availability of nutrients to plants. For example, phosphorus is available to plants at a pH range of 5.5 to 7.5. Even when present in the soil, phosphorus is not readily available if the pH is below 5.5 or above 7.5. Most plants prefer a soil pH range of 6.0 to 8.0.

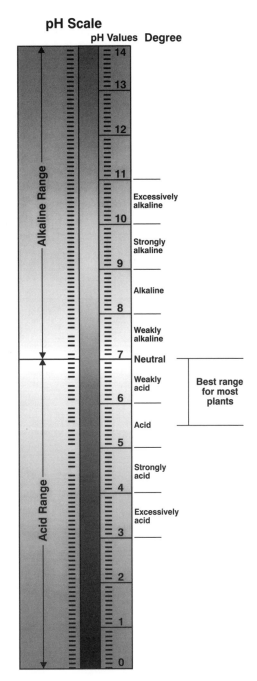

5-9. The pH scale.

NUTRIENTS

Plants need nutrients to grow. The proper nutrients must be present in the soil or added as soil amendments. **Nutrient analysis** is used to test the soil to determine the kinds and amounts of nutrients that are present.

The results of nutrient analysis are used to apply soil amendments. Soil amendments containing nutrients are known as **fertilizer**. Only the nutrients that are deficient in soil and needed by plants should be applied. Using too much fertilizer or the wrong nutrients is wasteful and can damage natural resources. Excess fertilizer can wash into streams and lakes or damage the soil.

Plants require 17 nutrients. The nutrients are often referred to as chemical elements. Ten nutrients are macronutrients because they are needed in larger amounts. Nitrogen, phosphorus, and potassium are the nutrients needed in largest amounts that are most likely to be deficient in the soil.

Table 5-1.
Essential Plant Nutrients

Macronutrients	Symbol	Micronutrients	Symbol
carbon	C	iron	Fe
hydrogen	H	zinc	Zn
oxygen	O	copper	Cu
nitrogen	N	boron	B
potassium	K	molybdenum	Mo
phosphorus	P	manganese	Mn
calcium	Ca	chlorine	Cl
magnesium	Mg	cobalt	Co
sulfur	S	vanadium	V
sodium	Na	silicon	Si

PHYSICAL NATURE OF SOIL

Soil is classified in several ways based on its physical nature: texture, depth, color, structure, consistency, and permeability.

SOIL TEXTURE

Soil texture is the proportion of sand, silt, and clay. Most soils are mixtures of materials. Very few soils do not have at least small amounts of all three. Sand on a beach may be nearly all sand; clay used in making brick may be nearly all clay.

Soils are named on the basis of texture. Loam is made of equal parts of sand, silt, and clay. Different names are used to indicate ranges of different materials.

Career Profile

SOIL PHYSICIST

A soil physicist studies processes in the soil. This includes how soil is formed and lost. The work may include studying pesticide residues and acid rain. Much of their work deals with water supply and movement in the soil.

Soil physicists have college degrees in soil science, horticulture, agronomy, geology, or related areas. Most have masters or doctors degrees in one of the same areas. Many have minors in areas of science to help gain understanding of soil processes and relationships. Taking high school courses in agriculture, chemistry, and physics is good preparation for college study.

Jobs are found with research stations, universities, government agencies, and selected private industries. (This photo shows a soil physicist simulating rainfall with irrigation equipment to study the movement and reactions of chemicals in the soil.) (Courtesy, Agricultural Research Service, USDA)

A *soil triangle* is a way of showing proportions of sand, silt, and clay in soil. The soil triangle indicates how soil textures are related to the materials found in the soil. It also shows how the different textures relate to each other.

Texture is important in using soil. Texture determines the kinds of practices that should be used. For example, sandy soil holds little moisture and may not be suitable for crops. Buildings, recreational fields, and other areas are also built using information about the soil.

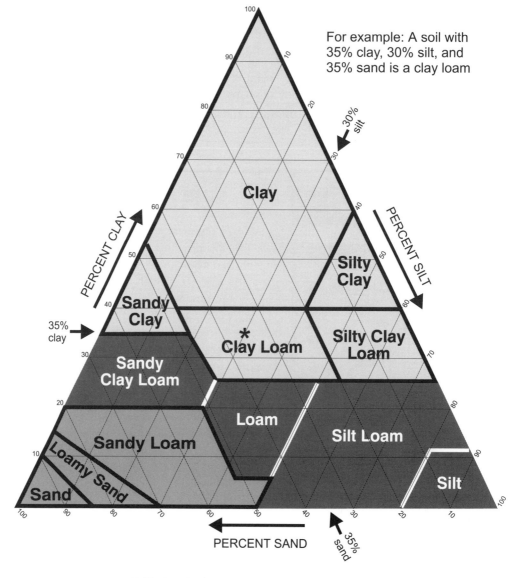

For example: A soil with 35% clay, 30% silt, and 35% sand is a clay loam

5-10. A soil triangle helps classify soil by texture.

SOIL DEPTH

Soil depth is the thickness of the soil layers. Very shallow soils are usually less than 10 feet (3 m) thick. Shallow soils are 10 to 20 feet (3–6 m) thick. Medium-depth soils are 20 to 40 feet (6–12 m) thick. Deep soils are more than 40 feet (12 m) thick.

SOIL COLOR

Soil color varies with the parent material and amount of organic matter. Soils that are gray to off-white are formed from a parent material of quartz. Darker soil contains more organic matter. Soils that are red have a high iron content. Soil that is wet often has a gray or whitish color. Soil color is also associated with the depth being studied.

STRUCTURE

Soil structure is the arrangement of soil particles into shapes and pieces. Soils can have eight different types of structure: granular, plate, subangular, blocky, prismatic, flat, single grain, or columnar. Structure influences the properties of soil. Water moves faster through a granular soil than through a

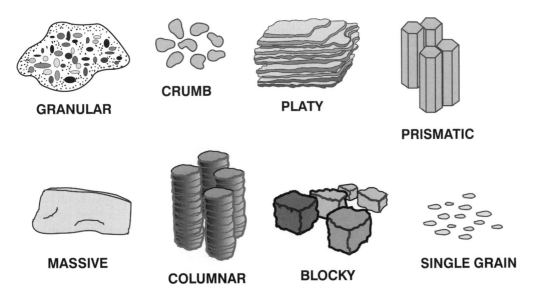

GRANULAR **CRUMB** **PLATY** **PRISMATIC**

MASSIVE **COLUMNAR** **BLOCKY** **SINGLE GRAIN**

5-11. Sample soil structures.

plate-structure soil. Root growth is better in granular than in prismatic structure soil.

CONSISTENCY

Consistency is how easy it is to work with a soil. Some soils, such as those high in clay, are hard when dry and sticky when wet. They are not easy to plow. Soils with sand tend to be loose and easy to work. Sandy soils do not form hard clods when dry. Consistency is also a factor in water movement.

The consistency of soil in a lawn, garden, or field can be altered to some extent. Adding sand or organic matter to clay will make the soil looser and easier to work. Organic matter is often added as leaf mold, composted manure, and peat. Using soil amendments to change the physical consistency of soil is too costly for large areas. It is most often used with flower beds and small gardens.

PERMEABILITY

Permeability is water movement in soil. It is known as internal drainage. Permeability depends on the texture and structure of the soil. Other factors in permeability are the presence of hardpans and mulch covering on the soil. Large rock formations also affect permeability.

5-12. Soils with poor surface and internal drainage may hold water on the surface after a rain.

A ***hardpan*** is a compacted layer of soil beneath the topsoil. Hardpans interfere with water movement and root growth. Hardpans may be naturally present or made by heavy equipment moving along the surface.

Based on permeability, soil is classified as very poorly drained, poorly drained, somewhat poorly drained, moderately drained, and well drained. Most very poorly and poorly drained soils are in bottom lands or swamps near creeks or rivers. Better drained soils are above the flood levels of streams.

Soils must have appropriate internal drainage for plants to grow. Most agricultural crops require moderately to well-drained soil. Rice, watercress, and a few others will grow on land with poor internal drainage.

SOIL PROFILES

Soil is formed in layers or horizons. In a typical setting, four or five layers, or horizons, are found. The thickness of each horizon varies. Construction activity, erosion, and farming activity may alter natural soil layers.

A ***soil profile*** is a vertical section of the soil at a site. The profile shows layers of soil for a depth of a few feet depending on the nature of the soil. As soil ages, more layers are developed.

- O horizon—With undisturbed soil, as found in forests or swamps, the top layer is known as the O horizon. This layer consists of leaves, roots, limbs, and decaying matter.

- A horizon—The A horizon is the topsoil. It is the first few inches of the most fertile soil. Organic matter is concentrated in the A horizon. This layer provides nutrients for plant growth. The thickness of the A horizon varies from none in a poor soil to eight inches or more in a good soil.

- B horizon—The B horizon is the subsoil. It is found beneath the A horizon. The B horizon accumulates some nutrients from the topsoil, but little organic matter. Plant roots penetrate and use the B horizon as a source of nutrients and to anchor the plant. Trees often have roots that go below the B horizon.

- C horizon—Parent material is found in the C horizon. Few roots, insects, or organic materials are found in the C horizon.

- R horizon—The R horizon is the bedrock layer and consists of solid rock. This forms the parent material in the C horizon.

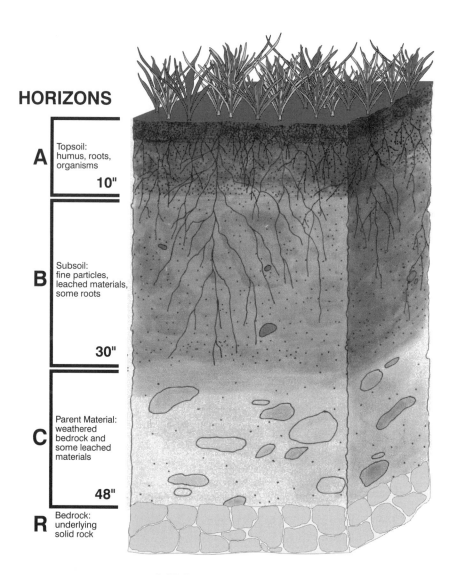

5-13. Layers in a soil profile.

Each horizon affects the quality of soil. Topsoil is formed from the layers beneath it and the materials that accumulate on the surface.

SOIL MOISTURE

Water in the soil is for plants to use in growing. Water is around and between soil particles. Some soils "hold" water better than other soils. The

Resource Connection

ROOTS GROW DEEP

Plant roots go deeper in the soil than people think. The roots are often deeper than the height of the plant! Root growth is related to soil properties, especially texture and depth. Loose soils allow more root growth. Deep soils allow roots to penetrate deeper. Compacted soils limit growth.

In good soils, root depth may be: corn, 8 ft. (2.4 m); wheat, 5 ft. (1.5 m); tomatoes, 5 ft. (1.5 m); alfalfa, 9 ft. (2.7 m); grain sorghum, 7 ft. (2.1 m); and pasture grasses, 5 ft. (1.5 m). Unfortunately, weeds grow root systems of the same size.

Good root growth is essential for plant growth. Compacted soils block root growth. Hardpans restrict the penetration of roots below the pan. Root systems that do not develop are unable to absorb needed nutrients and water. Roots also anchor plants so they do not fall over. This is especially important with trees, corn, and grain sorghum.

This shows a crab grass plant that is 7 inches (17.8 cm) tall above the soil with roots 22 inches (55.9 cm) long!

amount of water depends on the solid materials that makeup the soil. Soils must also have adequate air for plant growth. "Wet" soils hold too much water and not enough air for many crop plants.

WATER REQUIREMENT

Water requirement is the amount of moisture plants need. It is usually stated as the number of pounds of water needed for a plant to produce a pound of dry matter. Pounds of water are converted to acre-inches of water.

An acre-inch is the amount of water required to cover one acre to a depth of one inch. Wheat and oats typically need 18 acre-inches. Corn needs slightly more or about 20 acre-inches. Lawn grasses and ornamental plants need 24 or more acre-inches depending on the growth condition desired in the lawn. Fruit trees, clovers, and alfalfa have higher water requirements.

If the water for a crop is not naturally present in the soil, irrigation will be needed. Irrigation is the artificial application of water to the soil. The

5-14. The water table in this soil is about 20 inches (51 cm) deep.

amount of irrigation needed is determined by measuring available soil moisture. (More information on water is presented in chapter 7.)

WATER TABLE

Water table is the surface of the groundwater. Groundwater is where soil and rock formations are saturated with water. If a hole were dug downward into the soil, the water table would be the level at which water would rise in the hole. The distance from the top of the soil to the water table will vary. In some places, the water table is only a couple of feet deep. In other places, it may be many feet deep and below the depth of normal digging or boring.

Water table influences soil fertility and use of land. Water tables that are near the surface may make the land unfit for many crops. The soil may lack adequate drainage and air. Water tables that are a few feet downward can help provide water for crop growth. The water moves upward in the soil into the root zones of plants.

Climate, especially precipitation, is important for soil to have sufficient moisture for crop growth. In some cases, water may stand on the surface of the soil for days, weeks, or longer. Such land is not suitable for crops. Land with standing water on the surface is important in restoring groundwater and renewing aquifers.

WATER AVAILABILITY

Some of the water in soil is readily available to plants. Other water is held tightly by the soil particles and not readily available to plants. The amount of water soil holds and how it is held are related to soil texture.

Three forms of water are found in soil: gravitational, capillary, and hygroscopic.

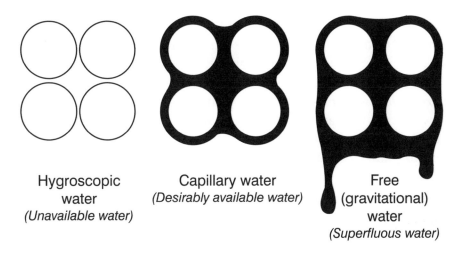

Hygroscopic water
(Unavailable water)

Capillary water
(Desirably available water)

Free (gravitational) water
(Superfluous water)

5-15. Forms of water in soil.

Gravitational water is the water that drains downward through the soil. It moves through cracks, spaces between particles, and other openings in the soil. Too much gravitational water can damage plants if it does not drain out of the zone where the roots grow. Gravitational water helps restore the supply of groundwater. Sandy soils typically have good gravitational water movement.

Capillary water is the water held between the soil particles. It moves from one particle to another by capillary action. Soils made-up of higher amounts of clay have more spaces between the tiny particles and hold more capillary water. Sometimes, they are poorly drained and are not good for

5-16. Freezing forces water from the soil. (This close-up shows ice formed from soil water. The ice crystals are about 3 inches (7.6 cm) long! Freezing loosens soil and results in water and soil loss. As the crystals melt, most of the water is lost from the soil because it enters the air as vapor.)

planting crops. On the other hand, soil high in sand has fewer, but larger, spaces between the particles. This results in the soil drying out quickly and not holding enough water for crop production. Capillary water is the most important water for terrestrial plant growth.

Hygroscopic water is the water that adheres to each soil particle. It forms a very thin film around the particles. Hygroscopic water is found even in the driest soils under natural conditions. Hygroscopic water is not readily available to plants because it moves only in vapor form.

REVIEWING

MAIN IDEAS

Soil is an important natural resource. It contains minerals, water, air, and organic matter. These provide nutrients for plant growth.

Soil slowly forms from parent material over many years through the process of weathering. The rate of soil formation depends on climate, living organisms, and topography. A soil profile shows the layered structure of soil.

The physical characteristics of soil include texture, depth, color, structure, consistency, and permeability. The texture of soil is determined by the proportions of sand, silt, and clay. A soil triangle is used to explain how these proportions relate to soil texture. Texture is more important than the other physical characteristics.

The chemical characteristics of soil include pH and nutrient analysis. pH is the degree of acidity or alkalinity of soil. Nutrient analysis indicates the nutrients present. The information is used to know the nutrients needed to enhance soil fertility.

Soil profiles are used to understand the layered character of soil. Profiles give information on hardpans, water permeability, and water tables.

QUESTIONS

Answer the following questions using complete sentences and correct spelling.

1. What are the reasons soil is important?
2. What are the four major components of soil?

3. What are the mineral materials in soil? Compare the materials based on particle size.

4. What are the sources of organic matter in soil?

5. How is soil formed?

6. What is soil pH?

7. What nutrients are present in soil?

8. What comprises the physical nature of soil?

9. What is a soil profile?

10. What are the ways water is held in soil? Classify each by availability of the water for plant use.

EVALUATING

Match the term with the correct definition. Write the letter by the term in the blank provided.

a. clay   e. mineral soil   i. permeability
b. organic matter   f. root zone   j. soil texture
c. water table   g. parent material
d. weathering   h. soil amendment

_____ 1. A soil that has more minerals than other materials.

_____ 2. The mineral and organic material from which soil is formed.

_____ 3. Water movement through the soil.

_____ 4. The smallest particle sizes in soil.

_____ 5. The relative proportion of soil components by particle size.

_____ 6. The level at which water saturates the ground.

_____ 7. The area in soil where roots are found.

_____ 8. Material added to soil to improve its productivity.

_____ 9. The process of materials becoming soil.

_____ 10. Decaying remains of plants and animals form soil.

EXPLORING

1. Determine the texture of a soil sample using the ribbon test. Follow these steps:

   a. Moisten a sample of soil to the consistency of putty.

   b. From this sample, make a ball about ½ inch in diameter.

   c. Hold the ball between the thumb and forefinger, and gradually press the thumb forward, forming the soil into a ribbon.

   d. If the ribbon forms easily, and is long and pliable, the soil is fine textured.

   e. If the ribbon forms, but breaks into pieces ¾ to 1 inch long, the soil is moderately textured.

   f. If no ribbon is formed, and the soil feels very gritty, the soil is moderately coarse textured.

   g. If the sample consists almost entirely of gritty material and leaves little or no stain on the hand, it is coarse textured.

2. Collect a soil sample and make a pH and nutrient analysis. If testing equipment is not available, send the sample to a testing lab for analysis.

6

SOIL CONSERVATION

Why is soil conservation important? The main reason is that we depend on the soil to grow the crops that provide food and clothing. That should be all the answer that is needed to the question!

Soil loss each year may run 10 tons or more of soil per acre. That is a lot of soil productivity! Once gone, it is impossible to get it back. Many years are required for more topsoil to form. Our best approach is to reduce soil loss.

Soil is damaged in many ways. Nearly all soil damage can be prevented. Following a few simple practices can protect soil and conserve it for future generations.

6-1. A soil scientist using a special camera to monitor soil processes. (Courtesy, Agricultural Research Service, USDA)

OBJECTIVES

This chapter covers the importance of conservation and practices used in maintaining soil productivity. The following objectives are included:

1. Describe how soil is lost and damaged

2. Describe the meaning and importance of wetlands

3. Describe practices to prevent soil loss

4. Explain the process of soil renewal

5. Name important soil amendments and describe the role of each

6. Collect soil samples and use appropriate tests in assessing soil condition

7. List examples of soil conservation practices in urban areas and with agriculture

TERMS

conservation practice
conservation tillage
contouring
crop rotation
grassed waterway
gully erosion
minimum tillage
mulch
no-till
rill erosion
sheet erosion
shelterbreak
silt fence
soil conservation
soil degradation
soil erosion
strip cropping
terrace
tilth
topsoil
vegetative cover
water erosion
wetland
windbreak
wind erosion

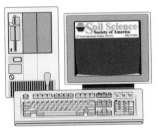

**Soil Science
Society of America
http://www.soils.org/**

HOW SOIL IS DAMAGED

Soil may be damaged in many ways. It may be lost because of erosion or degraded by human actions. People sometimes fail to think how soil is damaged by their actions. Merely driving an automobile onto the lawn at your home compacts the soil under the wheels. Compaction damages the soil.

EROSION

Soil erosion is the loss of soil. It is removed from the land and may add pollution to water or air. Erosion destroys the fertility of soil. Some erosion is natural. Big losses are caused by human actions, such as plowing, excavating, or otherwise leaving the soil unprotected.

Erosion begins with topsoil. *Topsoil* is the first few inches of soil with the greatest fertility. Losing topsoil results in the loss of important nutrients. Some erosion happens with the best managed soil. Erosion cannot be totally stopped but it can be reduced to a very low level.

6-2. Massive water erosion has resulted in a canyon washed in land that was once a forest. (Courtesy, Stephen J. Lee, North Carolina)

Causes of Erosion

Natural erosion results from the action of wind, water, glacial movement, and other natural events. When land is plowed or cleared of protective covering, it is much more susceptible to erosion.

■ Wind—*Wind erosion* is the loss of soil due to wind. It usually occurs in dry climates where the soil is loose. The wind picks up tiny particles of soil and moves them about. Strong winds can blow particles long distances. Very little wind erosion occurs where the soil is covered with vegetation or other materials. Most wind erosion is on newly plowed fields, construction sites, or where the vegetation has been grazed or cut short.

Wind erosion is particularly a problem in the plains states of North America. Texas has more land subject to wind erosion than the combined area in Ohio, Illinois, Indiana, and Iowa.

■ Water—*Water erosion* is the loss of soil due to water movement. It is the major cause of soil loss in North America. Excess rainfall creates runoff that carries large amounts of soil away. Controlling runoff reduces erosion.

Hard rain showers may result in runoff on newly plowed land. The runoff picks up soil particles. These particles are washed into streams and cause sediment and water pollution. The next time you see a stream, note the color of the water. If it is brown or black, the water has a high amount of soil material. Clear water is free of suspended soil particles.

Soil conservationists estimate that more than 63,000 tons of soil go down the Mississippi River each day. This is lost soil. It is the most fertile soil in states that feed the river. Upon reaching the Gulf of Mexico, the flow of the water slows and the soil particles settle out. The sediment forms a delta area. The passage of boats from the river may be blocked.

6-3. Muddy water in this river is due to suspended soil particles that have washed from unprotected land.

■ Glaciers—Glaciers were more active long ago than they are today. The front edge of a glacier may push soil, rocks, fallen trees, and other materials. Except in areas where glaciers occur, such as Alaska, they are of minor importance in soil erosion.

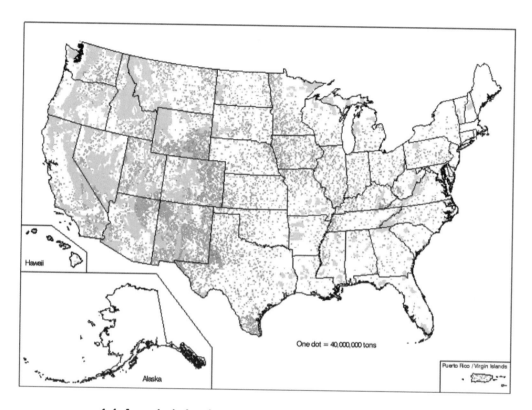

6-4. Annual wind and water erosion losses in the United States.

- Land Slippage—Land slippage (mud or rock slides) occurs on sloping land that is wet. The soil is saturated with water and slips down the hillside or mountain slope. Banks along highways, streams, and ocean fronts are often subject to slides.

Kinds of Erosion

Soil scientists have identified three kinds of water erosion. These are:

- Sheet—**Sheet erosion** is the loss of thin layers or sheets of soil. The process may be so slow that it is unnoticed. It usually occurs where no vegetation covers the land. Vegetation deflects the fall of raindrops. Raindrops that hit directly on the soil loosen tiny particles so they are easily washed away. Sheet erosion can occur on nearly level land and on hillsides. If the water running off an area is brown or black, sheet erosion is going on even if none of the soil appears to be gone.

■ Rill—***Rill erosion*** is the loss of soil on sloping land where small channels are formed by running water. The effects are obvious. The channels soon create small gullies that can grow larger. Rill erosion occurs on small slopes with little or no vegetation. Freshly plowed fields on hillsides frequently suffer from rill erosion following rain.

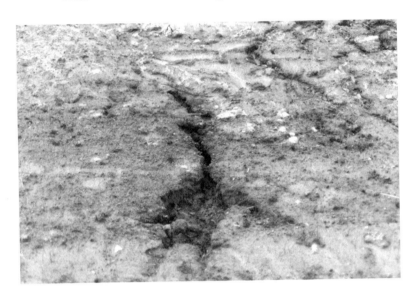

6-5. These tiny rills will soon become gullies unless the soil is protected.

■ Gully—***Gully erosion*** is a severe kind of erosion. It follows rill erosion if not controlled. Gullies form when rills continue to wash away. Gullies are easy to see in fields that have not been properly managed. Gully erosion is more likely on steeper slopes. The ability to farm land can be lost to gully erosion.

SOIL DEGRADATION

Soil degradation is any action or event that lowers the quality of soil. The soil is no longer as productive or useful as it once was. Many human activities degrade soil. Soil degradation occurs in two general ways:

■ Altering the physical nature of soil—Construction, landscaping, and agricultural work involve digging into the soil. The surface may be moved about or left unprotected and subject to erosion. Native grasses and trees are removed. The soil can be compacted by heavy equipment and mashed into deep ruts when it is wet. Digging deep into the earth brings up subsoil and parent material, which, when spread on the surface, lowers the fertility. Plowing the land for crops alters the soil.

6-6. Moving soil in constructing ornamental landscapes changes its physical nature.

■ Contamination—Contamination results when chemicals, oil, and other substances get onto the land. Some contaminants soak into the soil and destroy its ability to support plant growth. Other materials may pass through the soil and enter the groundwater supply.

Land once used as a dump, mine, or factory site may be rehabilitated. This involves removing contaminated soil and covering the remaining soil with noncontaminated soil. Contaminated soil is hard to clean up.

Soil can be contaminated by agricultural practices. Too much fertilizer can damage the soil. Excess chemicals on crops get into the soil. Irrigation water containing salt can result in the buildup of salt in the soil. Once the salt level is high, the land may stop being productive. It is best to remove salt from irrigation water or use water from sources that are salt-free.

6-7. Soil from a small chemical spill along a highway has been dug out and placed on plastic. (The contaminated soil will be hauled away. The area has been restricted because of danger.)

Resource Connection

SOIL COMPACTION

Equipment used to do work on land may weigh thousands of pounds. All of the weight is supported by a small area on each wheel. This creates pressure on the soil. A tire with a load of 2,000 pounds and an area that is 10x12 inches supporting the weight will create pressure 2 feet deep! (The tractor pulling the disk harrow in the photo may create pressure on the soil below the depth of tillage.)

Pressure on the surface of soil causes compaction. Hardpans are often found in soil that has had heavy equipment on it. In some cases, the surface of the soil can be compacted. Compaction stunts plant root growth. Roots simply cannot penetrate tightly compacted soil. Compaction is treated by using subsoil plows that break up compacted areas.

In some countries, soil has been degraded by land mines. These dangerous explosives are planted to deter military activity. People who use the land sometimes cause the mines to explode. This can cause personal injury or death.

WETLANDS

Wetland is an area where the soil is often saturated with water. Water may be standing on the surface for part or nearly all of the year. The wet condition determines the types of plants, animals, and other organisms that grow and the extent of soil development.

Wetland is typically near lakes, creeks, marshes, and swamps. Areas near the ocean may have saltwater. Most wetland areas have freshwater. About 100 million acres (40 million hectares) are now in wetlands in the United States. Millions of acres have been destroyed. Acreage in wetland is declining each year. Draining swamps, building new stream channels, and filling in low areas destroy wetland. Wetland is destroyed because people want to use

6-8. A wetland area.

the land for other purposes, such as highways, shopping centers, and airports.

IMPORTANCE

Wetland is important in maintaining productive soil and quality water. Here are three reasons wetlands are important:

- Renews groundwater—Wetland allows excess surface water to permeate into groundwater supplies. The soil and rock filter and renew the water. Wetlands are essential in maintaining groundwater. Every time a wetland area is destroyed, the area that replenishes groundwater supplies has been reduced.

- Waterfowl habitat—Wetland is the home of waterfowl. Fowl that migrate stop in wetland areas between their destinations. Summer breeding is in wetland areas (usually in the northern United States and Canada). As wetland is lost, areas for waterfowl are also lost.

- Fish nurseries—Many fish species reproduce in wetland areas. These include species that are commercially caught, as well as sport fish species. Without wetland, fish would not have a place to reproduce and for the young to grow until they swim to the ocean.

PROTECTION

Wetland is protected to prevent loss. Plans for construction projects must often meet approval of state and federal agencies. Destruction of wetlands is discouraged. Converting wetland to farm use is discouraged. Landowners

6-9. A basin near a highway traps runoff and helps restore groundwater.

who damage wetland are denied some benefits of the U.S. Department of Agriculture. Commercial sites that encroach wetlands must often build new wetland areas to compensate for any loss. Small reservoirs are built near parking lots and along highways to collect water.

PREVENTING SOIL LOSS

Soil loss can be reduced by using management practices to promote soil conservation. *Soil conservation* is using soil so damage or loss is very little or none. It includes both protecting and improving the soil. Several practices can be used in soil conservation.

PROPER LAND USE

Soil conservation begins with proper land use. Using land for its best use based on capability minimizes soil loss. This is a major factor in soil conservation. Land that is put to a use for which it is unfit is likely to have more erosion. Land capability classification helps people make good decisions about land use.

Opinions differ on land use. Some people feel that only land in the higher classes should be used for factories, businesses, and homes. Others feel that the better classes should be used for crops and not taken out of production.

A good way of looking at land for agriculture is to use flat land for row crops, rolling land for pasture, and steep land for trees and wildlife.

CONSERVATION PRACTICES

Soil damage and loss can be reduced by installing proper conservation practices on the land. A *conservation practice* is a structure, a vegetative measure, or an activity that protects, enhances, or manages soil and other resources. Some of the practices require skilled conservationists to install. Others are simple and easily done. The Natural Resources Conservation Service has developed standards that apply to planning, designing, and constructing structures and practices.

Terracing

A *terrace* is a long ridge of earth that follows the contour of land to slow runoff. Some terraces slowdown and divert water flow. Other terraces are designed for all water to soak into the ground. When properly designed and constructed, terraces reduce soil erosion and conserve water.

Contouring

Contouring is performing all field operations on the contour of the land elevation. Simply, this is plowing across a hillside rather than up and down. Contouring reduces the rate of runoff flow. Erosion is reduced. More water enters the ground. Survey instruments or lasers may be needed to guide the machinery in establishing a contouring pattern.

6-10. Plowing on the contour of land.

Strip Cropping

Strip cropping is planting crops of different types in strips across a hillside. The strips are contoured with the elevation of the land. Alternating strips are row crops and hay crops. This approach alternates plowed land with land that has a vegetative cover. Research has shown that production levels are maintained and may be increased with strip cropping.

6-11. Corn has been alternated with strips of perennial grass along the contour of this Virginia hill farm.

The width of strips varies with the kind of crop. Most strips need to be about 50 feet wide for effectiveness with crops such as corn and soybeans. Most producers prefer strips that are 300 or so feet wide. Strips can be narrower for small-growing crops, such as peanuts.

Ponds

Carefully designed levee ponds may be placed across small hollows or other sites to collect runoff. These ponds may catch water discharged by terraces. Ponds should be laid out by a trained conservation technician. Construction should follow proper procedures. A spillway is needed so excess wa-

6-12. This small pond has been built in a watershed to collect runoff from a terrace in Mississippi.

ter can drain out when the pond is full. Areas around the pond and the levee should have a vegetative cover to prevent erosion. Sport fish can be raised in the ponds. Some ponds provide drinking water for cattle.

Vegetative Covers and Grass Strips

Vegetative cover is a protective crop that is grown to prevent soil erosion. This is the most widely used approach to soil conservation. Vegetation helps control both water and wind erosion.

The plants used for vegetative cover should be close-growing with root systems that help hold the soil in place. Good plant covers catch rain, prevent loss by splashing the soil, and promote movement into the soil. The species planted should be adapted to the area. Perennial cover plants are more effective than annuals. Most vegetative covers must be seeded. This requires light tillage to have a seedbed and the use of properly applied fertilizer to promote growth.

Grassed waterways are used in some fields. A **grassed waterway** is a shallow vegetated ditch that carries runoff away. The ditch is planted with a perennial grass to slow the rate of runoff and prevent erosion in the waterway.

Trees are used on land where forestry is the highest use in terms of preventing erosion. Steep banks may be planted with grasses, herbaceous plants, and ornamental shrubs. Some areas of the South use a vine-type plant known as kudzu. Kudzu is a rapid-growing perennial plant that is killed back by cold weather. Some people view kudzu as a pest. Others know that it stops erosion in places where other control measures could not be implemented.

6-13. A grass strip between corn fields reduces runoff on this Indiana farm. (The strip is harvested for hay.)

6-14. Kudzu planted on this steep roadside bank in Georgia almost completely stopped erosion.

Windbreaks and Shelterbreaks

Windbreaks and shelterbreaks are similar. A **windbreak** is a row of trees or shrubs planted to slow the movement of surface wind. Windbreaks help reduce wind erosion and protect from blowing snow. They may also reduce wind around buildings and provide animal shelter.

A **shelterbreak** is a row or cluster of shrubs, trees, or combination of plants that help provide protection from the wind. Reducing wind prevents soil erosion and helps protect crops and livestock. Researchers have found that the height of the plants in a shelterbreak is important. Taller plants reduce wind movement more than shorter plants. A general rule is a shelterbreak provides protection downwind for a distance that is 20 times the height of the plants.

Windbreaks and shelterbreaks are long-term plantings. They should be located where they offer the greatest protection without interfering with the use of the land.

Conservation Tillage

Conservation tillage is using tillage practices that disturb the surface of the land very little.

No-till is producing a traditional crop without plowing. Herbicides are used to control weeds. Special planters are used to plant seed in soil that has not been prepared into a seedbed. No-till is sometimes known as zero-till.

Minimum tillage is plowing so the surface of the land is disturbed as little as possible. Special-shaped plows are used. These plows go underneath

6-15. A special planter is operating in soil that has not been plowed. (The planter opens a narrow trench, drops seed, and covers the seed through stubble from a previous crop.) (Courtesy, U.S. Department of Agriculture)

the surface and leave vegetative material on the surface. A finely prepared seedbed is not used. Planters with drill openers specially designed for minimum tillage land are used. Herbicides are applied to control weeds.

Special types of chisel plows may be used in the fall on harvested fields so the stubble and stalks of crop plants cover the soil. This reduces loss to erosion in the winter.

Crop Rotation

Crop rotation is alternating the use of land in producing crops. Rotation makes more efficient use of nutrients and helps maintain soil organic matter. This promotes soil tilth and moisture retention.

Rotations may be set to follow specific two- or three-year cycles. For example, a three-year rotation might be soybeans, wheat, and corn. Soybeans are legumes and fix nitrogen in the soil. Wheat produces considerable organic matter that helps prevent erosion. Corn promotes weed control due to more intensive cultivation practices. Rotation cycles are usually prepared based on local farm situations.

PRACTICE SELECTION

Conservation practices should be carefully selected. Assistance is available through local soil and water conservation districts that have an agreement with the Natural Resources Conservation Service (NRCS) of the U.S. Department of Agriculture. NRCS traditionally provides landowners with technical assistance on conservation practices. The practice selected must solve the problem, be reasonable to install, and allow use of the land.

TERRACES

Terraces are used to control runoff and reduce erosion. They are built on land where other soil conservation measures are impractical or not workable. Terraces are costly to install and may interfere with some uses of the land. With proper design, cost can be kept down and use of the land can be continued. Building terraces involves studying the land and selecting the approach that best meets your needs.

APPROACHES IN TERRACING

In terms of land contour, two approaches are used in building terraces:

- Level—A level terrace is parallel with the slope of the land. It does not divert runoff into a waterway. Level terraces are used on soil with good permeability—the water quickly soaks into the soil. Level terraces promote the retention of moisture and are more likely to be used in areas with moderate to low precipitation.

- Graded—A graded terrace has a gradual slope from one end to the other that follows the contour of the land. It collects and diverts the water into a water-

Career Profile

SOIL LAB TECHNICIAN

A soil lab technician conducts tests on soil samples. The work includes receiving and recording samples, running analyses, and reporting findings. A soil lab technician may also prescribe needed amendments for soil to improve fertility.

Soil lab technicians need college degrees in agronomy, soil science, chemistry, or closely related areas. Many have masters or doctors degrees in similar areas. Practical experience in growing crops, ornamental plants, and other work is beneficial. Experience working in a lab is essential.

Most jobs for soil lab technicians are found with universities, private soil-testing firms, and agricultural and horticultural supplies businesses. (Courtesy, Mississippi State University)

6-16. A new terrace with grass cover becoming established.

way. The amount of the grade may be only 1 percent. Graded terraces are used when all of the water will not soak into the soil. The soil may lack permeability. These terraces are often used on clay soils and in areas with high precipitation.

KINDS OF TERRACES

Several kinds of terraces are used. The kind to use depends on the soil erosion problems that exist or could develop. Variations are often made in terraces on the basis of site needs.

The most popular types of terraces are:

- Broad-base terraces—Broad-base terraces are used in large fields with gradual slopes. They are designed to accommodate the use of farm machinery. The distance between terraces is based on the width of the machinery that is used. Machinery should never be operated across terraces.

- Grassed back-slope terraces—This type of terrace is used in land with more slope than the broad-based terrace. The back slope of the terrace is not tilled but is seeded to permanent grass. Land to form the terrace is pushed up from its downside on a hill. This reduces the slope below the grassed part of the terrace. The channel and ridge are planted to grass. The grassed area further slows the flow of runoff and keeps soil in place.

- Narrow-based terraces—The narrow-based terrace is used on land with somewhat more slope than the first two types. Both the front and back of the narrow-based terrace have permanent grass. Less soil is needed for this type of terrace. The front and back of the terrace cannot be planted to crops.

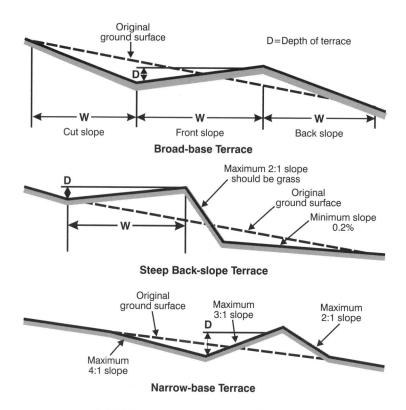

6-17. The most popular types of terraces.

Other types of terraces include:

■ Bench terraces—Bench terraces are used on steeper hillsides. Their structure makes it possible to grow certain crops on and between the terraces. Bench terraces are named because of the retaining wall of stones or grass on the lower side. Most bench terraces have very little slope.

■ Ridge terraces—Ridge terraces are used to hold water in place rather than drain it away. They are used in areas with less precipitation and where water conservation is important. Soil from below the terrace is used in building the ridge.

■ Diversion terraces—Diversion terraces are built on steep slopes of more than 10 percent grade. They are designed to quickly carry away water from heavy rains. These terraces cannot be easily crossed with machinery because of the deep channel.

■ Lister terraces—Lister terraces are small terraces often used on a temporary basis. The terrace is small and often constructed with a plow that throws up a small dam. Land may be smoothed out prior to planting and more lister terraces constructed later.

GENERAL CONSTRUCTION DETAILS

Terracing is based on the characteristics of the site, including slope and soil texture. How the land will be used is important in terracing.

Leveling instruments are used to lay out the contour of a terrace. Lasers and laser-guided equipment are often used to establish the channel and other details of a terrace. In the past, a terracing level and rod were used. The location of terrace structures is often marked with stakes or flags. Equipment operators use the stakes or flags to guide movement of the soil.

Most terraces (except lister terraces) require 15 to 25 feet of land for the entire length of the structure. The depth of a terrace channel is usually no more than 10 inches. Bulldozers are used to build terraces.

6-18. Using a laser to establish elevation points.

With graded terraces, the lower end serves as the outlet for water. Provisions must be made for disposal of runoff. This may be into a grassy area or a pond. Outlets should have good vegetative covers to prevent erosion. Seeding approved grasses will usually provide sufficient cover. Unprotected outlets can be washed away by heavy rain. Tiles are sometimes used to carry the water away. Excess water must be disposed of without damaging the land. A qualified soil conservationist should be involved in surveying terraces.

SOIL RENEWAL

Soil renewal is used when moderate to severe loss has occurred. The purpose is to restore productivity of the soil. In some cases, the soil will need to be used in different ways from past uses. Renewal may include using nutrients, lime, or organic matter; installing drainage and control structures; and, with severe pollution, bioremediation.

DETERMINE THE PROBLEM

Renewal should be based on the problem that has resulted in soil damage. Why has the soil been damaged? Treating symptoms is not adequate. The cause of damage must be identified and dealt with. For example, using a silt fence at the bottom of a plowed hill does not stop erosion. (A silt fence keeps silt from getting into streams and being totally lost.) Another example is soil pollution in a lawn. (The cause is excess use of pesticide on grass and flowers.)

THE SOLUTION

Once the problem causing soil damage has been identified, possible solutions are determined. Each possible solution is investigated. The approach to be used is selected. Good information is needed in selecting the soil renewal approach. Study the practices used on other sites. Determine if the practices have worked well. Compare the characteristics of sites. Select a solution that appears most promising in solving the problem.

SPECIAL PURPOSE SEEDING

Some kinds of plants have the ability to remove pollutants from the soil. Careful investigation is needed of the pollutant and the ability of a plant species to remove substances. Heavy metals and other materials may be absorbed by the roots of plants and moved to the leaves and stems. The plants

6-19. The *Thlaspi* **plant has the ability to remove heavy metals from the soil. (Courtesy, Agricultural Research Service, USDA)**

can be cut, raked up, and hauled away. This removes the heavy metal or other pollutant from the site.

SOIL SAMPLING AND ANALYSIS

Soil analysis involves having soil samples tested to determine the presence of pollutants, as well as nutrient levels.

SAMPLING

The results of analysis are no better than the quality of the sample. A sample is a very small amount of soil–often no more than two or three ounces! The sample must be representative of the area being studied. Areas that are different should be sampled separately. For example, a creek-bottom field would be sampled separately from a hillside.

A sample should involve collecting soil from ten to fifteen sites in a field. Samples are collected 4 to 6 inches below the soil surface, though some may be deeper. The small amounts from each site are mixed together in a clean bucket or carefully placed in a bag. Labs may provide special containers for shipping soil samples. Be sure to label all samples.

6-20. Collecting a soil sample to send for laboratory analysis.

ANALYSIS

Analysis is using chemical tests to determine the nutrients in a soil sample. Analysis also determines the pH of the sample. Once the results of analysis are known, fertilizer and lime are used to assure adequate soil conditions for the plants that are being grown. Nutrient and pH needs vary among crops.

Analysis may involve using test kits or sending the sample to a laboratory. Laboratory analysis is most needed to determine the presence of residues that may degrade the soil. Kits should be used according to the instructions. Always use care with chemicals and avoid contact with skin and eyes. Wear goggles and rubber gloves for protection.

USING SOIL AMENDMENTS

Soil amendments are used to improve the physical, chemical, and biological nature of soil. Using some kinds of amendments with large fields may be impractical. Common soil amendments are organic matter, fertilizer, and innoculants.

- Organic matter—Organic matter is used to promote tilth. *Tilth* is the physical condition of soil that makes it suitable for crop production. A soil with good tilth is easily cultivated and prepared into a seedbed. Leaf mold, manure, or humus may be added to soils that lack organic matter. These materials improve the tilth of soil. In areas where poultry is produced, litter cleaned from houses may be spread over pasture or cropland. Well-decomposed organic matter is most often used with lawns, flower beds, and small areas. Poultry litter and animal manure that is not composed creates an unpleasant odor around homes, parks, and businesses.

- Fertilizer and lime—Fertilizer and lime may be needed to improve the chemical nature of soil. Soil test results should be followed in determining the kind and rate of application. Some fertilizer is from natural sources, such as manure and materials from wastewater facilities. Much of the fertilizer used today is synthetic and is manufactured in large plants. An example of a synthetic fertilizer is ammonium nitrate. It has 33 percent nitrogen. A complete fertilizer is one that has nitrogen, phosphorus, and potassium. The amounts

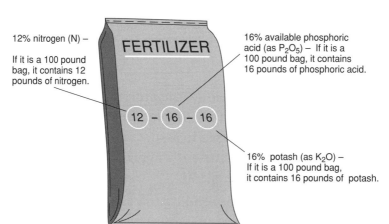

12% nitrogen (N) –

If it is a 100 pound bag, it contains 12 pounds of nitrogen.

FERTILIZER

16% available phosphoric acid (as P_2O_5) – If it is a 100 pound bag, it contains 16 pounds of phosphoric acid.

12 – 16 – 16

16% potash (as K_2O) – If it is a 100 pound bag, it contains 16 pounds of potash.

6-21. A 12-16-16 fertilizer has 12 percent N, 16 percent P_2O_5, and 16 percent K_2O.

of these elements are listed on labels of fertilizer bags. Agricultural lime is used to raise pH and make soil less acidic. In some cases, amendments, such as ammonium sulfate, are used to make the soil more acidic.

■ Innoculants—Innoculants are sometimes used to improve the biological nature of soil. Seeds may be innoculated before planting. An example is using nitrogen-fixing bacteria on the seed of legumes, such as soybeans. Other microbes may be used to breakdown pollutants in the soil, such as microbes degrading oil spilled on the land.

CONSERVATION IN URBAN AREAS

Urban areas have unique soil conservation needs. The general approach is to keep the soil covered and control water runoff. This applies to building sites, roads and parking lots, and recreational areas. Paved areas and building roofs do not absorb water. This may result in huge amounts of water that need to be quickly handled by storm sewers and ditches.

Here are a few practices to conserve soil:

■ Use mulch—*Mulch* is a layer of straw, burlap, or other material placed on the top of soil to protect it from wind and water. Mulch helps hold water and reduce the impact of water flow.

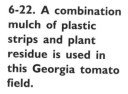

6-22. A combination mulch of plastic strips and plant residue is used in this Georgia tomato field.

■ Construct silt fences—A *silt fence* is a structure placed at the bottom of a slope to allow water to flow through but to hold back the soil particles. This

6-23. Two types of silt fences are shown here. Bales of hay are held in place by wooden stakes (left) and plastic silt fencing has been attached to a wooden frame fastened to posts (right).

keeps sediment out of streams and lakes and prevents the loss of soil. Silt fences may be made with bales of hay, plastic strips, or other materials.

■ Plant cover crops—Vegetation can be planted on excavated soil to hold it in place. For example, winter grass can be planted in the fall on new lawn areas to prevent erosion until a permanent sod is established.

■ Build on the contour—Streets, buildings, and other structures can be located on the contour of the land. This allows the structures to slow the flow of water.

■ Stabilize stream banks—Creeks, roadsides, and other places often have banks that will quickly erode. Riprap, fabrics, straw, vegetation, and concrete are used to stabilize banks.

■ Plant trees and shrubs—Trees and shrubs can be planted in areas where erosion is likely. The roots hold the soil, the limbs and leaves on the trees slow the impact of rain, and fallen leaves cover the ground.

■ Manage storm water—Curbs, ditches, and other structures may be installed to manage excess precipitation. These prevent soil loss and reduce sediment in water.

6-24. Covering newly prepared lawn area with straw helps prevent erosion.

CONSERVATION IN AGRICULTURE

Many agricultural activities use the soil. Growing crops creates loose soil that can be easily lost. Many producers use conservation practices to prevent soil loss.

Here are a few practices to reduce soil erosion due to agricultural practices:

- ■ Plant on the contour—Contour planting slows the flow of water and allows it to soak into the soil.

- ■ Rotate crops—Planting different crops on land each year. The residue from crops helps hold the soil in place. It is especially good if legumes are a part of the rotation. Rotation makes better use of nutrients in the soil because different crops have different nutrient needs.

- ■ Build terraces—Terraces prevent the rapid flow of water and help hold the soil in place. Terraces must be designed and constructed properly. If not, they will fail to properly manage runoff.

- ■ Plant grass strips—Small strips covered with grass may be left near plowed areas. These strips are often located at the lowest elevations in a field. The strips slow the flow of water and keep gullies from forming. The water is diverted to a safe outlet.

- ■ Build diversion ditches—Small ditches may be built across slopes to slow the flow of water and divert it into a safe outlet. These are similar to grassed waterways, but may be lined with riprap or other material.

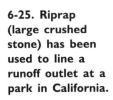

6-25. Riprap (large crushed stone) has been used to line a runoff outlet at a park in California.

- Use strip cropping—Planting alternating strips of row crops and hay crops is effective. The strips of hay slow the flow of water from rain and hold the topsoil in place.

- Plant vegetative cover—Cover crops are quite effective. Using legume varieties also adds nitrogen to the soil. Some vegetative covers are used in the winter; others are used in the summer. Fields may be planted in winter cover crops, such as vetch and clover, after the fall harvest. The cover crop adds fertility and protects the soil from erosion.

- Practice conservation tillage—This involves planting crops without plowing or with little plowing. Crop residue from the previous year is left on the surface to protect the land. Depending on how conservation tillage is implemented, various versions are used: no-till, mulch-till, and strip-till.

- Plant windbreaks—Rows of trees may be planted to slow blowing wind and help prevent wind erosion. These are frequently used in the plains area of North America.

- Keep livestock out of streams—Livestock damage stream banks, cause erosion, and muddy the water in streams. Watering facilities should be used. Bridges or crossing structures should be located where livestock cross a stream.

REVIEWING

MAIN IDEAS

Soil is damaged by erosion and other actions or events that cause degradation. Erosion results in the loss of topsoil. Soil fertility is reduced by erosion.

Making wise use of land helps curtail erosion losses. This begins by knowing the best use of the land. Land should be used to conserve soil and moisture. In some cases, land includes wetland. Wetland is important in renewing groundwater.

Soil loss can be reduced but never completely stopped. Conservation practices should be used. These include terracing, contouring, strip cropping, using ponds, using vegetative covers, installing windbreaks and shelterbreaks, practicing conservation tillage, rotating crops, and using protective covers. Terraces have been widely used. Good terrace design meets the needs of the site, as well as allows continued use of the land.

Damaged soil may be renewed. The process may be costly and time consuming. Practices can be used in both urban and agricultural areas to renew and protect soil. Some of the urban practices are: use mulch, construct silt fences, plant cover crops, build on the contour, stabilize stream banks, plant trees and shrubs, and manage storm water. Practices in agriculture include plant on the contour, rotate crops, build terraces, plant grass strips, build diversion ditches, use strip cropping, plant vegetative cover, use conservation tillage, plant windbreaks, and keep livestock out of streams.

QUESTIONS

Answer the following questions using complete sentences and correct spelling.

1. What is erosion? How does erosion damage soil?
2. What are the kinds of erosion? Which is most prevalent in the area where you live?
3. What is soil degradation?
4. How is use related to soil conservation?
5. Why is wetland important?
6. What soil conservation practices may be used? Briefly describe each.
7. How does conservation tillage help prevent erosion?
8. What is the difference between a level terrace and a graded terrace?
9. What is soil renewal?
10. List one practice that can be used to conserve soil in urban areas and one in agricultural areas. Explain why you selected the two practices.

EVALUATING

Match the term with the correct definition. Write the letter by the term in the blank provided.

a. topsoil
b. soil erosion
c. soil degradation
d. tilth

e. wetland
f. soil conservation
g. terrace
h. contouring

i. conservation tillage
j. mulch

_____ 1. Using tillage practices that disturb the surface of the land very little.

_____ 2. A layer of straw, burlap, or other material that covers the soil.

_____ 3. First few inches of soil high in nutrients.

_____ 4. Loss of soil by movement to another location.

_____ 5. Actions or events that lower the quality of the soil.

_____ 6. An area where the soil is often saturated with water.

_____ 7. Using soil so loss or damage is very little or none.

_____ 8. The physical condition of soil that makes it suitable for crops.

_____ 9. Long ridge of earth that follows the contour of the land to prevent soil and water loss.

_____ 10. Performing land use operations on the contour of the elevation.

EXPLORING

1. Invite a resource person from the Natural Resources Conservation Service to speak to the class. Have them explain erosion control programs and the assistance available.

2. Study an eroded area near your home or the school grounds. Assess what could be done to stop erosion and renew the soil. Prepare a report on your observations and recommendations.

3. Collect a soil sample and make an analysis to determine the nutrients present and needed.

4. Prepare an oral presentation on an area of soil conservation. Choose a topic that you can cover within the guidelines of the Prepared Speaking Event of the National FFA Organization. Deliver the speech to your class or other group.

7

WATER

Water is used in many ways. Think about your uses of water—drinking, cooking, cleaning, swimming, and others. There are many uses! You would have a long list if you included all of your water uses. Add to your list the water used in factories, offices, and agriculture. The list is even longer!

Humans need water. The human body is 65 percent water. Blood plasma is 92 percent water. Muscle tissue is 80 percent water. Body functions require water. Adults drink about 2.5 quarts (2.4 liters) of water a day. About half of this is in food and half is as liquid. The body tries to keep needed water content. Death results if more than 20 percent of the water is lost. That is why it is important to drink plenty of water.

7-1. Water activities are fun to many people.

OBJECTIVES

This chapter covers the meaning and nature of water and how we can help assure an adequate supply of quality water. The following objectives are included:

1. Describe the importance of water

2. Analyze the physical states and chemical components of water

3. Explain water salinity

4. Identify sources of water

5. Diagram the water cycle

6. Explain the importance of watersheds and wetlands

7. Identify the major water quality factors

8. Select and use appropriate methods to assess water quality

9. Identify practices to conserve and protect water

TERMS

aquifer
brackish water
desalination
distillation
evaporation
flood plain
freshwater
hardness
ice
irrigation
pathogen
potable water
saline water
saltwater
stream
stream channel
streamflow
transpiration
turbidity
water distribution
water quality
watershed

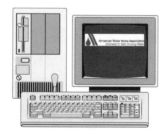

American Water Works Association
http://www.awwa.org/

THE IMPORTANCE OF WATER

Water has important roles. It supports all life and shapes the landscape of our world. Water creates power when it changes from liquid to gas (vapor or steam). Water expands when it freezes and cracks rocks, highways, and the water pipe at your home if it is not protected in cold weather.

Here are several uses that show the importance of water:

- Life Processes—Living organisms must have water. It is essential for organisms to carry out life processes. Plants use water in photosynthesis and temperature regulation through transpiration. Animals use water in metabolism and making body fluids. Most animal bodies are 60 to 70 percent water. Most plants are 70 to 95 percent water.

- Daily Living—Many of the things we do require water. The average person in the United States uses 100 gallons (380 liters) each day for bathing, washing, cooking, and sending wastes from the home. Taking a bath uses 20 to 30 gallons (76 to 114 liters). About 15 gallons (57 liters) are used to wash the dishes for a day. The water is made dirty. Renewal is required. The earth has natural processes to renew water. In some cases, water is so dirty that nature needs help. Cities and factories often have treatment facilities to renew water.

- Food and Fiber Production—Water is needed to produce crops and animals. Nature provides much of the needed water. Plant roots take moisture from the soil. Dry areas may not have enough water for plants to grow and the land is irrigated. *Irrigation* is the artificial application of water to crops. Producers carefully regulate their use of water. To avoid waste, they apply no more water than is needed.

- Climate—Water influences our climate by regulating and transferring heat. Cities near large bodies of water have climates moderated by the water. Extreme temperature changes are on

7-2. Water is essential for animals, such as this moose. (Courtesy, U.S. Fish and Wildlife Service)

land far away from water. Large areas of water are places where storms develop. Hurricanes develop over oceans and may move onto land. High winds and rain can cause property damage.

■ Manufacturing—Water is used in manufacturing many products. For example, making steel, refining oil, producing paper, and food processing require large amounts of water. Efficient methods can reduce water requirements. Most plants use water efficiently and recondition it after it is used.

■ Transportation—Ferries, boats, ships, and barges travel on water. Rivers, oceans, and canals are used to transport raw products and manufactured materials. One nice thing about using water for transportation is that the water is not dirtied just by riding on it. However, boat operators need to be careful to avoid polluting the water with engine oil and other materials.

■ Recreation—People use water to have fun! Swimming, boating, and fishing are obvious uses. But, there are uses that are not as obvious, such as on golf courses and athletic fields. In some cases, reconditioned water from other uses is applied on recreational areas, such as golf courses.

WATER COMPOSITION AND STATES

Water is a tasteless, colorless, odorless, and clear liquid. If it is not, it contains substances that have made it impure. All water from natural sources contains substances that make it impure, but these do not usually make it unusable. If the wrong things get into water, it is polluted and unfit to use.

Water can be made pure by *distillation*. The process is to boil water and collect the vapor from it. The vapor is cooled and becomes liquid. Any solid

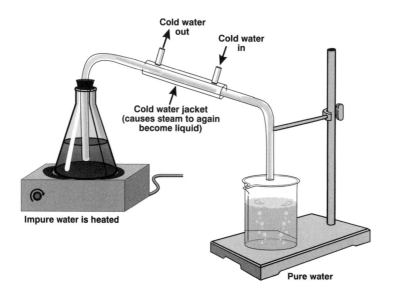

Cold water out

Cold water in

Cold water jacket
(causes steam to again
become liquid)

Impure water is heated

Pure water

7-3. A simple setup for distilling water.

materials in the natural water are left behind in the water or as residue. Gases are released into the air. The liquid that collects from the vapor is pure. Distillation is not practical on a large scale.

WATER COMPOSITION

Water is a chemical compound made of hydrogen and oxygen. Two atoms of hydrogen combine with one atom of oxygen to form one molecule of water: H_2O. Any variation in water is due to substances in it rather than to water as a compound.

Water molecules have a positive charge on one end and a negative charge on the other. This means that they are polar molecules. This "polarity" makes water good for cleaning and mixing to form other solutions.

STATES OF WATER

The three states of water, as introduced in Chapter 1, are solid, liquid, and gas or vapor. Both temperature and atmospheric pressure help water change from one state to another.

The solid state of water is *ice*. Ice forms at the freezing point of 32° F (0° C). Some impurities are forced out of water when it freezes. Impurities also cause water to freeze at slightly different temperatures. Antifreeze may be added to water in the cooling system of an engine to lower the freezing point. This keeps the water from freezing and damaging the engine.

The liquid form is between freezing and boiling temperatures. For many purposes, this is the most useful state. It is also the most common form of water.

7-4. Glaciers store a lot of freshwater. (This is the Mendenhall Glacier in Alaska. The more than a century-old snow compacted into this glacier contains impurities that reflect geologic activities through the years. For example, dust from a faraway erupting volcano may have collected in the glacier.)

Water vapor forms when water boils or evaporates. Water molecules escape from the surface of the water into the air. The boiling point at sea level is 212° F (100° C). As elevation increases, the boiling point goes down. On a mountain, water may boil at 190° F (88° C) because the atmospheric pressure is lower. Foods must be cooked longer.

WATER SALINITY

Water varies widely. Only about 1 percent of all water on the earth is available for use as freshwater. Why is the other 99 percent of water not available? How does this affect our supply and how we conserve water? Salinity is a major factor with water supplies.

Saline water is water that contains salt. Different kinds of salt are in water. Sodium chloride (NaCl) is best known. Salinity is measured as parts per thousand (ppt). A level of 10 ppt means that the water has 1 percent salt. Salt content limits the use of water. Water with high salinity is unfit for drinking and many other uses. Salt at low levels in irrigation water can build up and damage land. Never use water with high salinity for irrigation. In some cases, salt can be removed from water before it is applied to the land.

FRESHWATER

Freshwater has little or no salt. The salt content is less than 3.0 ppt. Salt levels higher than 3 ppt may damage land, destroy living organisms, and destroy property.

7-5. Irrigation applies water and whatever the water contains. (The contents of the water will build up in the land and can destroy productivity.)

The reason for conserving freshwater is simple: The supply is limited. Only 3 percent of the earth's water is freshwater. Of this, 2 percent is not readily available because it is frozen in the polar caps or in deep aquifers. Only 1 percent is readily available freshwater.

Freshwater is from wells, streams, surface runoff, and most lakes. Precipitation is freshwater.

BRACKISH WATER

Brackish water is a mixture of saltwater and freshwater. It is found where freshwater flows into saltwater at oceans and lakes. Freshwater is "lighter" than saltwater. The specific gravity of saltwater is 1.025, which means that the freshwater floats on the saltwater. Mixing freshwater and saltwater together may take a while.

Resource Connection

MAGICAL WATERS

Some water is thought to have "magical" powers. People say that it will heal disease and keep people from getting old. Some people question whether it really works.

Hot Springs National Park in Arkansas is one place with "magical" water. The park contains hot mineral springs at the base of Hot Springs Mountain. People travel long distances to drink the water and take special baths in the bathhouses. Some people bring jugs and take the water home with them!

What is special about the water? It naturally flows from the earth in springs. The water has a high mineral content. It is not cold like most groundwater but is 143° F (62° C). The region was first set aside in 1832 to protect the springs though it did not become a national park until 1921. Today, the park has 47 hot springs, a number of bathhouses, and convenient ways of getting the water.

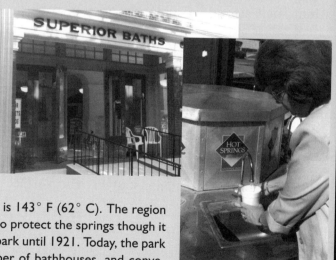

7-6. A saltwater diver is stroking a grouper fish.

Some plants and animals prefer brackish water. Examples include fish, such as mullet, and crabs. Many plants grow in these areas and provide food for animals.

SALTWATER

Saltwater is water with more than 16.5 ppt salt content. The water in oceans and seas is often 33 to 37 ppt salt. Some aquifers have water with high salinity.

About 97 percent of the earth's water is saltwater in lakes, seas, and oceans. This water supports marine aquatic life. Freshwater changes as it flows into saltwater. Care is needed to prevent freshwater from becoming saltwater. Reducing runoff is a good step because it helps water soak into the soil.

Desalination is the process of removing salt from water. The cost of desalination often prohibits its use. Desalination is not practical when large amounts of freshwater are needed, such as to irrigate a golf course. Mineral byproducts from desalination, such as sodium chloride, may also be useful in manufacturing.

WATER SOURCES AND STORAGE

Having plenty of quality water available requires a good source and the ability to store the water until it is needed.

SOURCES

Water is from two major sources: the surface of the earth and underground.

Surface Water

Surface water is found in lakes, streams, reservoirs, and oceans. Most of it is saline, such as in the ocean, and has limited use unless desalinated.

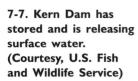

7-7. Kern Dam has stored and is releasing surface water. (Courtesy, U.S. Fish and Wildlife Service)

Streams, reservoirs, and lakes usually have freshwater. Half of all drinking water is from surface water.

Where we find surface water is related to watersheds. Watersheds collect surface water as it is running off. Since surface water is from precipitation, it is low in dissolved salts and pollutants. Surface water is good for drinking and agricultural uses except when it gets polluted. Surface water should be treated and made ready for use.

Groundwater

Groundwater is from within the earth. It may be located only a few feet (meters) to hundreds or thousands of feet (meters) below the surface. A cross-section of the earth tells about geologic materials. Some of the materials

7-8. An electric pump is used to lift groundwater for irrigation.

form aquifers. An *aquifer* is an area of porous sand, gravel, and limestone that is saturated with water in spaces between particles and in cracks. Wells are bored into aquifers to get water.

Most of the freshwater we use is from groundwater. It is often pumped to the surface for use. In some cases, it naturally flows as springs from the earth. Taking too much groundwater lowers the groundwater level. Some wells no longer produce water because the water level is below the pipe from the pump. Groundwater is often of good enough quality to use without treatment.

STORAGE

Water is stored so it will be available when needed. Storage facilities for water must keep it clean and prevent loss. Some evaporation often occurs during storage. With earthen facilities, both evaporation and infiltration cause loss. Natural water storage is in lakes, seas, oceans, aquifers, and other natural bodies of water. Tanks, reservoirs, and other structures are built for water storage. Many municipal water systems use elevated tanks for storage and to provide pressure so the water goes through the distribution system. Huge reservoirs are made by placing dams across streams and watersheds.

Water distribution is moving water from its source to where it is needed. Distribution systems must be leakproof to prevent the loss of water. A hazard of leaky systems is that, in case of pressure loss, polluted water and other materials from the ground can be sucked into a pipe through a break. This makes the water hazardous to use.

7-9. The Hetch Hetchy Reservoir near Yosemite National Park collects and stores water for San Francisco, which is some 130 miles away. (A system of large pipes carries the water for treatment and use.)

THE WATER CYCLE

The water cycle is a natural process of water going from the earth to the atmosphere and back to the earth. The process renews water. The sun is a part of the cycle by warming the water and turning it into vapor.

Water is continually moving through the water cycle (also known as the hydrologic cycle). The cycle does not create water—it cleans and restores water. Remember, the amount of water never changes. Its state and availability change.

WATER IN THE AIR

Water gets into the air by evaporation and transpiration. *Evaporation* is the process of water going from liquid to gas by exposure to air or heat. It is a natural process from any open water container.

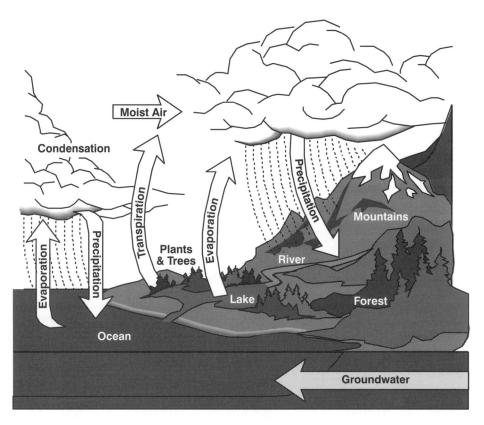

7-10. The water cycle is a continual process of circulating water in the atmosphere and to the earth.

WATER SECURITY OFFICER

A water security officer guards water supplies and protects them from contamination. They monitor water reservoirs and the facilities for treating water. The work involves patrolling areas where water is stored and treated.

Water security officers need training in law enforcement and introductory water quality training. They are usually deputized law officers that work for government agencies though some may be employed by private security agencies. Most have college degrees in an area related to law enforcement. Practical experience with water systems is beneficial.

Jobs are found where water security is needed. Reservoirs and aqueduct systems may have water security officers. This photo shows a water security officer on duty at a reservoir that provides water to a large city.

Transpiration is the release of water from the leaves of plants. Transpiration is greater on a hot, windy day.

Some water gets into the cycle through combustion (such as from an engine) and respiration. The air you exhale contains moisture. You can see it on a cold day when you exhale and the tiny particles form a thin visible fog.

WATER RETURNS TO THE EARTH

Water vapor forms clouds, mist, or fog when it reaches the atmosphere. Changes in temperature cause the tiny vapor particles to join and form raindrops. When the drops get too large to stay suspended in the air, they fall to the earth.

Precipitation is freshwater. On the earth, it may evaporate, infiltrate the soil, or become runoff. The goal is for a high amount to infiltrate the soil. Aquifers are "recharged" when water goes into the groundwater. Terraces, ponds, and other structures slow the rate of runoff so more water will soak into the earth. Runoff enters streams, lakes, and oceans. If runoff goes into a body of water containing saltwater, it becomes saltwater.

WATERSHEDS AND WETLANDS

A *watershed* is an area that provides runoff for a stream or reservoir. Watersheds include land, parking lots, roads, farms, factories, forests, fields, pastures, and any other artificial or natural part of the landscape. Precipitation that does not infiltrate the earth flows to a downhill location. Some watersheds are large; others are very small.

Watersheds need to be clean and free of pollutants. Anything in a watershed might be carried away in runoff to a creek or river. This may contaminate the water so it cannot be used. Activities in some watersheds are restricted to assure good water downstream.

STREAMS

A *stream* is a flowing body of water. Most streams have freshwater. Studying the interactions between water and the aquatic environment it creates is stream hydrology. This includes properties of the water and surrounding area. Stream hydrology helps understand the aquatic environment and the organisms that live in it.

Streamflow is the movement of water in a stream. It includes both volume and velocity of water movement. Velocity is the rate of flow and volume is the amount of flow. Small streams at higher elevations may have a high velocity of flow, but a small volume. Larger streams may have slower velocity,

7-11. The watershed for Lake Tahoe is all of the surrounding land area from which runoff flows into the lake.

7-12. Using a flowmeter to measure streamflow.

but larger volume of flow. Velocity suddenly stops when a stream flows into a lake or ocean.

Streams determine how water moves through a watershed. Streams have structures that help understand how they work. A ***stream channel*** is the sides and bottom of a stream. A channel is the conduit through which the water flows. Channels may be formed of earth or rock. The bottom of a channel is the stream bed. The edges or sides form the stream bank.

The common kinds of streams are:

- *River*—A river is a large stream that has high streamflow. River size and importance vary. Some rivers are long and wide; others are short and narrow.

- *Creek*—A creek is a stream that is smaller than a river. Creeks may flow into rivers, lakes, or oceans. Many people associate creeks with muddy, polluted water.

- *Brook*—A brook is a small stream. They are often associated with cool, clear freshwater. Brooks flow into rivers, creeks, lakes, or oceans.

- *Canal*—A canal is an artificial waterway. Canals are built for transportation, to relieve flooding, or to divert water to where it is needed.

Stream channels usually hold the streamflow. Heavy rain or melting snow may result in the water overflowing the channel. The area along a stream that may be covered with overflow is the ***flood plain***. Flood plains are covered only when a stream overflows. Materials in flood water settle out. Deposits of soil in flood plains from distant places have created fertile land, such as the Mississippi River delta.

Flooding can destroy homes, businesses, crops, and other things. People need to know the flood history of an area before building on it. Construction is often based on a 100-year history. Building should be above the 100-year flood plain.

NONFLOWING WATER

All streams flow into oceans, lakes, or marshes. Some may flow into other streams beforehand. Changes occur in the water and ecosystem the water provides. Freshwater may suddenly flow into saltwater. Cool water may flow into warmer water. Nonflowing water has distinctive characteristics from flowing water.

The kinds of nonflowing bodies of water are:

- *Ocean*—The ocean is a large body of saltwater that covers nearly three-fourths of the earth's surface. Though divided into sections by names, such as Atlantic and Pacific, the earth has only one large ocean.

- *Lake*—A lake is a body of water surrounded by land. Some lakes are quite large; a few smaller lakes are artificial and created for a particular need, such as flood control.

- *Pond*—A pond is a body of water that is smaller than a lake and is often artificial. Many are built for watering livestock or to raise aquacrops, such as fish.

- *Reservoir*—A reservoir is a large body of stored water. The water is from streams or runoff and may have a particular use, such as to generate electric power. Many reservoirs are artificial.

- *Slough*—A slough is an area of shallow water located on low-lying, nearly level land where streams overflow. Sloughs may have thick muddy areas. Some sloughs may have water only during rainy times of the year.

- *Marsh*—A marsh is similar to a slough. Marshes are areas of waterlogged land without trees and may be covered with cattails and other plants that grow best in wet areas.

7-13. Water in this small wetland pond is nonflowing.

■ *Estuary*—An estuary is the general area where streams join oceans. Estuaries are connected with the open oceans. They are where freshwater and ocean water mix.

WETLANDS

Wetlands are low areas that are wet most of the year. The ground may be covered with water or the soil saturated with water. Wetland areas, as described in Chapter 6, are important in restoring groundwater. Wetlands provide areas for water to move from the surface into the deep soil and replenish aquifers.

Watersheds typically include one or more wetland areas. Maintaining wetland is important in preserving a watershed. Wetland may include sloughs, marshes, estuaries, and playa lakes. A playa lake is a type of lake found in the plains states with internal drainage.

WATER QUALITY FACTORS

Water quality is the condition of water for a particular use. A quality problem exists if water for a particular use has an unfavorable condition. It is easy to know that some water is poor quality. In other cases, water quality is difficult to know without accurate tests.

The water that people use in daily living is known as potable water. *Potable water* is water that is safe to use for drinking, cooking, and washing. Most municipal water systems provide potable water. Potable water is not pure water. It often contains a variety of minerals.

QUALITY FACTORS

Some factors in water quality are:

■ Odor and Taste—Some water does not smell nor taste right. The odor and taste start with the water source. Normal processes in the earth may result in water having an earthy- musty odor. Pollution, leachate, organic sulfur, and microorganisms can contribute to a bad odor or taste.

■ Color—Sparkling clear water is most desired. Water that has a rusty or yellowish-brown color is objectionable. Color may not mean that the water is unfit to drink. Water may sometimes contain iron, magnesium, calcium, and other minerals that alter its color. Sediment, organic matter, and plankton may alter the color of surface water.

- pH—Most water has a pH between 4.0 and 9.0, with between 5.5 and 8.6 being most common. A pH higher than 7.0 tells the presence of carbonates and bicarbonates. Acid rain can lower pH to below 7.0. Water treatment may be used to modify pH. A pH of 7.0 to 7.8 causes the least amount of damage to pipe and pumps. Water pH is often measured with a meter.

7-14. Bottled water is increasingly used to assure safe drinking water.

- Hardness—**Hardness** is the presence of calcium and magnesium ions in water. It is often reported as calcium carbonate, though magnesium is also present. As the amount of calcium carbonate in water increases, the harder the water. In washing, more soap is needed with hard water. Hard water leaves a residue known as scale in hot water pipes and water heaters. Laboratory analysis is often needed to determine hardness. Excessive hardness can be removed by a "softening" process.

- Turbidity—**Turbidity** is suspended solid material in water. The materials may give water a cloudy or muddy appearance. The water is not clear. Turbidity is caused by tiny particles of suspended clay, silt, plankton, and other microscopic materials. The particles block light passage through the water. Turbidity is removed by filtering and allowing the materials to settle.

- Heavy Metals—Heavy metals may pose hazards in water. Mercury and lead are more common. Lead gets into water from older plumbing systems where lead was used to seal joints. Samples of water should be tested for lead. If it is present, replace the plumbing system.

- Chemical Residues—Water should be checked for chemical or pesticide residues. If found, get water from another source. Using bottled water in drinking and cooking can reduce the associated risks. The risks of drinking water with very small amounts of chemical residues are not well known but the materials may be associated with cancer.

- Coliform Bacteria—Water that contains fecal coliform bacteria is contaminated with human and animal wastes. The presence of *E. coli* is a strong indication that human excrement is getting into the water. The water is not fit for consumption. Simple tests for coliform bacteria are available. Water should be tested for coliform bacteria. Boiling water will destroy coliform bacteria.

7-15. Dead fish floating on the surface is a likely sign of bad quality water. (Courtesy, W. L. French, U.S. Fish and Wildlife Service)

POLLUTANTS

Water is polluted by a wide range of materials. Some are hazardous to the health of humans, plants, animals, and other organisms.

Here are some ways water is polluted:

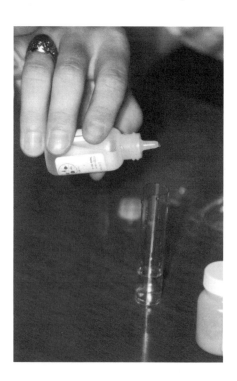

7-16. Conducting a test on water to determine if it contains a pollutant.

■ Sediment—Tiny soil particles and other materials may be suspended in water. The soil particles are from soil erosion. In some cases, soil is by far the biggest source of water pollution. Sediment clouds the water and reduces the quality of the environment of aquatic species. Light does not pass through the water. This reduces photosynthesis by water plants. When the sediment settles on the bottom, feeding and spawning areas for some animals are destroyed.

■ Pathogens—A *pathogen* is a living or nonliving thing that causes disease. Parasitic worms, bacteria, viruses, and protozoa are the major living pathogens in water. Coliform bacteria are often in polluted water. Disease and death may result from drinking water containing pathogens.

■ Organic Wastes—Organic wastes are materials being decomposed by bacteria. High organic waste requires a lot of bacterial activity for decay. Large numbers of bacteria tie up the oxygen in the water. Water in ponds with rotting hay or wood may have low dissolved oxygen.

■ Inorganic Substances—Water is damaged by acids, salts, heavy metals, and plant nutrients, such as nitrates and phosphates. The nutrients cause excessive plant growth in the water. Other inorganic substances damage the soil, equipment, and injure wildlife. The presence of certain inorganic substances makes water unfit to drink.

■ Organic Chemicals—Detergents, oil, solvents, paint, plastic, pesticides, and other organic compounds are hazardous to humans and wildlife. When people are careless in using or disposing of these products, such as used engine oil, they may enter the water.

■ Thermal Pollution—Thermal pollution is altering the natural temperature of a body of water. Organisms living in the water may be killed. It happens when warm or cold water is released in large enough amounts to change the temperature of the aquatic environment in a stream or lake.

WATER QUALITY MONITORING

Water quality monitoring is checking water for changes in quality. Regular monitoring helps determine changes that are taking place. Steps can be taken to correct problems.

PHYSICAL MONITORING

Physical monitoring is observing the characteristics of a stream, ocean, or lake. What we see may show that tests are needed.

Here are some things to do in physical monitoring:

■ Visual Inspection—Looking at water helps identify changes that indicate problems. A brown color may indicate sediment; a green color may indicate the growth of algae; and an orange-red color may be a sign of iron residues in the water. Foam bubbles on the water are signs that a substance has gotten in it or that gas is being produced by de-

7-17. The tag on this faucet warns against drinking the water.

composition. Dead fish or other aquatic animals floating on the surface are a sign of water problems.

■ Odor Detection—Odors indicate problems, such as a rotten egg smell indicates a high level of sulfur. Chlorine, sewage, and oil pollution can often be smelled. Careful testing is needed to determine the exact problem. Remember, an odor is a symptom and it is not the problem.

■ Note Course Changes—Most streams have a definite channel. Flowing water can change its course. Erosion of the bank may need attention. Riprap or other materials can be used to deter erosion.

WATER TESTING

Testing is analyzing samples from a water supply. Sometimes analysis can be done on the stream bank. Other times, a sample will need to be collected and sent to a laboratory. The results of a test are no better than the quality of the sample.

Water samples should represent the water being tested. Do not collect the sample just from the cleanest nor dirtiest water. Samples should be collected in clean containers. A dirty container will contaminate the sample and give inaccurate results.

7-18. Using a meter to determine the level of dissolved oxygen in water.

Kits and Meters

Kits are used for stream bank analysis. They tell important information about water and if a sample should be collected for additional analysis. The procedures must be followed to have reliable test results. All kits have detailed instructions. Some people question the reliability of results with kits. Laboratory analysis can be used to verify the results with the kit.

Meters speed the process of making water tests. Meters are often used to measure pH and dissolved oxygen. Meters must be properly calibrated for accuracy.

Laboratory Testing

Laboratory testing uses a sample of water from the supply being tested. Most laborato-

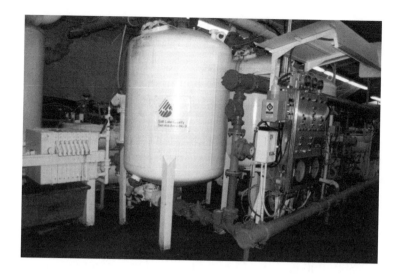

7-19. Water monitoring and filtering equipment at the Wasatch Tunnel treatment facility near Salt Lake City.

ries charge fees for their services. Laboratories provide a printed report on their findings.

Testing drinking water is typically to check for bacteria (especially coliform), heavy metals, and chemicals and pesticides. The tests may also check pH, ammonia levels, and turbidity. Hardness and alkalinity tests are important in some uses of water, such as aquaculture.

Use reputable laboratories. Most land-grant universities may have testing services. Local health departments can help with information on testing. Private labs are often appropriate. One example is the National Testing Laboratories, Inc., of Cleveland, Ohio. Analysis reports should be signed and certify that methods approved by the Environmental Protection Agency were used.

CONSERVING AND PROTECTING WATER

Water supplies will serve more people by wise use and good management. Every person has the responsibility to conserve water in daily living. Manufacturing, agriculture, and other commercial ventures should also conserve water.

Several approaches in using water are:

■ Avoid waste—Everyone can make better use of water in their daily lives. Simple things add up when done by many people. Taking shorter showers and brushing your teeth with the faucet off (turning it on briefly to rinse) save water. Just think of the water that could be saved each day if every person in your school used one gallon less water for a shower!

- Avoid Polluting—Pollution makes water unfit for use. Renewing takes time and nature may not be able to renew it if the pollution is bad. Properly dispose of oil so it does not get into water. Use pesticides sparingly. Use no more detergent and soap than is essential.

- Dispose of properly—Proper disposal of wastewater helps protect natural supplies. Wastewater can be partially renewed in lagoons and other treatment plant facilities.

- Install conservation practices—Many approaches can be used to conserve water supplies and quality. Approaches that conserve soil also conserve water. Terraces, ponds, and mulches can be used to reduce water runoff. Factories can seek more efficient ways of using water. An example is a paper mill. Some mills use 40,000 gallons (152,000 liters) of water to make a ton of paper. Others make the same amount of paper with much less water.

- Have good equipment—Pipes, pumps, and other facilities should be free of leaks. Leaky equipment wastes water. It also costs more to operate a leaky system because more water must be pumped just to have enough to do what is needed. More energy is needed to power the pumps.

- Reuse—Water used for one purpose can often be used for other purposes before it is released. The additional uses may help clean the water. An example is using wastewater to raise fish and grow hydroponic crops. Both activities remove nutrients in wastewater from food manufacturing operations.

- Renew used water—Renewing wastewater is helping nature do its job. It may involve filtering to remove solid materials. In holding reservoirs, it might include promoting the growth of microbes so processes occur, such as the nitrogen cycle.

7-20. A hydroponics lettuce production facility reuses water from a food processing plant in Illinois.

REVIEWING

MAIN IDEAS

Water is important in many ways. Life processes require water. Water is used in daily living and to produce food, clothing, and manufactured goods. We use water for recreation and transportation.

Water is a tasteless, colorless, odorless, and clear liquid. If it is not, substances have gotten into it. Some of the substances are safe and others may be harmful. Water is made of hydrogen and oxygen that bond to form H_2O. Water may be in a solid, liquid, or gas form, depending on the temperature and atmospheric pressure.

Salt is a particular problem in water. Many living organisms need freshwater to survive. Unfortunately, most of the water on the earth is saltwater. Desalination is used to remove salt from water, but the process is not practical on a large scale.

Water used in homes, factories, and other places is freshwater. It is obtained from surface water or groundwater. After it is used, water should be prepared for release into the natural water cycle. The water cycle is the movement of water throughout the atmosphere and earth. This cycle includes activities in watersheds.

Water quality is the condition of water for a particular use. The water people use in their homes is known as potable water. Water quality factors include odor and taste, color, pH, hardness, turbidity, and the presence of heavy metals, chemical residues, and microorganisms. Water can be monitored to detect changes. Tests may be needed to determine exact quality.

QUESTIONS

Answer the following questions using complete sentences and correct spelling.

1. What are the important uses of water?
2. What is the chemical formula for water? Explain the formula.
3. What are the three states of water? When does water move from one state to the other?
4. What is salinity? Why is it a problem?
5. How is salinity measured?
6. What are the major sources of water? Briefly describe each.
7. What is the water cycle? Why is it important?

8. What is a watershed? Why is it important to keep watersheds free of pollution?
9. What are the kinds of streams?
10. Why is flood plain information needed before building a home?
11. What is water quality? What factors indicate quality water?
12. What is physical monitoring of water?

EVALUATING

Match the term with the correct definition. Write the letter by the term in the blank provided.

a. distillation
b. desalination
c. freshwater
d. brackish water
e. saltwater
f. aquifer
g. evaporation
h. watershed
i. flood plain
j. potable water

_____ 1. Water with very little or no salt.
_____ 2. Water containing more than 16.5 ppt salt.
_____ 3. The process of removing salt from water.
_____ 4. The process of making water pure.
_____ 5. Underground areas where water fills pores between sand and rock.
_____ 6. Water that is a mix of saltwater and freshwater.
_____ 7. Water that is suitable for drinking and other household use.
_____ 8. The movement of water molecules from liquid into the air.
_____ 9. The area that provides runoff for a stream or reservoir.
_____ 10. The area along a stream that may be covered with overflow water.

EXPLORING

1. Investigate the source of water for your school. Determine how the water is prepared for use and treated after it is used.

2. Use a kit and test a sample of the water at your school or home. Be sure to properly carry out the test. Interpret the findings of your test and take actions to make any improvements.

3. Study a stream in the local area. Observe the kinds of plants and animals that grow in and around the stream. Use a plankton net to collect a sample from a local stream or lake. Use a microscope to identify the kinds of plankton (phytoplankton or zooplankton) in the water. Collect samples from several sites and compare what you find.

8

WILDLIFE

Wildlife makes our world fun! Think about the wildlife near your home or school. What kinds of wildlife do you see? What does it do that is important to you? You no doubt see much wildlife and may know how it helps us.

People are important to wildlife. We can do things that make more food and shelter for wildlife. We can also do things that damage the environment in which wildlife lives. With a little knowledge, we can be more responsible in our actions toward wildlife.

Most people think they know the meaning of wildlife. There are many different wildlife species. What does wildlife mean to you?

8-1. A desert big horn ram.

157

OBJECTIVES

This chapter explains the meaning and uses of wildlife and provides information on wildlife needs. The following objectives are included:

1. Explain the meaning of wildlife

2. Identify common wildlife species

3. Identify the benefits of wildlife

4. List and explain the uses of wildlife

5. Explain habitat and its establishment

6. Classify wildlife in relation to habitat

7. Explain the meaning of endangerment and other threats to wildlife

8. Describe how wildlife is protected

9. Identify recreational uses of wildlife

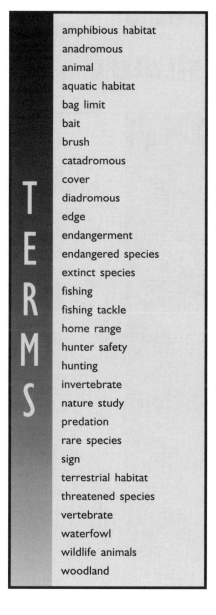

T E R M S

amphibious habitat
anadromous
animal
aquatic habitat
bag limit
bait
brush
catadromous
cover
diadromous
edge
endangerment
endangered species
extinct species
fishing
fishing tackle
home range
hunter safety
hunting
invertebrate
nature study
predation
rare species
sign
terrestrial habitat
threatened species
vertebrate
waterfowl
wildlife animals
woodland

National Wildlife Federation
http://www.nwf.org/

WILDLIFE CLASSIFICATION

We classify wildlife as all the things that live in the wild and that have not been domesticated. People differ in their definitions of wildlife. Some people only view wildlife as animals that live on the land. Wildlife includes plants, animals, and other living things. Many people fail to include aquatic animals and plants. The focus of this chapter is on animal wildlife.

CLASSIFICATION OF WILDLIFE

Wildlife can be classified based on the kingdoms used by biologists—animals, plants, fungi, Monera, and Protista. Further classification is based on such things as habitat, body structure, and reproduction.

Animals

An *animal* is an organism that gets its food by consuming materials and can usually move about. Animals have bodies made of organ systems consisting of many cells. Their cells have flexible membranes. The major groups are vertebrates and invertebrates.

VERTEBRATES. A *vertebrate* is an animal that has a backbone. Vertebrates also have two pairs of appendages, bodies with three segments (head, neck, and trunk), and a spinal column that is enlarged to form a brain. Vertebrates are further divided into:

- Mammals—Mammals are those whose young are born live and are nourished by milk from their mothers. Examples include deer, elk, squirrels, and rabbits. The mammals are among the most popular wildlife. Most are terrestrial though some are aquatic.

- Birds—Birds are vertebrates that fly. They have light bones and bodies covered with feathers. Birds lay eggs and incubate the eggs until the young are

8-2. A red fox is a mammal.

8-3. A yellow warbler with two nestlings (baby birds in a nest).

hatched. Common birds are sparrows, crows, quail, ducks, and geese. Birds are sometimes known as Aves.

■ Reptiles—Reptiles are animals with skin covered with scales and a body temperature regulated by their environment. Examples of reptiles include snakes, lizards, alligators, and turtles.

8-4. A Texas alligator lizard is a reptile.

■ Amphibians—Amphibians typically live on land and reproduce in water. They have thin skin that secretes mucous. Amphibians have appendages for walking, climbing, and jumping. Examples include salamanders, frogs, and toads.

8-5. The green tree frog is an example of an amphibian.

■ Fish—Fish are aquatic vertebrates. Nearly 22,000 species of fish have been classified. Some fish prefer freshwater. Other species grow in saltwater and brackish water. Some are covered with scales, while others only have skin. Examples include trout, catfish, tuna, swordfish, and barracuda.

Here are a few examples of how people distinguish among areas of wildlife. Wildlife biologists focus primarily on terrestrial animals, fishery biologists focus on aquatic animals, ornithologists focus on birds, and waterfowl biologists deal with migratory waterfowl. This chapter concentrates on terrestrial animal wildlife.

8-6. The white crappie is a sport fish.

INVERTEBRATES. An *invertebrate* is an animal that does not have a backbone. The exteriors of their bodies are typically made of hard materials

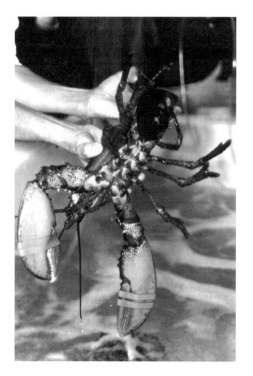

8-7. The lobster is an invertebrate.

that give the body shape and offer protection. Examples include insects, worms, shrimp, spiders, and lobsters.

Plants

Plants that grow in natural environments without human effort are wild. Plant wildlife makes food by photosynthesis. Many kinds of plants are found in the United States. Some grow quite large; others are small. Plants include trees, grasses, shrubs, vines, and wildflowers. Any plants that are cultured in fields, lawns or flowerbeds, or on farms are domesticated.

Fungi

Fungi absorb food from their surroundings. Many are small and require magnification to be seen. Other fungi are larger and easily seen. Mushrooms, mold, and mildew are three examples of fungi. Many people hunt wild mushrooms—though some mushrooms are cultured. If you hunt mushrooms, be sure to go with a person who can distinguish between those that are good to eat and those that are poisonous.

Monera and Protista

The Monera and Protista are two kingdoms of small, single-celled organisms. They perform important functions in the environment; however, they can cause disease. Some provide nutrients for other organisms, such as the bacteria (Monera) used as food by oysters. Protista include algae, amoeba, paramecium, and protozoa. Algae are often seen as the seaweed in a body of water.

DOMESTICATION

Domestication is removing living things from nature and raising them in an environment that is more or less controlled. The organisms have been tamed by humans and are raised and bred in captivity. All domesticated organisms were once wild.

Most domesticated animals depend on humans for food and care. Domesticated animals include cattle, horses, dogs, cats, and some birds. Humans often have close relationships with their animals. Domestication is a long, slow process.

WILDLIFE ANIMALS

Animals that have not been domesticated are *wildlife animals.* They have not been tamed. Wild animals live in a "free" condition and get food from their habitat. People sometimes put out food, such as a squirrel feeder or a salt block for deer.

Wildlife animals must be able to live, survive, and reproduce on their own. One member of a species might appear tame, for example in a zoo, but never should be regarded as domesticated. Animals in zoos revert to their natural instincts and attack when people get too close.

Career Profile

ENDANGERED SPECIES BIOLOGIST

An endangered species biologist studies and develops solutions to problems that endanger wildlife. The work is often outside tracking and identifying the habitat of animals. It may involve capturing and transporting animals. The animals may be moved to a new location. (This photograph shows a sedated female wolf being backpacked out of a remote area.) (Courtesy, U.S. Fish and Wildlife Service)

Endangered species biologists need college degrees in biology, wildlife management, or related areas. Many have masters or doctors degrees in similar areas. Practical experience working with wildlife and an appreciation of the outdoors are beneficial.

Jobs are with government agencies or associations that promote the protection of endangered species.

People sometimes capture wild animals and try to tame them. Often, this is unsuccessful. Do you know of people who have caught a raccoon, wild bird, or squirrel and tried to tame it? What was the outcome? (Note: In some places, it is illegal to confine or keep wildlife. A game warden can provide information.)

SPECIES IDENTIFICATION

Wildlife is known by its scientific taxonomy and common name. Scientific identification is based on similarities and differences in species. Names are based on scientific classification. Most wildlife has a scientific and a common name. Common names tend to vary by region or local custom. Scientific names are consistent worldwide.

People use common ways of identifying wildlife. These are the things to look for when identifying species. People often compare what they see to pictures or mental images. With experience, species are identified at a single glance.

Elk
(wapiti)

Caribou

Moose

White-tail deer

8-8. Antler shape and size can be used to identify animals.

Here are some questions when identifying animal wildlife:

- What is the body covering? Feathers, scales, hair, or skin are common. Compare the exterior you observe with that for a species. Feathers go with birds, scales with fish and reptiles, skin with amphibians and a few others, and hair with mammals.

- What is the body shape? Shape deals with conformation. Snakes are long, frogs are stocky, deer are sleek, and birds are angular.

- What body appendages are present? What is the shape of the appendages? Deer have long legs for running, snakes do not have legs, frogs have strong hind legs for jumping, and water birds have long legs for standing in water. Determine the number of legs, such as insects have six legs, spiders have eight, and squirrels have four.

- What are the features of the head? Some have antlers, such as deer, and others have antennae such as insects. Look at ear presence and shape.

- What are the features of the mouth? Birds have beaks that vary with the kind of food they eat, such as hawks have strong beaks and pelicans have large

8-9. Four signs of wildlife are the squirrel nest in a tree (top left), kildeer eggs on the ground (top right), food remains left by a squirrel (bottom left), and a beaver dam across a stream (bottom right).

8-10. A deer has left foot prints in the mud.

beaks. Some have mouths suited for grazing and others have mouths for eating flesh.

- What is the habitat of the species? Some live on land, others live in water, and others use both land and water.

- How does the species reproduce? Some give birth to live young and others lay eggs. Mammals and a few other species give birth to young. Birds, most snakes, most fish, insects, and frogs lay eggs.

- What are the signs of a species? A **sign** is evidence that an animal is or has been in the area. It is evidence that the animal left behind. Foot prints, manure, burrows and other digging activity, nests, hair, skin, feathers, and evidence of feeding activity help identify animals.

BENEFITS OF WILDLIFE

Some benefits of wildlife are easy to see; other benefits are not as obvious. The benefits are important in the lives of people and in striving for balance in nature. (Note: Nature is never balanced. It is continuously changing and evolving. Some situations can be more stable than others.)

The five major areas of benefit from wildlife are:

- Aesthetic benefits—The aesthetic benefits are those that people place on wildlife for beauty and appeal. People will travel long distances and invest in equipment to observe wildlife. Moose, wildflowers, fall leaf color, deer, bear, ducks, and song birds are a few examples. Some people go to national and state parks, refuges, and forests.

■ Game benefits—Some wildlife animals are hunted as game or otherwise taken. Deer, rabbits, squirrels, quail, and ducks are hunted. Fish, crabs, and frogs are captured. Each is taken for food or other purposes that humans value. Sports enthusiasts also cite the pleasure of being outside and going hunting or fishing.

■ Economic benefits—People spend money to enjoy wildlife. This ranges from eating wildlife foods in restaurants to buying guns, shells, and travel to hunt or observe wildlife. Millions of dollars are spent on clothing, equipment, and other items. Some landowners get income by leasing their land for hunting.

■ Scientific benefits—Wildlife is important for research. Some provide useful information. For example, lichens can be used to determine air pollution. Others can be used to seek cures for human disease. Wildlife is needed to assure biodiversity, which is preserving species to have their genetic material.

■ Ecological benefits—Each species makes important contributions to nature. Interactions among species are important. Some species are food sources for other species. Other species are important in cleaning the earth and assuring a good environment. The ecosystem must have a diversity of wildlife to provide a place for species to survive.

USES OF WILDLIFE

Some uses consume the animals, and are known as consumptive uses. Other uses are said to be nonconsumptive. (Refer to Chapter 2 for an explanation of consumptive and nonconsumptive uses.) Important uses include food, clothing, ornamentation, medicine, and recreation.

■ Food—Using wildlife for food is a consumptive use except for bird eggs. Most food, such as venison from a deer, involves killing the animal. Wildlife is important in the diets of many people. Common foods from animal wildlife include oysters, clams, calamari (squid), tuna, squirrel, rabbit, elk, and pheasant. Some of these may be cultured, such as elk, rabbit, and oysters. The eggs of a few birds are used as food. Caviar, the eggs from fish, is food that may result in destroying the fish to get the eggs.

■ Clothing—Some animals are used to make clothing, such as fur, leather, and fasteners. Animals trapped for fur include beaver, mink, fox, and rabbit. Leather is from kangaroo, lizard, alligator, and snake skins. Making clothing from wildlife is a consumptive use. Fasteners include buttons made from shells or bones.

■ Ornamentation—Wild animals have been taken to make ornaments. These are used on clothing, jewelry, household furnishings, and other places for their appeal. Everyone has seen large mounted heads of wildlife on walls. These are often referred to as trophies. Pearls from oysters are used in jewelry. Ivory from elephant tusks has been used in making piano keys. This activity has stopped. Sea shells are used for necklaces and other decorations.

■ Medicine—Human medicines often use substances taken from wild animals. Some wild species are used in research to identify new treatments and medical procedures. For example, the armadillo is used to study ways of treating leprosy. The armadillo is the only identified animal that has leprosy—a dreaded disease of humans. Some products are used to make dietary supplements.

■ Recreation—Hunting is popular with some people. Animals are also caught with traps, such as mink, or with hooks, such as fish. Hunting has a valuable role in wildlife management. Populations that are too big can be reduced by hunting to a level that can be supported by the available food. Recreation includes watching animals and enjoying nature. Whale-watching expeditions and birding (bird watching) are examples.

8-11. A hunter proudly displays a trophy elk.

HABITAT

A habitat is the area in which animal wildlife live. Habitat needs vary by species. A habitat for a bear is different from a habitat for a pheasant. Habitat must meet the needs of an animal. If it does not, the animal will die or move to another location.

To support the well-being of animals, habitat should have four major components: food, water, shelter, and space. These must be naturally present or can be initiated or supplemented in wildlife management.

FOOD

Food provides the nutrients animals need to carry out life functions. The food varies with the species. Some species eat plants; some species prey on other animals.

Typical wildlife food of plant origin includes the following:

- Leaves—Leaves are the vegetative portions of plants. They are particularly important to ruminant animals, such as deer and bison.

- Flowers—Flowers contain nectar that is particularly important to some insects, such as bees and butterflies. Other insects and animals eat buds, petals, and stamens.

- Fruit—Fruit matures following the flowering of a plant. Fruit contains seed as well as other edible parts. Fruit includes blackberries, mulberries, gooseberries, and plums.

- Nuts—A nut is the seed of some trees, such as acorns, pecans, and hickory nuts. Most nuts have a hard shell around the seed.

- Seed—Some seeds are not in nuts or fruit. They are in pods similar to beans and peas. Herbs, grasses, and other plants produce seed.

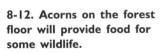
8-12. Acorns on the forest floor will provide food for some wildlife.

■ Twigs and bark—Woody plants have stems and bark. Examples include dogwoods, maples, huckleberries, and oaks. Some wildlife, such as insects, burrows into bark. If an area is overpopulated with deer, they may strip the bark off trees.

■ Roots—Roots are the underground foods of some wildlife. Some roots are more desirable than others as food. Nematodes often destroy plants by burrowing into them. Rodents may dig in the ground to uncover roots.

WATER

Water is an essential nutrient for life. A habitat must have adequate quality water year round. Springs, creeks, standing pools, dew, and succulent tissues provide water for most animal wildlife. Of course, aquatic animals, including water birds, live in or in association with a water habitat.

Water quality must be satisfactory. Salty water is not appropriate for most terrestrial animals. Polluted water can injure or kill wildlife.

COVER

Cover is an important part of habitat. *Cover* is the protection animals gain from their habitat from predators and weather. Cover offers a safe place for animals to rear their young.

Cover varies with the species of animal. Hollow trees and standing dead trees offer cover for squirrels, woodpeckers, and owls. Piles of brush provide cover for rabbits and snakes. People sometimes use artificial cover to attract

8-13. A Canada goose sits on her nest. (The nest is on the eastern shore of Virginia in cover designed to camouflage her presence.)

wildlife. Examples include bird houses and hummingbird and squirrel feeders. When planning to enhance cover, learn the needs of the animals that you wish to attract and establish cover accordingly.

SPACE

Space is the size of the home range an animal needs. The area over which an animal travels is its *home range*. The area the animal will defend is its territory. Worms do not travel far nor need much space. Birds need more space, with some traveling long distances. A wild turkey needs 500 acres of range; a deer needs about 650 acres; and a squirrel needs less than one acre.

HABITAT CLASSIFICATION

Animal wildlife is adapted to specific habitats. Each, to a certain extent, has its own unique habitat. For example, the habitat of an eagle might cover an area of several miles, while that of a salamander might be the closest small rock pile near water. Three general classifications based on habitat are aquatic, terrestrial, and amphibious.

AQUATIC HABITAT

An *aquatic habitat* is a water-based habitat for animals that live in water and/or depend on it for their food and reproduction. Species are adapted to different water environments. Three factors in an aquatic environment are:

■ Salinity—Aquatic species vary in adaptation to water salinity. The types of water based on salinity are freshwater, saltwater, and brackish water. Fish in most streams require freshwater. Those in oceans require saltwater. A few species, such as salmon, may live in freshwater and saltwater, depending on their life stage. Fish that live in saltwater and spawn in freshwater are known as *anadromous* fish. Fish that migrate between freshwater and saltwater are *diadromous* species. Freshwater species that go to saltwater to spawn are *catadromous*. In general, most aquatic species live their entire lives in one kind of water.

■ Temperature—Most species prefer temperatures within certain ranges. Three ranges are used: cold, cool, and warm. Cold water is 38 to 58° F (3 to 14° C). Most cold water species cannot survive in water above 68° F (20° C). Warm water is between 73 to 86° F (23 to 30° C). Cool water is between the

8-14. Sandhill cranes are wading birds with long legs.

cold and warm water temperatures. The temperature ranges often overlap. The salinity of the water is also a factor in tolerance of temperature extremes. Fish will not survive well in a temperature that does not suit them.

■ Movement or Flow—Water movement varies from rapidly flowing mountain streams, to slow- flowing rivers, and nonflowing lakes and oceans. Some species, such as trout, prefer the rapid-flowing clear water from melted snow. Other species prefer murky water in slow-flowing streams, such as water moccasin snakes. Species in oceans and lakes are adapted to nonflowing water. Examples include fish, snakes, and shrimp.

AMPHIBIOUS HABITAT

An *amphibious habitat* is a habitat for animals that require both land and water. They use land at one stage and water at another. Some animals get their food in the water and live on land. Other animals live in the water and get their food from the land or both land and water. Reproduction may be in water or on the land, depending on the species. This group includes the amphibians as well as some mammals, birds, and reptiles.

Water mammals, such as beavers and otters, live largely in or near water. Whales do not go on land as do the beaver, otter, and sea lions. Some water mammals spend much of their time sunning on rocks and dive in the water for food. Each species has unique habitat requirements. The beaver, for example, prefers fresh, flowing water with small trees and shrubs growing nearby.

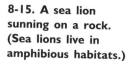

8-15. A sea lion sunning on a rock. (Sea lions live in amphibious habitats.)

Waterfowl are swimming birds that live in water habitats. Common waterfowl are ducks, geese, and swans. Some are game birds and are popular with hunters. Cormorants are non-game swimming waterfowl that are often pests on fish farms. Swimming birds must have water areas that are open and deep enough for swimming. Wading birds stand in water searching for food. They have long legs for wading and long necks and bills for capturing small fish in the water. Wading birds include cranes and herons. The habitat for wading birds is relatively shallow water.

Water birds typically reproduce on land and in marshes. Some water birds nest in trees or in thick grass. Conservationists may put up nesting boxes for water birds.

Water reptiles typically spend their lives in water but do occasionally leave the water for land. Depending on the species, some especially like creek banks for food or reproduction. Reptiles like logs, rocks, and grassy bank areas in their habitats. Water reptiles include alligators, turtles, crocodiles, and some species of snakes.

TERRESTRIAL HABITAT

A terrestrial habitat is a habitat for animals that live on the land. The habitat varies within an ecosystem. Some animals dig into the earth, such as the muskrat. Others primarily live in the canopies of trees, such as some species of birds. Regardless, food, water, shelter, and space must be available.

The major kinds of terrestrial habitats are:

8-16. Mule deer live in terrestrial habitat.

- Woodland—**Woodland** is an area of trees, shrubs, vines, mosses, and fallen limbs and tree trunks. These areas are natural forests though some are tree farms. The trees include oak (acorns), hickory (nuts), and some evergreens, such as pine (cones). Tree canopies are used for bird and squirrel nests. Fallen trees and limbs on the ground are habitats for insects and toads. Gnarled and hollow trees are habitats for some, such as woodpeckers.

    The forest floor, with its leaves, twigs, and small plants, is habitat for insects, rabbits, and other species. Deer may use the cane and vines in the forest for browse. Some species like standing dead trees for a habitat. Owls, hawks, wrens, fox, and chipmunks may use standing snags or the decaying base as a den, nest, or food source.

- Brush—**Brush** includes shrubs, scrub trees, vines, herbaceous plants, and dead plant materials. These provide a habitat for rabbits, some birds, rats and mice, lizards, opossums, insects, and many other animal species.

- Grassy Areas—Grass provides the habitat for many animal species. Grass areas near woods, in fence rows, and as pastures serve as habitat for different species. Grass areas are attractive to some birds, rodents, fox, and other animals. The prairie land area of North America is well known for grass habitats. These habitats are important as are the grass areas near fields, factories, and residential developments.

- Rock and Soil—Some animals burrow into the soil, hide under rocks, and crawl into crevices. Rock piles are habitats for chipmunk, skunks, rodents, snakes, and ants. Those that live in and around rock piles attract predators.

- Edge—**Edge** is the area where two habitats meet. For example, edge is where woods and grasslands join or where wetlands and woods meet. Edge is the place for wildlife that lives in one kind of habitat and seeks food in another.

Rabbits, fox, quail, turkeys, deer, and raccoon are examples of wildlife that thrive along the edge.

WILDLIFE ENDANGERMENT

Endangerment is a condition in the ecosystem that threatens the continued existence of a species. Fish, birds, mammals, and other species can be endangered. The ability of a species to reproduce and maintain its population is related to endangerment.

The long-term consequences of losing a species are unknown. Scientists estimate that at least 100 species are lost from the earth each year.

- Extinct Species—An *extinct species* is one that no longer lives on the earth. It has disappeared. Extinction results when a species does not reproduce itself and dies out. Once extinct, a species cannot be brought back. The passenger pigeon is an example of an extinct animal. Better-adapted species may rise to take the place of one that becomes extinct.

- Endangered Species—An *endangered species* is one that is threatened with becoming extinct. The species is not reproducing itself sufficiently to maintain its population. About 400 species are on the endangered species list in the United States. Steps are taken to protect endangered species. Examples of endangered species are grizzly bears, whooping cranes, and gray wolves.

- Threatened Species—A *threatened species* is one that is facing serious dangers and likely to become endangered. The danger is not great enough to classify the species as endangered. Many species are threatened by hunting, trap-

8-17. The Florida manatee is an endangered aquatic species.

ping, and other harvesting. More than 125 species are now listed as threatened in the United States.

■ Rare Species—A *rare species* is one that exists in small numbers and could become threatened. Rare species are often kept in refuges, zoological parks, and other places for protection. As long as a few members of the species exist, there is still hope to restore adequate numbers of the wildlife.

PROTECTING WILDLIFE

Wildlife populations can be promoted with good wildlife management practices. These practices are based on the biological needs of the species that are being promoted.

THREATS

Wildlife populations are faced with several threats. Solving the threats helps protect a species.

■ Loss of Habitat—The greatest threat to wildlife is the loss of habitat. Factories, homes, cropland, schools, and other facilities destroy habitat. Often, ways can be found to promote habitat growth. New habitat can compensate for that removed for development purposes.

■ Health and Age—Wildlife that is healthy and disease free is more productive. It is less likely to decline in population. Good nutrition is related to health. The lack of food reduces the vigor of wildlife. Food shortage may be due to overpopulation of wildlife or not enough food. Inadequate food makes wildlife more likely to get disease. As animals age, they are less able to defend themselves and find food. They are more likely to be attacked by predators or get disease.

■ Predation—*Predation* is the capture and consumption of one animal by another. Predators have important roles. Big populations of predators can threaten a population of prey. For example, cormorants are large water birds that prey on fish. One cormorant can consume many fish in a summer. A fish population in a small pond could be wiped out by a number of cormorants.

■ Pollution—Pollution can threaten wildlife. Most pollution is from human activity. Controlling pollution prevents this cause of wildlife loss. For example, large fish kills may occur in streams that are polluted by factories or cropland.

■ Hunting—Hunting can be a tool in wildlife management or it can threaten its existence. Laws have been established to regulate hunting. These are intended to protect wildlife. All hunters should know and follow the laws.

WILDLIFE MANAGEMENT

Wildlife management is using practices that promote wildlife. Knowing what to do is essential. Get the assistance of a trained wildlife biologist.

Here are a few activities in wildlife management:

■ Promote Habitat—Wildlife prospers if it has good habitat. Take steps to establish habitat to promote the target species. This begins with developing a habitat management plan. The plan includes an inventory of what is on the site, the goal to be achieved, and the ways and means of reaching the goal. Planting trees, seeding grass, building brush piles, establishing food plants, and assuring that water will be available are steps in promoting habitat.

■ Introduce/Reestablish Species—It is sometimes necessary to bring in and release wildlife. These should be species that are suited to the area and will not pose problems. The best success is with reestablishing a wildlife species. Trying to establish species that are not naturally in the area is more difficult.

■ Prevent Pollution—Having a good environment for wildlife promotes its well-being. Keeping streams free of pollution and removing hazards from land promotes wildlife.

8-18. Putting up houses for nesting promotes wildlife.

■ Take Properly—People should follow all rules when hunting and fishing. Do not take more than the bag limit. As a tool in management, hunting can be used to remove excess populations. This provides more food for the remaining population.

RECREATIONAL WILDLIFE

Wildlife is used for recreational purposes in several ways. Some people enjoy sports involving wildlife. Some people gain pleasure from helping improve wildlife habitat and the contact with nature this activity gives.

HUNTING

Hunting is killing game for food or sport. Game is animal wildlife that is hunted, such as rabbits, squirrels, deer, and quail. Laws regulate hunting. People must usually have a hunting license for the state in which they hunt. A hunter should know the regulations on the species being hunted. For example, it is legal to hunt some species only at certain times of the year, known as hunting season. *Bag limit* is a restriction on the number of animals that can be taken in one day or one hunt. Laws may also specify shooting hours, which is the time of the day when hunting can take place.

The devices a person uses when hunting are known as hunting gear. Most hunting is with primitive devices and firearms. Primitive devices include

8-19. A quail hunter uses a Pointer dog to locate birds.

bows and arrows, crossbows, and muzzleloading guns. Firearms include shotguns, rifles, and handguns.

Hunter safety is using hunting gear and practices to prevent accidents and injury. Hunters must demonstrate safe behavior. They must follow the rules of using firearms. All hunters should complete a hunter education program. Such programs instruct in safety and about laws related to game.

FISHING

Fishing is capturing fish with hooks, nets, seines, traps, and other means. Fishing is a popular hobby. Some people make their living as commercial fishers. Sport fishing is capturing for enjoyment.

Laws relate to sport and commercial fishing much as they do to hunting. Game fish are regulated. A fishing license is usually required except on fish farms that raise fish and offer fishing for a fee. Laws regulate the species that can be caught, the number caught, the size of the fish that can be kept, and the season of the year when fishing can take place.

Resource Connection

LET'S GO FISHING!

Millions of Americans enjoy sport fishing. Sport fishers carefully study the species they want. They select fishing tackle and bait to catch the "big one." Applicable laws are learned and carefully followed.

Safety is always important. All equipment should be used properly. Care is essential around water. It is always a good idea to wear a life jacket. Hooks, knives, and other tools should be used carefully to prevent injury.

When you catch one, what do you do? If the fish is small, it can be carefully removed from the hook and returned to the water. If it is a "keeper" for food, save it to prevent deterioration until it can be dressed and placed on ice. If it is a trophy-size fish, save it on ice and have it mounted for a fond memory of your fishing experience. This photo shows a fish being unhooked. (Courtesy, Jim Palmer, U.S. Fish and Wildlife Service)

8-20. A sport fisher catching a small fish.

A wide range of fishing gear is used. The equipment used in sport fishing is known as *fishing tackle*. The simplest tackle is a line with a baited hook on a cane pole. The kind of bait and hook depend on the species and size of fish being sought. *Bait* is live or dead material placed on a hook to attract fish. Fish eat the bait and, in doing so, take the hook into their mouth.

Water safety is important in fishing. Watch for water snakes. Carefully walk and stand to prevent falling into the water. If a boat is used, operate it safely.

NATURE STUDY

Nature study is learning about things in nature. It includes all species of wildlife as well as natural phenomena of waterfalls, streams, and rock formations. Wildlife is observed in its habitat. Some wildlife species are present on a seasonal basis, such as migratory birds. It is important to know the daily habits of wildlife. Some are out in the early morning, some midday, some late afternoon, and others at night.

REVIEWING

MAIN IDEAS

Wildlife is any living thing that has not been domesticated. Some people use "wildlife" only when referring to animals. Wildlife is in each of the five kingdoms used in scientific classification. Animal wildlife that is hunted for sport and food is known as game. Wildlife has a number of uses and provides important benefits.

The two major classes of wildlife animals are vertebrates and invertebrates. The vertebrates include mammals, fish, birds, reptiles, and amphibians. The invertebrates include insects, crustaceans (shrimp and crawfish), mollusks (oysters and clams), and worms.

The area where an animal lives is its habitat. The major habitat components are food, water, shelter, and space. Human efforts to improve wildlife populations must consider these components. Wildlife lives in three kinds of habitats: aquatic, terrestrial, and amphibious.

Some species of wildlife are endangered. Wildlife that once was on the earth but is now gone is extinct. Those species that are threatened with becoming extinct are endangered species. A species that exists in small numbers and could become endangered is a threatened species. Rare species are those that exist in small numbers and often in zoological parks. Proper protection can help preserve wildlife numbers.

Wildlife has important recreational uses. Hunting, fishing, and nature study are three large areas of interest. All laws and safety practices should be followed with recreational uses of wildlife.

QUESTIONS

Answer the following questions using complete sentences and correct spelling.

1. Distinguish between vertebrate and invertebrate animal wildlife.
2. What are the five groups of vertebrates?
3. In identifying wildlife, what is a sign?
4. What are four benefits of wildlife?
5. What are five uses of wildlife?
6. What four components are found in habitat?
7. What is cover? Why is cover important?
8. What are the three major classifications of habitat? Briefly describe each.
9. What is wildlife endangerment?
10. What are the threats to wildlife?
11. What activities may be used in wildlife management?
12. What are the three major recreational uses of wildlife? Briefly explain each.

EVALUATING

Match the term with the correct definition. Write the letter by the term in the blank provided.

a. bait
b. bag limit
c. hunter safety
d. vertebrate

e. home range
f. anadromous fish
g. waterfowl
h. woodland

i. extinct species
j. nature study

_____ 1. Learning about things in nature.

_____ 2. A group of animals that have backbones.

_____ 3. The area in which an animal travels.

_____ 4. A fish that lives in saltwater and spawns in freshwater.

_____ 5. Live or dead material used to attract animals.

_____ 6. Using hunting gear in a way to prevent accidents and injury.

_____ 7. Swimming birds that live in water habitats.

_____ 8. Land areas covered with trees, shrubs, vines, mosses, and fallen limbs and tree trunks.

_____ 9. A species that is no longer found on the earth.

_____ 10. Restriction on the number of animals that can be taken in one day or one hunt.

EXPLORING

1. Compile a list of the game animals found in your area. Interview hunters, game wardens, and naturalists to get the common names. Classify the list by habitat requirements. Select one species and make an in-depth study of it. Take photographs and construct a bulletin board about your findings.

2. Investigate the game laws in your area. Be sure to include species, seasons, bag limits, and license requirements. Prepare a written report on your findings.

3. Make a tour of a wildlife refuge or zoological park. Determine the major species and how the needs of the species are met. Interview the caretaker or superintendent about their work.

9

FORESTS

Forests provide many of the things we need. Wood and paper are major products we use each day. These are from the trees that grow in forests.

Examine the book you are using. You will see two or three different kinds of paper, such as the cover is different from the inside pages. How long did it take a tree to grow the pulp to make the paper in this book? A new pine seedling would need at least five years to grow big enough to make this book. (It would still be too small to harvest!) A larger tree—say 15 years old—would possibly grow enough pulp in a year for several books.

Since early times, forests have provided housing, tools, and a wide variety of foods, ranging from maple syrup to hickory nuts. Native forests are important to wildlife. In addition, forests provide recreation for outdoor enthusiasts.

9-1. Forestry in urban areas may involve using ropes to climb into tree tops to prune and otherwise promote tree health.

OBJECTIVES

This chapter introduces the importance of native forests. It has the following objectives:

1. Contrast and compare native forests with tree farming

2. Identify uses of forests

3. Explain the physical structure of forests

4. Identify the major parts of a tree and explain the functions of each part

5. Identify common species of forest plants

6. Outline the major forest regions of the United States

7. Describe relationships between species that live in forests

8. Apply important management practices in forests

TERMS

canopy
common name
conifer
crown
dendrology
diameter breast high
dominant species
forest
forest region
hardwood
lichen
log
native forest
old-growth forest
pulpwood
regrowth forest
root
scientific name
seedling
shrub
silviculture
stand
story
tree
tree farm
trunk
urban forestry
vine

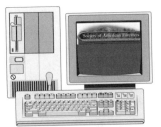

**Society of
American Foresters
http://www.safnet.org/**

FORESTS AND TREE FARMS

A *forest* is an area where trees and other plants grow in an ever-changing community. Plants dominate the land area. Animal wildlife may live in association with the forest community. The study of forests and associated communities is known as forestry.

A **native forest** is one in which the species are voluntarily growing and are naturally present in the area. Native forests often have a variety of species and provide wildlife habitat. Native forests are contrasted with tree farms.

A **tree farm** is an area that has been planted to selected and improved tree species. Undesirable native species are not allowed to grow in improved timber stands on tree farms. Practices are used to protect the trees and promote rapid, desirable growth.

Commercial forestry is caring for a forest to improve the quality and quantity of wood when it is marketed. Regular harvest schedules are followed with tree farms but may not be used with native forests. Wood production is usually higher on tree farms.

9-2. The redwood trees of California are among the largest plants.

ORIGINAL NATIVE FORESTS

Forests once covered North America. This vast natural resource promoted the growth of our nation. Today, millions of acres are still in forests and many have native species.

The availability of quality timber was a major factor in the colonization of the United States. England depended on the shipping trade and American forests provided tall, straight timber for building ships.

The original forests in the United States covered 822 million acres of land (1,284,975 square miles). More than 200 million acres have been cleared for crops and pastures, factories, and residential areas. Another 489,555,000 acres of the original forestland remain as forest. It is estimated

9-3. Three stages of growth are shown here on a tree farm. (The foreground shows young six- to eight-year-old pine trees. The midground shows two- to three-year-old pine seedlings. The background shows 14- to 18-year-old pine trees approaching pulpwood harvest size.)

that 247,126,000 acres of forest are farm wood lots and small wooded areas scattered in the original forest areas.

The majority of the forest area east of the Rocky Mountains has been cut one or more times. This area is known as **regrowth forest** because it regrows every quarter century or so after cutting. Some regrowth forests are managed to protect the trees and promote growth.

Only a few areas of uncut forests remain. An uncut forest is known as an **old-growth forest**. Most old-growth forest is in the Pacific coast states. National parks and national forests protect much of the old-growth forest. Old-growth forests are studied for their nature and diversity of plant life.

URBAN FORESTRY

Urban forestry is establishing and caring for trees in urban areas. Most cities have plantings with species that are normally found in forests. These may be in parks, landscapes around factories and office buildings, along streets, and in residential areas. Trees must be properly planted, pruned, and otherwise cared for in urban settings.

Trees have a number of benefits in urban areas. A major benefit is soil and water conservation. Trees also help modify the temperature in cities. The presence of trees results in lower summer temperatures on streets and parking lots. Shade on buildings reduces the energy consumed for air conditioning. Trees also help people like urban areas and enjoy life. Trees provide places for wildlife to live in urban areas.

USES OF FORESTS

Forests have many uses. Products from the trees that grow in forests are used in many ways by people. But, the uses of forests are far greater than just trees!

ECONOMIC BENEFITS

Economic benefits are the commercial uses made of forests. Raw materials are used for manufacturing useful products. Here are a few examples:

- Logs—A *log* is a segment of the main stem, or trunk, of a tree that is suitable for sawing into lumber. Trees are cut down and into logs that are 12 to 20 feet (3.66 to 6.1 m) long. Logs should be straight, free of knots, and without rotten places. The small end of a log must be large enough to make products of the desired size. For example, a board that is 8 inches (20.32 cm) wide will require a log that is at least 8 inches (20.32 cm) in diameter after the bark has been removed. Shorter logs are used to make plywood.

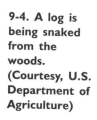

9-4. A log is being snaked from the woods. (Courtesy, U.S. Department of Agriculture)

9-5. Harvested pulpwood is on a rail car for hauling to a paper mill.

- Pulpwood—*Pulpwood* is the wood that is used to make paper and similar products. Smaller trees can be used for pulpwood. The trees can also be crooked and have knots.

- Other products—Forests provide a large number of other products including fence posts, maple syrup, nuts, berries, and many specialty wood materials. Trees also influence property values. Homeowners like to have trees near their homes and are willing to pay more for the property if trees are present.

ENVIRONMENTAL AND AESTHETIC BENEFITS

Forests provide a number of important benefits to the environment. A few examples are:

- Influence local climate—Trees can cool small areas in warm weather and reduce wind movement throughout the year.

- Conserve moisture—Trees reduce the loss of water to runoff and help retain snow as it is melting. This helps maintain groundwater supplies and reduces the chance of flooding.

- Habitat—Forests provide habitat for wildlife. Many trees produce nuts or berries that are used as food by wildlife. Some wildlife species use leaves, holes in trees, and other places as nesting or bedding areas.

- Pollutant removal and detection—Trees remove some pollutants from the air. For example, small amounts of sulfur dioxide may be used by a tree. Trees reduce particulate in the air by holding it on leaf surfaces. Some leaves

9-6. A biker enjoys the structure of this forest.

absorb gases from the air. These can be analyzed in a laboratory for the presence of pollutants.

- Noise reduction—Trees are used for noise abatement (reduction). Trees are often planted along roads to abate the noise from passing vehicles.

Resource Connection

MEASURING STANDING TIMBER

Measuring standing timber uses a process known as cruising. The dbh of a tree is determined followed by an estimate of the height of the tree in terms of useable wood. Special devices or scales are used to make the measurements.

Information from the measurements is used to calculate board feet. Board feet is the standard measure of timber for making lumber in the United States. One board foot is a piece of lumber that is 1 inch thick, 12 inches wide, and 1 foot long. Simple formulas can be used to convert lumber of any size to board feet.

This photo shows an altimeter being used to measure the height of a tree. Along with dbh, knowing height allows the amount of wood in a tree to be determined.

■ Recreation—People often enjoy hiking in forests and observing tree growth and wildlife. Some people, known as "leaf-lookers," travel to forests to see the leaves in the fall as they turn to yellow, orange, and red.

PHYSICAL STRUCTURE OF FORESTS

Individual trees and other plants form a forest community. They support each other and help make the overall community stronger. Good evidence of how trees support each other is demonstrated when some trees are cut and others are left. Those that are left cannot resist wind and ice as well as when the community of trees was untouched.

PLANTS IN A FOREST

Forests are made of trees and other plants that form a fairly definite structure. The size, age, and species that are present influence forest structure.

The common kinds of plants in a forest are:

9-7. Poison ivy is a vine that often grows on tree trunks. (Poison ivy contains an oil that causes small, itching blisters on the skin.)

■ Trees—A *tree* is a perennial plant more than 15 feet (4.5 m) tall. Some may be more than 100 feet (30 m) tall. Trunks near the ground may be 30 inches (76 cm) or more in diameter. A tree has one woody stem that supports a crown. The crown is the top part of a tree that includes branched limbs. Common trees include the oaks, pines, and maples.

■ Shrubs—A *shrub* is a perennial plant that grows no more than 15 feet (4.5 m) tall. Shrubs have woody stems, with some having several stems. Examples include buttonwood, huckleberry, and sumac.

■ Vines—A *vine* is a plant that creeps or climbs on other plants, rocks, or the ground. The stems of vines do not offer support as do the stems of trees and shrubs. Vines may have tendrils or other growth structures that attach and hold them to their support. Common vines include poison ivy, blackberry, and Virginia creeper.

■ Herbs—An herb is a plant with roots, stems, and leaves but without a definite structure. They grow from a few inches to a few feet (cm or m) tall. Herbs may be annuals, biennials, or perennials, depending on the species. Examples include wild strawberries, violets, daisies, and horse nettle (sticker weed).

■ Mosses and ferns—Mosses are very low-growing plants that do not have flowers. They are often seen covering rocks, the ground, or tree stems. They may form a mat-type covering in moist, shady places. Ferns are nonflowering plants that reproduce with spores. They grow in shady, moist places underneath the cover of trees and shrubs.

9-8. Ferns are often in shaded areas near small streams, springs, or wet areas.

PLANT-LIKE SPECIES

Lichens are found in many forests. A *lichen* is an organism made of a fungus and an alga that live together as a single unit. Lichens grow on the

9-9. A large lichen from an old-growth area is being examined in Mt. Hood National Forest.

bark of trees, the ground, decaying wood, or on rocks. Some 20,000 species of lichens have been identified.

Lichens have no roots and grow only where moisture is present. Pigmentation in the alga part allows photosynthesis to take place. The fungus part absorbs water for the alga. Color varies from green to yellow, brown, and gray.

Lichens are used in many products, such as perfumes, soap, and to make litmus paper. (Litmus is used in a chemistry lab to determine if a substance is basic or acidic.) Environmentalists use lichens to help monitor pollution. Lichens absorb substances in the air, such as metals. Lab analysis determines the presence of some substances in a lichen and, therefore, in the air.

CANOPY AND STORY

Some forests are composed of a single tree species that spreads large, dense canopies. A *canopy* is formed by the upper part of trees by limbs and foliage. Many kinds of wildlife use the canopy as their habitat.

Career Profile

FORESTER

A forester works to improve forest production. The work may involve planning forests, overseeing planting, using silviculture practices, harvesting trees, and other work. They are also concerned about wildlife and environmental quality.

Most foresters have bachelors degrees in forestry. Many have masters degrees. Those in research or higher levels have doctors degrees in forestry. Practical experience with trees and in the outdoors is beneficial. Prepare to study forestry by taking courses in agriculture, biology, and similar areas in high school.

The work is found where forestry is important. Many jobs are with large commercial forestry companies. Some jobs are with government agencies at the federal and state levels. This photo shows a forester reviewing specialty timber with a millworker. (Courtesy, U.S. Department of Agriculture)

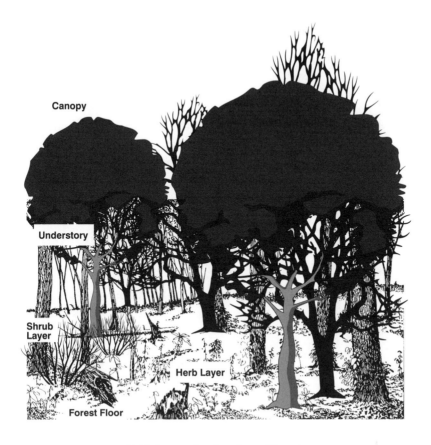

9-10. Layers in a hardwood forest.

The physical structure of a forest is known as story. A *story* is a horizontal layer of growth. The layers are often easy to see. Layers are based on the species and age of the plants that are growing. Story is often in three layers: understory, mid-story, and upper story. Understory is the layer on or near the ground. It is underneath the mid-story. The upper story is at the top of the canopy.

Forests with mixed species of different ages and sizes have greater story. Some forests have openings in the top canopy that allow sunlight to reach the forest floor. These forests have a variety of grasses, vines, and small trees and shrubs growing at or near ground level to form an understory.

PARTS OF A TREE

Trees have three major parts: crown, trunk, and roots. These three parts carry out life processes for a tree.

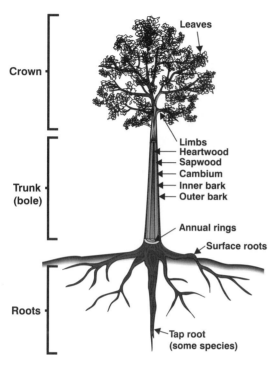

9-11. Major parts of a tree.

The **crown** is the top part of a tree with limbs, leaves, and, perhaps, flowers and fruit. A major role of the crown is to hold leaves up to collect sunlight so photosynthesis can occur. Damaged crowns may result in weakened or diseased trunks or roots. The crown often serves as a nesting site for animal wildlife, such as squirrels and birds. The nature of the growth in a crown varies with tree species.

The **trunk** is the main stem connecting the crown with the roots. It performs important roles in transporting raw materials upward to the crown for photosynthesis and manufactured food downward to the roots. Stems are often strong and valued for the wood products they can produce.

Examining a cross section of a trunk will tell much about a tree—age, damage by fire or disease, nutrient deficiency, and insect damage. Cross sections have annual rings, which reflect the amount of growth that occurred each

9-12. Diameter breast high (dbh) is measured with a diameter tape (also known as a d-tape). (This is a special type of tape that converts circumference measurements to diameter measurements.)

year. Trunk diameter is measured 54 inches (1.37 m) above the ground. This height is **diameter breast high** (dbh).

The **root** is the part of a tree that is in the ground. Most trees have large root systems. Root systems are of two types: tap and fibrous. A tap root system has one large root with a number of small roots. A fibrous root system has many roots that spread and branch in the soil. Roots take water and nutrients from the soil. They store manufactured food for the plant. Roots hold a tree in position and help it withstand wind and other weather conditions. Some trees have shallow root systems and fall over easily. Others have deep root systems that allow them to resist more wind.

TREE SPECIES

More than 250 species of trees have been identified in North American forests. The study of tree identification is known as **dendrology**. The major focus is to identify trees based on easily seen external features.

TWO MAJOR GROUPS

Trees are in two major groups: conifers and hardwoods.

A **conifer** is a tree that has needles (instead of broad leaves) and produces seed in cones. Scientifically, conifers are in the Gymnospermae class. Many conifers are evergreen trees and retain needles year round. They are known as trees that grow rapidly and produce soft wood. Because of the ease of work-

9-13. This small limb of blue atlas cedar shows the traits of a conifer: cones and needles.

9-14. Red oak are important hardwoods in some locations.

ing with the wood from conifers, they are predominantly used in making lumber, plywood, and other construction materials. Pines, spruces, and firs are examples of conifers.

A *hardwood* is a tree that has broadleaves and has wood that is hard and of fine grain. The hardwoods are in the Angiospermae class. Seeds are produced in fruit, berries, and nuts. Hardwoods are deciduous, meaning that they lose their leaves each fall. Common hardwoods include the oaks and gums, as well as walnut, cherry, and maple.

FOREST STANDS

A *stand* is the number of plants distributed over the ground. Native forests vary in spacing and number. Tree farms have relatively uniform stands in terms of number, spacing, and species.

Tree species may vary in a stand. A stand made of one species is pure. In practice, a pure stand is 80 percent or more of the same species. If the stand has more than 20 percent of one or more species other than the dominant species, it is a mixed stand. Most native forests are mixed stands with a predominate species. A hardwood stand may have oak, hickory, and maple.

DOMINANCE

Some species of trees outgrow other species. Those that grow the largest and shade the other species are known as *dominant species*. A dominant species has a large canopy that deprives smaller, less-dominant species of sunlight, water, and space.

In general, hardwoods are dominant over conifers in mixed forests. The first trees to grow in some forests are the conifers. The hardwoods will grow later and become dominant over the stand. The conifers will be unable to survive.

NAMES AND IDENTIFICATION OF TREES

Working in forestry requires the ability to identify common trees found locally. This involves distinguishing between species and using the correct names.

TREE NAMES

Trees have common and scientific names. A **common name** is the one used by people in their every-day work. Homeowners typically select trees for their lawns using a common name.

Common names are sometimes confusing. People in different places may use different common names for the same species. For example, water oak is

Table 9-1.
Common and Scientific Names of Selected Species

Common Name	Scientific Name
black walnut	*Juglans nigra*
blue spruce	*Picea pungens*
California sycamore	*Plantanus racemosa*
eastern hemlock	*Tsuga canadensis*
jack pine	*Pinus banksiana*
loblolly pine	*Pinus taeda*
noble fir	*Abies nobilis*
Pacific mountain ash	*Sorbus sitchensis*
pin oak	*Quercus palustris*
ponderosa pine	*Pinus ponderosa*
red maple	*Acer rubrum*
sugar maple	*Acer saccharum*
sweet gum	*Liquidambar styraciflua*
sycamore	*Platanus occidentilis*

Note: For a more complete listing, refer to: *Forests and Forestry* (5th edition) by I. I. Holland and G. L. Rolfe, published by Interstate Publishers, Inc., Danville, Illinois, 1997.

known as possum oak, red oak, pin oak, swamp oak, and spotted oak. The name used depends on where you live and this can be confusing. Scientists know this species as *Quercus nigra*—a name that communicates the exact species.

Scientific names avoid confusion. A ***scientific name*** is the name of a species based on its scientific classification. Scientific names are written in italics or underlined. The first part of a scientific name is the genus, with the first letter capitalized. The second is the species, which is not capitalized.

TREE IDENTIFICATION

Most trees are fairly easy to identify. The major identifying characteristics of trees are leaves, twigs, bark, flowers, and fruit. All of these may not be present when you look at a tree. Bark and twigs are usually always present. Evergreen trees always have leaves.

With leaves, shape, type, size, arrangement, color, and odor are used in identification. Some leaves are long, slender needles. Other leaves are large, flat, and have lobed or serrated edges. Flowers, fruit, and nuts are helpful in identification. For example, the leaf of a post oak has distinct shape differences when compared to the white oak.

More information on local species of trees is available from the forest service or the Cooperative Extension Service near you.

9-15. The tulip poplar is easily identified by its flower and the dried seed head that follows.

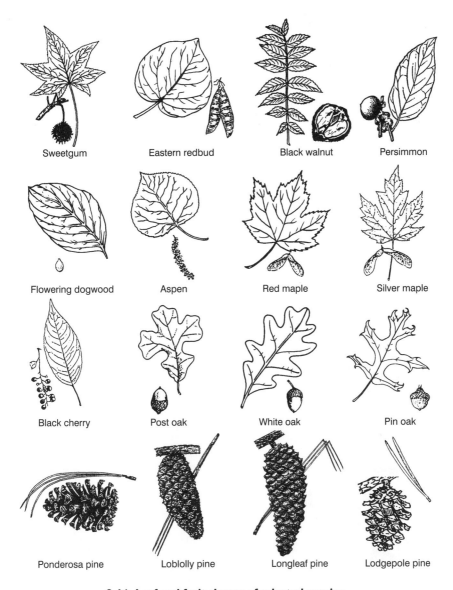

Sweetgum   Eastern redbud   Black walnut   Persimmon

Flowering dogwood   Aspen   Red maple   Silver maple

Black cherry   Post oak   White oak   Pin oak

Ponderosa pine   Loblolly pine   Longleaf pine   Lodgepole pine

9-16. Leaf and fruit shapes of selected species.

FOREST REGIONS

Forest industries often develop around the type of forest in an area. Some industries prefer softwoods; others prefer hardwoods. For example, the fine-wood furniture industry developed from North Carolina into Pennsylvania and northward because walnuts, cherries, and maples grew in the area.

Moisture, temperature, and soil influence the types of forests that grow. For example, forests in North Carolina are quite different from forests in Texas and Idaho. This is because the temperature and moisture in North Carolina are different from those of Texas and Idaho.

Forest regions vary within and between states. Some areas have very mild winters, relatively flat land, and deep soils saturated with water. Other areas may have steep land that is mountain-like, dry soils, and low winter temperatures.

The United States can be divided into six major forest regions. A *forest region* is an area with a predominance of related tree species present. Regions are also based on the climate that promotes the forest growth.

1. NORTHERN FOREST REGION — The Northern Forest Region is the largest of the six forest regions. It extends from northeastern Georgia, along the Appalachian Mountains, to New England and the northern portions of the Lake States. This region extends through Canada and the interior of Alaska.

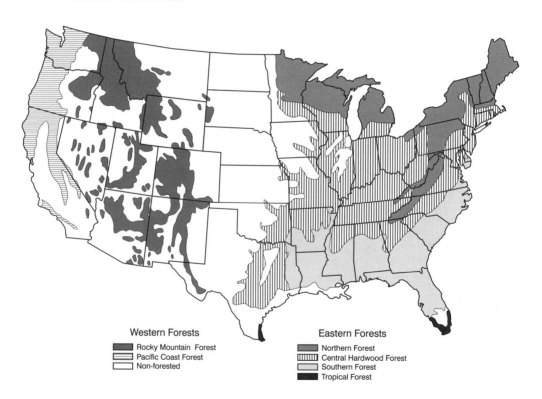

Western Forests
- Rocky Mountain Forest
- Pacific Coast Forest
- Non-forested

Eastern Forests
- Northern Forest
- Central Hardwood Forest
- Southern Forest
- Tropical Forest

9-17. Locations of forest regions in the forty-eight contiguous states.

The northern portion of this region produces small-size trees that are primarily black and white spruce, balsam fir, larch, paper birch, aspen balsam, poplar, and willows. The southern portion is characterized by highly valuable timber species, such as spruce, birches, beech, basswood, maples, and red oak.

2. SOUTHERN FOREST REGION — The Southern Forest Region covers the coastal area from Texas to Maryland. It extends north from Texas along rivers into Oklahoma, Arkansas, and Missouri and eastward across the southern states. This forest region is one of the most important timber producing areas in North America. This region produces seven species of pine, bald cypress, tupelo gum, sweet gum, beech, ashes, elms, oaks, hickories, and others.

3. CENTRAL HARDWOOD REGION — The Central Hardwood Region covers the central portion of the eastern United States, with the exception of the Appalachian Mountains, and extends into Canada. Oaks are the dominant species. Other important species include hickories, ashes, elms, maples, gum, beech, yellow poplar, walnut, cottonwood, sycamore, and dogwood.

4. TROPICAL FOREST REGION — The Tropical Forest Region is found in Arizona, California, southern Florida, and extreme southern Texas. Trees are small and often lack commercial value. Florida and Texas represent the extreme northern range of plants from the deep tropics of Central and South America. Arizona and California provide a desert climate with brushy plants capable of living under extremely dry conditions. Palms, ebony, mesquite, and other thorny species are typical of this region.

5. ROCKY MOUNTAIN FOREST REGION — The Rocky Mountain Forest Region is spread over the mountains and high plateaus from Mexico into northern Canada. It is bordered on the east by the Great Plains and on the west by the Pacific Coast Forest. The primary tree species are spruce, lodgepole pine, aspen, poplar, ponderosa pine, Douglas fir, oaks, pinyon pine, junipers, and cottonwood.

6. PACIFIC COAST FOREST REGION — The Pacific Coast Forest Region includes the Pacific coast states and is bounded on the east by the Rocky Mountain Forest and on the west by the Pacific Ocean. This region supports the largest and tallest trees in the world (giant sequoia and redwood). The single most important timber species in the world is

Douglas-fir and it is in this forest region. Trees tend to grow in dense stands. This region has considerable saw timber.

FOREST SPECIES

Forests provide habitat for animal wildlife. The species present is influenced by the kinds of trees that are present. Trees produce food for wildlife. An example is an oak tree that produces acorns which deer may eat.

MAMMALS

Forests are habitats for many mammals. The larger mammals include the white-tail deer, elk, and moose. Most of these animals prefer areas in forests near openings along lakes and streams. Squirrels (grey and fox squirrels) prosper in hardwood timber stands where trees are at least 60 years old or older.

The cottontail rabbit does well in forest openings and along edges of standing timber. Most fur-bearing mammals are near or in forests, including the raccoon, mink, opossum, weasel, otter, beaver, and skunk. Red and gray fox populations are highest in forest areas. Bobcats and lynx are also in forested areas.

Larger predators, such as wolves and bears, are in forests. Bears remain almost entirely in forests. Wolves have a large range and often go outside the forest. Originally, the coyote was a predator of open areas and brush land. In recent years this mammal has done well in forested areas of Texas and Louisiana.

A number of less-visible small mammals are found on the forest floor. These include wood rats, moles,

9-18. Cougars live near forests and use them for cover.

mice, ground squirrels, and flying squirrels. Many of these small mammals forage for food and burrow among root systems. Some use tree cavities or fallen logs for cover.

BIRDS

Only a small number of bird species spend their lives completely in open land. Most depend to some degree on forested areas. Birds use wooded areas for nesting, feeding, and roosting.

Woodpeckers prefer maturing forests. They nest in cavities and get food from older diseased and insect-laden trees. Most birds prefer to periodically use openings and margins of wooded areas. This is especially true of turkeys, quail, and doves.

Eagles build huge nests in tall trees and generally return to the same nest each year. They often hunt for food around rivers, lakes, and streams and are often seen perching in trees.

9-19. A bald eagle is perched in a cottonwood tree.

Mallard ducks have a strong tendency to use flooded oak forests during winter where they feed on acorns. They rest during the day under the dense canopy. Wood ducks are strongly oriented to forest areas. They nest in tree cavities in the spring and summer and frequent dense woods in winter.

Nongame birds are in forests with openings and small streams. Warblers, nuthatches, chickadees, jays, hawks, owls, and others rely on the vegetation and insects found in forests.

FISH, REPTILES, AND AMPHIBIANS

With the exception of the desert portion of the Tropical Forest Region, forests are associated with water. Southern forests generally have an abundance of slow-moving streamflow. Northern forests have running water from mountains or hilly terrain that is clear and cold. Southern waters are more likely to be warm and turbid.

Trout streams are in clear, cold water with high levels of dissolved oxygen. In warmer forest areas, black bass, sunfish, and catfish are the major fish species where the water is more turbid (less clear) and warmer.

Alligators, snakes, turtles, frogs, and small amphibians are in warm, slow-moving streams, lakes, and swamps. The organic material in these areas from decaying woody vegetation results in a good environment for these animals.

FOREST MANAGEMENT

Commercial forests are managed to promote tree growth. Income is from selling wood. Additional income may be from hunting, mineral leases, and oil and gas production. In some cases, forest areas are used for livestock grazing, but this is not an approved practice in most commercial forests.

SILVICULTURE

Silviculture is managing tree stands to increase productivity. Several cultural practices may be used. These often begin with planning and scheduling the practices that are used.

Major areas of silviculture are:

9-20. Forest areas often require measurement in planning silviculture practices.

■ Planting—Planting is preparing the land, choosing the species to plant, and properly planting the seed or seed-

9-21. Cutting is used to thin, clean, liberate, and harvest trees.

lings. The land may be cleared for planting. The trees planted should be of the desired species. Many people prefer to plant seedlings. A **seedling** is a young tree 15 to 18 inches tall. It is set in the ground so the roots are properly covered. Most trees are planted in winter or early spring. Moisture must be available for a seedling to live. In some cases, native forests are managed so mature trees are left to produce seed. The seed will germinate and produce new trees. The stand may not be spaced properly with natural seeding.

■ Thinning—Thinning is reducing the number of trees in a stand. In some cases, the trees are large enough for posts or poles. Trees may be removed to promote the growth of understory for wildlife.

9-22. This tree has been killed by a lightning strike and should be cut. (Part of the bark was ripped off by the lightning.)

- ■ Cleaning—Cleaning is removing diseased or defective trees. It may be done at the time of thinning or as a separate process. The species of animal wildlife desired should be considered in cleaning. Some animals prefer to live in dead or defective trees.

- ■ Liberation—Liberation is cutting that removes older, dominant trees so younger trees can grow. Trees with large canopies can shade much ground and prevent the growth of young trees.

- ■ Harvesting—Harvesting is cutting trees for poles, logs, or other uses. Partial or complete harvests may be used. Clear-cutting is removing all trees on a tract of land. Soil and water problems are associated with clear-cutting. However, clear-cutting results in more efficient production of forest crops when replanted.

- ■ Protecting forests—Trees need to be protected from insects, disease, fire, and weather. In some cases, trees that are diseased or that have been damaged by insects need to be removed. A common practice is to remove trees infested with borers in an attempt to keep the borers from attacking other trees. Removing diseased trees tends to protect other trees from the disease or insect problem. Trees damaged by ice, wind storms, and lightning may also need to be removed. Lightning strikes may damage a tree so severely that the wood is of little commercial value.

9-23. The round structure on the post oak leaf is a gall. (The gall was caused by an insect larvae and pupae developing inside the "bubbled" leaf. The insect will emerge at maturity. Several species of insects cause galls.)

PROMOTING WILDLIFE

Forests can be managed to promote wildlife production with little sacrifice in wood production. Many practices that promote wildlife can be a part of growing trees.

Several wildlife management practices with forests are:

- Avoid clear-cutting practices that involve the harvest of all trees on a given site.

- If clear-cutting is used, reduce the size of clear cuts and use a checkerboard configuration of clear-cut and mature forest.

- Do not clear-cut along streams. This helps prevent erosion and silting of the water. Provide stream-side belts of mature trees.

- Quickly replant clear-cuts with a mixed stand of trees rather than a pure stand. A mix of trees will result in better food variety for wildlife.

- Use selective cutting in harvesting timber. Some desirable trees should be left to produce seed and help provide wildlife habitat.

- Avoid cutting den trees during timber harvest. A den tree is typically an older tree with dead limbs, hollow areas, and other places where animals might nest and hide.

- Limit livestock grazing activities to well-planned grazing programs. Grazing might be used to control vegetation and improve both timber and wildlife production. In most cases, grazing a forested area is a poor practice and is not recommended.

- Use well-planned burning programs. Fire can be used as a management tool to improve both timber and wildlife production.

- Limit the harvest of game species to keep population numbers in check. Overpopulation of some game species results in damage to trees and other plants as they search for food.

- Leave diverse natural areas in and around the forest area. This includes leaving some timber that would protect marshes, bogs, deep sands, and steep slopes.

9-24. Widespread efforts are made to protect forests from fires. (A fire in a forest also destroys wildlife.)

REVIEWING

MAIN IDEAS

A forest is where a stand of trees is growing. Some forests are native; others are planted to improved species. Tree farms are planted to grow trees for harvest. Some native forests and all tree farms are commercial forests. A commercial forest is one that is managed to produce timber and other wood products. Most forests are regrowth forests. Only a few areas of old-growth forest remain. Trees have benefits in urban areas that make life more appealing and satisfying to residents.

Forests have a number of uses. Economic benefits are certainly important. Environmental and aesthetic benefits are important in maintaining a quality of life.

Forests are organized as a community of plants and other species. Trees, shrubs, vines, herbs, and mosses and ferns are plants found in forests. Lichens serve useful roles in forest and environmental technology. Forests are characterized by story: understory, mid-story, and upper story.

Trees are living organisms with roots, trunks, and crowns. Most tree stands are either conifers or hardwoods. Trees may be known by common or scientific names. Scientific names are preferred because they tend to be the same worldwide.

Six major forest regions are in the United States. Each region is an area with predominant species of trees present. Forests support a wide range of animal life. Mammals, birds, fish, reptiles, and amphibians are found in forests.

Silviculture is used to improve forests so they will be more productive. It includes planting, thinning, cleaning, liberating, harvesting, and protecting forests. Wildlife can be promoted as part of silviculture work.

QUESTIONS

Answer the following questions using complete sentences and correct spelling.

1. What is a forest? Distinguish between native forests and tree farms.

2. How were forests important in the development of the United States?

3. What is urban forestry? Why is it important? *pg. 187*

4. What are the major products harvested from forests? *logs, pulpwood, pg. 188*

5. What are the environmental and aesthetic benefits of forests? *pg. 188*

6. What common kinds of plants are found in forests? Distinguish between the kinds. *pg. 190*

7. What is story? What kinds of story are found in a forest? *pg. 193*

8. What are the major parts of a tree? What are the functions of each part? *pg. 194, notes*

9. What are the two general groups of tree species? Distinguish between the groups.

10. What are the major things to look for in identifying a tree? *pg. 198*

11. What is a forest region? How many regions are there in the United States? *pg. 201*

12. What silviculture practices are used to improve forests? *pg. 205-206*

EVALUATING

Match the term with the correct definition. Write the letter by the term in the blank provided.

a. native forest   e. lichen   i. stand
b. log   f. canopy   j. seedling
c. urban forestry   g. story
d. shrub   h. conifer

___i___   1. Number of plants distributed over an area of land.

___j___   2. A young tree no more than 15 to 18 inches (38-45 cm) tall.

___b___   3. The stem of a tree harvested for making lumber.

___a___   4. A forest where the species are voluntarily growing.

___c___   5. The care and management of trees in cities.

___d___   6. A perennial plant that does not grow as tall as a tree.

___f___   7. The upper part of a tree comprised of limbs, leaves, etc.

___g___   8. The horizontal layer of vegetative growth in a forest.

___e___   9. A nonplant organism that is a combined fungus and alga.

___h___ 10. A tree that produces seed in cones.

EXPLORING

1. Visit a forest area near your home or school. Classify the plants: trees, shrubs, vines, herbs, and ferns and mosses. Also, determine if lichens are present. Further classify the species of trees as to conifers and hardwoods. Have a forester help identify the trees using both common and scientific names.

2. Prepare a dendrology notebook with ten of the most common trees in your area. This is a notebook with leaves of the trees attached to paper. Each leaf has the name (common and scientific) of the tree it is from and descriptions of growth characteristics.

3. Visit a lumberyard or large hardware store and make a list of items for sale that originated in the forest. Observe wood products from different species of trees. Describe the appearance of the various products in a written report.

10

AIR

Air is all about us. We live in it. We use it to help do work and for recreation and travel. Living things must have air. Sometimes, we fail to consider just how important air is to us!

From birth to death, people breathe–the process of inhaling and exhaling air from the lungs. A sign of life is movement in the lungs. People never stop breathing because the body must have air. A few minutes pause can result in a deficiency of oxygen and damage to the brain or death.

In breathing, a person takes into the body whatever is in the air. The body has a few means of filtering air, such as cilia in the nose that remove some dust. Overall, the body's filters cannot remove many of the harmful substances in the air. If the air contains exhaust substances from an engine, our body receives these substances.

10-1. Air pollution collection using a wet-dry system.

OBJECTIVES

This chapter covers basic information on air quality. The following objectives are included:

1. Explain the meaning of air

2. List the components of air

3. Describe air pollution and identify pollutants

4. Explain the meaning of air quality

5. Explain how air pollution is tested

6. Identify the effects of air pollution on living organisms

7. Describe approaches in preventing air pollution

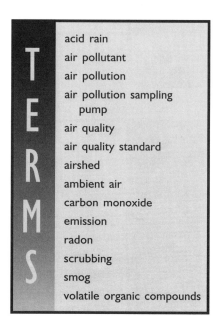

TERMS

acid rain
air pollutant
air pollution
air pollution sampling
   pump
air quality
air quality standard
airshed
ambient air
carbon monoxide
emission
radon
scrubbing
smog
volatile organic compounds

Environmental Protection Agency (EPA)
http://www.epa.gov/

THE MEANING OF AIR

Air is the mixture of gases that surrounds the earth. It is invisible, tasteless, and odorless. Air that can be smelled or seen is polluted. Polluted air may contain substances that are hazardous to the health of living things.

Air is never pure. It always contains substances in amounts that may vary slightly from one time to another. When we think of "pure" air, we are usually thinking of air that is good to breathe and is free of harmful substances. Natural processes on Earth create some pollution, such as the release of methane by decaying vegetation.

Air forms the atmosphere. This creates weather conditions that lead to cold fronts, rain, and storms. As wind, air movement creates power that can be captured to do work. Even though it is made of gases, air can support weight. Just think how much a large airplane weighs!

It is important to remember that the gases in the air form a mixture–not a chemical combination. The gases can be identified and separated. However, some gases do react with pollutants to create compounds, such as when we have acid rain.

10-2. The air over this city is polluted. (The pollution is greater near the ground and decreases with altitude.)

AIR CONTENT

The air contains a relatively consistent mix of gases in all places. Some variation may be found based on the local environment. It may contain sub-

Components of the Atmosphere

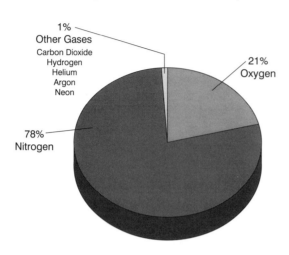

1%
Other Gases
Carbon Dioxide
Hydrogen
Helium
Argon
Neon

21%
Oxygen

78%
Nitrogen

10-3. Major components of the air.

stances that reflect local factories, natural resources, and way of human life. In some cases, materials that get into the air in one place may be carried long distances by wind.

The greatest concentration of gases is near the surface of the earth. As elevation increases, the air becomes "thinner." Air in the atmosphere decreases in density as the distance from Earth increases. About 95 percent of the total air mass is within 12 miles of Earth. Beyond that, density decreases so by 250 miles the atmosphere merges into "empty space."

Driving up a mountain helps demonstrate the change in air pressure—your ears may feel uncomfortable.

Gases in the air are nitrogen (78 percent), oxygen (21 percent), carbon dioxide (.03 percent), argon (less than 1 percent), and several others, including hydrogen. The air often contains materials other than air gases. Smoke, dust, and water vapor are often in the air we breathe. These materials make breathing difficult and may injure the lungs. A good example is riding down a dusty road behind another vehicle. It is hard to breathe dust-filled air. The nostrils try to clean the air but the amount of dust is too great.

AIR POLLUTION

Air pollution is the entry of materials into the air that damage its quality. Some pollution can be reduced or prevented. Other pollution cannot be stopped.

MAJOR SOURCES OF POLLUTION

How does the air get polluted? Routine life processes create some pollution. Events on Earth create pollution. Some sources can be controlled and some sources cannot be controlled.

Air pollution is from two major sources:

- Human Activities—Factories; engines in boats, automobiles, and lawn mowers; home heating and cooling systems; and many other activities produce substances that pollute the air.

- Natural Processes—Many natural events and processes on Earth create air pollution. These include volcanic action, decay of organic materials, plant pollen, wind erosion, and natural fires.

POLLUTANTS

An ***air pollutant*** is a material that causes air pollution. Pollutants include gases, dusts, and droplets of materials. Some materials are much more dangerous than others. For example, smoke is more dangerous than steam when released into the air.

Some air pollution is seasonal. Pollen, which causes hay fever, is released when flowers are blooming. Dust is more often created during dry seasons of the year. Other air pollution results from home heating units, food and fiber processing plants, and climate conditions. The decomposition of plant materials is greater in warm, humid weather.

The air is continually being changed. Every time you breathe, oxygen is removed from the air and carbon dioxide is added to it. Nature has a way of keeping the air clean and in good balance. The carbon dioxide you exhale is used by plants in photosynthesis, with oxygen being given off by plants.

Sometimes, materials get into the air that are dangerous and hard to remove. Many of these result from our daily lives and the manufacturing processes to meet the demands of people.

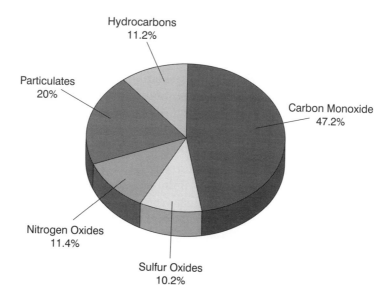

10-4. Air pollutants in the United States.

Hydrocarbons
11.2%

Particulates
20%

Carbon Monoxide
47.2%

Nitrogen Oxides
11.4%

Sulfur Oxides
10.2%

10-5. This electrical power generating plant is releasing pollutants into the air. (Courtesy, Mollee Thomas, Danville, Illinois)

Gases

Gas pollutants sometimes have an odor but are usually less obvious than particulate. Most pollutant gases are similar to the gases normally found in the air. An exception is nitrogen dioxide (NO_2), which has a brownish color. Gases do not readily settle out of the air as does particulate. A gas can remain in the atmosphere for years.

The most damaging chemical elements found in gases in the air are sulfur, carbon, nitrogen, oxygen, fluorine, and hydrogen. These elements are not problems themselves, but the compounds they form can be hazardous. In addition, various gases and dusts from waste decomposition, manure, and sewage may create unpleasant odors. Some of these are not hazardous to the well-being of plants and animals. They are just not pleasant to smell.

- Carbon—In the air, carbon combines with oxygen and hydrogen to form various compounds. It may combine only with oxygen to form carbon monoxide (CO) or carbon dioxide (CO_2). These two forms result primarily from the use of fuel and respiration. Carbon may combine with hydrogen and oxygen to form hydrocarbon compounds.

  The hydrocarbons form **volatile organic compounds** (VOC). A VOC is any compound, such as unburned fuel, containing carbon that is a part of the photochemical reactions in the atmosphere. Photochemical reactions are initiated by the sun, such as the creation of smog. **Smog** is a mixture of dense radiation fog and gaseous pollutants, such as carbon dioxide and sulfur dioxide.

  Some carbon substances can build up in the atmosphere and create a condition known as the greenhouse effect. The greenhouse effect is the trapping of infrared radiation underneath carbon gases in the atmosphere. The gases form a shield similar to the roofs on greenhouses. If the layer of gases were not present, the radiation would move to higher levels in the atmosphere. The greenhouse effect is often associated with emissions from engines and heating systems.

■ Sulfur—Sulfur may combine with oxygen, hydrogen, and other elements. Most often it combines with oxygen to form various oxide compounds. The normal atmosphere contains 0.2 to 0.4 ppb sulfur. The EPA standard is a maximum of 0.14 ppm sulfur over a 24-hour period. Industrial cities may reach higher levels of sulfur. The odor of sulfur becomes obvious at 0.5 to 1.0 ppm and this is the level at which humans begin to notice the effects.

10-6. Burning trash releases carbon, particulate, and other materials into the air.

Sulfur dioxide is produced when fuels containing sulfur are burned in the presence of oxygen. Sulfur is found in coal and oil. Burning these two fuels, especially high-sulfur coal, can release large amounts of sulfur. Smelting metal ores releases some sulfur. Sulfur may be attached to particulate.

In the air, sulfur trioxide combines with water vapor to form sulfuric acid (H_2SO_4). This is a strong acid that can quickly react with materials. Rain containing sulfuric acid is ***acid rain***. Acid rain is any precipitation that is more acidic than normal. Acid rain can damage plants and property when it comes into contact with them. Nitrogen can also form acid rain.

■ Nitrogen—Several nitrogen compounds may be found in the air. Ultraviolet radiation may form nitrogen into nitric acid (HNO_3). In precipitation, this acid can damage property and organisms. Some benefit may be gained when it falls to the ground. The nitric acid may soak into the soil and serve as a small source of nitrogen for crops.

The nitrogen cycle is a natural process for using nitrogen. Organisms circulate nitrogen through the atmosphere, soil, and water. Decomposers in the soil act on decaying plants and animals and release nitrogen. The nitrogen gas is released back into the atmosphere. Rain and other precipitation return the nitrogen to the earth for use by plants. However, plants cannot use the

THE NITROGEN CYCLE

10-7. The nitrogen cycle illustrates the continuous movement of nitrogen from the earth to the atmosphere and back.

gaseous nitrogen form. Nitrogen fixing bacteria convert gaseous nitrogen to nitrates that plants can use. Nitrogen in water also undergoes a similar cycle.

■ Ozone—Nitric acid and hydrocarbons react in the presence of sunlight to produce ozone (O_3). Ozone in the atmosphere protects the earth by screening out ultraviolet (UV) radiation from the sun. If the unscreened UV reaches the earth, the chemistry of living organisms can be changed. Cancer and other diseases will increase among humans. The ozone layer in the stratosphere is being damaged by pollutants. The region over Antarctica has lost most of its ozone. Scientists have labeled this area the ozone hole.

Particulate

Particulate includes tiny pieces of dust and droplets of liquid. Depending on location, particulate may be acid droplets, the salts of metals and sulfate, carbon and silica particles, pollen, mists, dusts from manure, and other substances. Smoke from factories, burning trash, and forest fires, as well as dust from roads and mines, are sources of solid particles.

Rain helps clean particulate from the air. Some of the small particulate does not settle out of the air. The moisture it collects is not sufficient to cause it to fall to the earth.

About half of the dust in the air is due to natural events on the earth. People can take steps to reduce some of this by protecting soil from erosion. In other cases, people cannot stop particulate pollution. People can control the particulate they create, such as eliminating fires, removing particles from factory smoke, controlling dust, and reducing all emissions into the air.

Factories use a process known as scrubbing to remove particulate. *Scrubbing* is using methods to remove particulate from exhaust. Some smoke stacks have large bags made of a fine mesh material. The smoke passes through the fine mesh. Particulate is filtered from the smoke. Another approach is to spray a fine mist of water through smoke. The water collects on solid particles and causes them to settle out of the smoke. Electrostatic equipment is used to remove fine particulate by electrically charging the particles that are collected on oppositely charged electrodes.

Lead and mercury are metals that sometimes cause air pollution. Lead is a heavy metal with a low melting point. Paint containing lead is dangerous. Tiny particles can be inhaled in dust when the paint is sanded. Chips of paint can get on food and be eaten. Some lead is retained in the body. Brain cells and bone marrow are particularly sensitive to lead. Small children exposed to lead may have brain damage. Lead has been used to seal pipe, in gunshot, and fishing tackle weights. These uses are being discontinued.

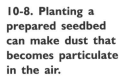

10-8. Planting a prepared seedbed can make dust that becomes particulate in the air.

10-9. Aerial application of pesticides produces tiny droplets of chemical solution in the air.

Mercury is also a heavy metal that is declining in use because of mercury poisoning. Mercury gets into the air as a vapor, into water droplets as dissolved mercury, and in particulate. Mercury poisoning symptoms include irritability, loss of memory, birth defects, gum disease, and involuntary shaking of the body.

Resource Connection

ENGINES GULP AIR

Internal combustion engines use a lot of air! These are the engines that provide the power for four-wheelers, trucks, boats, and chain saws. The good air they use is changed and released in exhaust.

The ratio of air to fuel is 9,000 to 1. That means that 9,000 gallons (or liters) of air are needed for 1 gallon (liter) of fuel! Engines that use gasoline, diesel, or other fuels take oxygen from the air and release gases into the air. Engines that are not operating properly may be releasing even greater pollution!

Cut back on engine pollution. Use engines less. Install devices that reduce pollutants in the exhaust. Use fuels that contain fewer harmful substances. Use clean air filters and properly adjusted fuel systems. This photo shows an air filter on a tractor engine being serviced to allow efficient movement of air.

AIR QUALITY

People want to breathe good quality air. They are sometimes unsure about the meaning of air quality. *Air quality* is the suitability of air for a particular use. In most cases, air quality refers to how suitable it is for use by living organisms. It is the purity of the gases that comprise unpolluted air.

High quality air is free of pollution. Low quality air contains hazardous substances. Air quality applies to the air outside our homes, schools, and other structures as well as within the structures.

AMBIENT AIR

Ambient air is outside air. Most people have access to ambient air. This is the air that is most important in air quality. The Environmental Protection Agency (EPA) has standards for the maximum amount of pollution that can be in ambient air.

Ambient air is affected by the materials released into it. The smoke from a factory or the exhaust from an automobile engine affects the quality of the ambient air. We sometimes open windows in our homes to let in "fresh" air. We want ambient air free of pollution.

INSIDE AIR

Most people are inside buildings, automobiles, or other places much of the day. With closed windows, there may be very little exchange of air with the outside. Some places have fans that exchange the air. These should be used only if they improve the quality of the inside air. Most inside air should have some exchange with ambient air for human use.

Inside air may be more polluted than ambient air. Exceptions are in times of high ambient air pollution. When this occurs, people are advised to stay inside. Some scientific evidence indicates that substances in inside air react with outdoor air pollution and diminish its hazards.

Filters are sometimes used on inside air. Most filters remove dust particles and help

10-10. Air filters in heating and air-conditioning systems should be changed frequently to prevent clogging, as has happened with this filter.

keep down dust on the furniture in our homes, schools, and businesses. Some things are hard to remove from air. Filters must be kept clean to work efficiently.

Carbon Monoxide

Carbon monoxide (CO) is a poisonous gas produced when certain materials burn. Fumes from automobiles and heaters contain carbon monoxide. Since it is colorless, odorless, and tasteless, it can get into our environment and we won't know it. People who breathe it fall asleep without realizing what is happening. It gets into the blood and blocks the ability of the hemoglobin to carry oxygen.

Engines, heaters, and other users of fuel should be properly ventilated. Many are now equipped with devices that remove the carbon monoxide. Never operate an internal combustion engine in a closed building without plenty of ventilation. All home, office, and factory heaters should be vented. Vents carry the carbon monoxide to the outside air and keep inside air safe.

Radon

Radon is an invisible, tasteless, and odorless radioactive gas. It comes from the natural decay of uranium in the soil. Radon (Rn) causes few problems outside because the gas quickly dissipates into the air.

Radon can be a problem inside buildings, especially older buildings. It is more likely a problem in basements and crawl areas under a building where there are cracks in the floor. Radon in the soil enters through cracks in the floor and walls. To reduce the chance of this happening, the ground under buildings may be covered with a sheet of plastic material. Radon is sometimes found in well water. People in buildings with high levels of radon may have health problems, such as lung cancer.

Other Inside Pollutants

Inside air quality is affected by what is released into it. Tobacco smoke pollutes the air. Cooking; using aerosol sprays, perfumes, and detergents; and other activities pollute inside air. Some materials used in building construction and furnishings pollute. An example is the use of formaldehyde in manufacturing materials, such as carpet and draperies. Dizziness, vomiting, and nosebleeds have been tied to the use of formaldehyde.

Schools, factories, and offices have other materials that pollute the air. In schools, chemistry experiments and welding in the school shop are two ex-

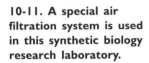

10-11. A special air filtration system is used in this synthetic biology research laboratory.

amples of activities that contribute to poor quality air. Most manufacturing processes in factories lower air quality. People who work in these areas often wear protective masks. Offices are subject to many of the same pollution problems as homes. The added pollution in an office area may stem from fumes from copy machines and cleaning solvent. Fans and other devices may be used to remove noxious fumes and air from buildings. The work environment is covered by standards of the Occupational Safety and Health Administration (OSHA).

Having proper air exchange helps maintain the quality of inside environments and reduces the amount of pollution in the air. People need to have good air quality where they live, study, and work.

POLLUTION MOVEMENT

Air movement in the atmosphere can carry pollutants thousands of miles. Wind currents can move polluted air

10-12. Assess the airshed that begins at the top of a waterfall in the Blue Ridge Mountains. Are major sources of pollution present in the area? How would you rate the quality of the ambient air?

across continents and over oceans. The air will carry pollutants greater distances than water or soil will carry them.

Some air pollution travels around the planet Earth. The pollutants may be lifted into the upper atmosphere and moved long distances by air flow and weather fronts.

Land areas release materials into the air. An *airshed* is the area of land that contributes to the air. Airsheds are geographic areas that may release pollution into the air. Some places may have many factories. Others places may have large forests. Airsheds do not follow the boundaries of nations or states. Controlling air pollution is difficult when governments fail to cooperate.

AIR QUALITY STANDARDS

An *air quality standard* is the maximum level of pollution allowed at one time in a geographical area. Standards are set by the federal government. States and local governments can also set standards that meet or exceed those of the federal government.

The EPA has established National Ambient Air Quality Standards (NAAQS). These standards are designed to set limits on the amount of pollution allowed in the air and to force those who pollute the air to stop.

Two sets of standards are used: primary and secondary. The primary standards deal with safe limits of pollution from the standpoint of human health. The secondary standards deal with limits on nonhealth effects, such as damage to crops, property, and wildlife. The major air pollutants covered by the NAAQS are ozone, sulfur dioxide, particulate matter, nitrogen dioxide, lead, hydrocarbons, and carbon monoxide.

TESTING AIR QUALITY

Air can be tested to determine if pollutants are present. Since the materials that create air pollution are very small, special procedures are needed for the testing.

AIR MONITORING

Air monitoring involves collecting air samples and testing the samples for the presence of pollution. An *air pollution sampling pump* is used to collect samples. This device collects and measures air. The sample is passed

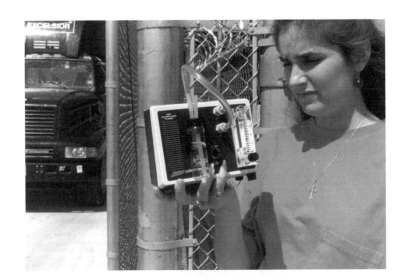

10-13. Using an air sampling pump near the loading dock of a warehouse. (This pump bubbles air through a chemical solution. The solution removes substances in the air that cause pollution. The solution is analyzed in a laboratory to determine the presence of specific pollutants.)

into a special absorbing solution. The solution is chemically analyzed to see if a pollutant is present. Different pollutants require different solutions.

Specially designed kits are available to use in testing for hazardous materials. These often provide step-by-step procedures to conduct the tests.

EMISSIONS MONITORING

An *emission* is a gas-borne pollutant that is released into the air. Smoke, fumes, and other gaseous substances are emissions. Factories that produce air pollutants are usually required to monitor what is produced. They are known as point source air pollution.

Monitoring factory emissions involves using complex sampling techniques to collect information. The EPA has specific methods of emissions monitoring based on the kind of factory and the pollutant emitted.

AIR QUALITY MEASUREMENTS

Air quality measurements must be carefully done. Volume measurement is often used. It is the number of parts of a pollutant in a given volume of air. Parts are usually expressed as parts per million (ppm) or per billion (ppb). In polluted air, a sample is tested to determine the number of parts of the pollutant in a million (or billion) parts of air. For example, if a measurement indicates that the air has 5 ppm this means that 1 million parts of air contain 5 parts of the pollutant and 999,995 parts of air. The pollutant and the air total 1 million parts.

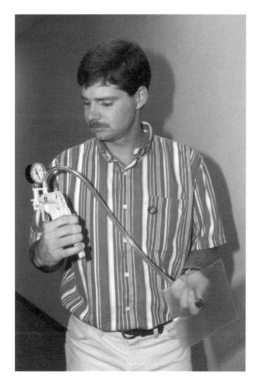

10-14. An air sampling device that collects a sample in a bag that is sent to a laboratory for analysis.

Weight is also in an air quality measurement. Weight is the weight of a pollutant in a cubic meter of air.

The actual size of solid particles may be measured, such as dust or pollen. Most particulate is quite small. A measurement known as micrometers (μm) (one-millionth of a meter) is used. Particulate ranges from 0.005μm to 100 μm. Fine particulate of less than 2.5μm is often more dangerous to health than larger particulate.

PREVENTING AIR POLLUTION

Air pollution can be reduced and, in many cases, prevented. Some of the procedures are easy to implement; others are more difficult. People can assess how they go about their everyday life and take steps to lower pollution. Finding a way to have modern conveniences and keep pollution down is a challenge.

CONTROLLING EMISSIONS

Stopping or reducing emissions will reduce pollution. Factories can use scrubbers on smoke stacks to remove gases and particulate. Fuels that produce less sulfur and other wastes can be used. Emissions control devices, such as catalytic converters, can be installed on engines. The converters should be kept in good operating condition so they are effective.

Sometimes, simple activities reduce emissions. Watering dusty roads or fields helps keep down dust. Using less electricity lowers demand for power generation and lowers the emissions that go into the air at fuel-powered generation plants. Reducing the amount of fuel used in automobiles can help reduce emissions. For example, walking one block saves fuel and reduces emissions. Also, walking may be good for an individual's well-being.

REUSING AND RECYCLING

Manufacturing often releases pollutants. Reusing and recycling eliminate some manufacturing and reduce the release of pollutants. Many products can be reused with only minimal preparation. Others can be recycled. Recycling likely releases more air pollution than reusing. Recycling does not release as much as initially manufacturing a product. Reusing and recycling also conserve limited natural resources.

USING NEW METHODS

New materials and methods have been developed for many activities that once polluted the air. New kinds of refrigerants have replaced freon in most appliances and equipment. No-till farming reduces plowing and keeps down dust. Not plowing also saves fuel and eliminates the emission of exhaust into the air. New approaches to agricultural pest control involve using fewer hazardous pesticides. Building construction materials that reduce hazards can be used.

Use safe construction materials. Paint and pipe without lead reduces the likelihood of lead pollution. Avoid asbestos materials. Tiny particles get into the air and threaten human health when inhaled.

Career Profile

AIR QUALITY TECHNICIAN

Air quality technicians monitor air quality and pollution. They devise or recommend methods of reducing pollution. They must have skills in collecting, testing, and interpreting test results of air samples.

Air quality technicians need college education in environmental science or a related area. Some gain two-year technical training rather than a college degree. Those who advance to higher levels have college degrees and some have masters degrees.

Jobs are found with government agencies, universities, research stations, and large corporations. This shows an air quality technician working for a research station setting up a device to measure methane from cattle. (Courtesy, Agricultural Research Service, USDA)

10-15. Growth chambers at Auburn University are used to study the effects of changes in the atmosphere on plant growth. (An environment similar to that predicted by scientists for the earth in future years is set up in each chamber. For example, carbon dioxide levels are raised in some chambers. Temperatures are raised slightly higher to reflect global warming in other chambers. Plant growth is carefully monitored to see the effects of the changes.)

PRACTICING SAFETY

Some protection from hazards of air pollution is possible. Closing windows and staying inside when outside pollution is high will help protect from hazards of pollutants. Exposure can also be reduced by wearing protective masks and respirators. Be sure masks are used properly and that respirators are operating properly. Installing and using fans and vents will remove polluted air from a closed area in a home, office, or factory. Avoid using and breathing pollutants in the home. These and other safety practices can help prevent breathing polluted air.

Be sure to use products in appropriate ways. Never use a product in a situation where it has not been approved.

REVIEWING

MAIN IDEAS

Air is the mixture of gases that surrounds the earth. There is no such thing as pure air—just air that is free of harmful substances. Living organisms need oxygen from the air to carry out life processes. They get oxygen by taking air into their bodies.

Substances get into the air and cause pollution. This damages its quality. Some of the substances in air chemically react with other elements creating new, more dangerous compounds. The major air pollutants are gases, particulate, metals, and others, including radioactive materials and foul odors. Sunlight causes some reactions to occur.

Air quality standards have been set to assure at least a minimum level of air quality. Air pollutants are measured in volume, dimensions, and weight bases. The Environmental Protection Agency was set up by the federal government to help assure good air quality.

Good quality air is important to the health of humans, other animals, plants, property, and the well-being of the planet Earth. Air quality is the suitability of air for use by living organisms. Ambient air is particularly important, since it is the air to which everyone has access.

Pollution is from natural events and human activity. Pollution can be reduced by using devices to remove pollutants, reusing and recycling materials, and using alternative methods in production. People need to use personal protective equipment, such as particle masks and respirators, in some situations to protect their lungs.

QUESTIONS

Answer the following questions using complete sentences and correct spelling.

1. What is air?
2. What are the major components of air?
3. What is air pollution?
4. What are the two major sources of air pollution?
5. What is an air pollutant?
6. What are the major air pollutants?
7. What are the effects of carbon, nitrogen, and sulfur in the air?
8. What is particulate? What materials are found in particulate?
9. What is air quality?
10. How is air tested?
11. What can be done to reduce air pollution?
12. What personal protection may be used to reduce exposure to pollution?

EVALUATING

Match the term with the correct definition. Write the letter by the term in the blank provided.

a. air quality
b. ambient air
c. airshed
d. μm

e. carbon monoxide
f. radon
g. air pollutant
h. greenhouse effect

i. air quality standard
j. acid rain

_____ 1. Outside air.

_____ 2. A poisonous gas with the chemical structure of CO.

_____ 3. A condition caused by the trapping of radiation underneath layers of polluted atmosphere.

_____ 4. The suitability of air for a particular use.

_____ 5. Rain that has higher than usual levels of acid.

_____ 6. Any material that causes air pollution.

_____ 7. The area of land that contributes to the contents of air.

_____ 8. An invisible radioactive gas that may get into buildings from the ground.

_____ 9. A regulation on the amount of pollution that can be in the air.

_____ 10. A unit of measurement often used with air pollutants representing one millionth of a meter.

EXPLORING

1. Form a team of three to five people and make a survey of your school or home to identify sources of air pollution. Identify both inside and outside sources of pollution. Prepare recommendations to reduce or eliminate the pollution. Provide an oral report to class on your findings. Submit a written report to the school administrator.

2. Use air sampling and testing equipment to monitor the air in your classroom or home. Collect samples and information each hour for an eight-hour period. Compare your findings with those of your fellow students. Prepare a report that includes graphs to illustrate air quality and how it changes throughout the day. Relate air quality to the events that are taking place in the area, such as cooking in your home or the conduct of an experiment in your classroom. Note: Always be careful in any air that contains materials hazardous to human health.

11

LAND

"Land For Sale" is the caption for an advertisement in a newspaper. The ad goes further, "250 acres, with 175 acres gently rolling with improved pasture, fenced, two watering ponds, and 75 acres mixed hardwood timber bottomland near creek; on gravel road . . ."

What will the buyer of this land get? How much is the land worth? What would you pay for it? Would a bank be willing to make you a loan to buy it? What is needed to be sure you own the exact property you bought? A number of questions should be answered before land is purchased.

People have different ideas about land. Land varies widely in value and productivity. What is land?

11-1. A farmstead that makes efficient use of land based on capability. (Courtesy, U.S. Department of Agriculture)

OBJECTIVES

This chapter is about the meaning of land, how the features of land influence its use, and how land is legally described. The following objectives are included:

1. Define land and relate land to renewable natural resources

2. Describe the role of quality in land use

3. Identify land capability factors

4. Explain land capability classification

5. Describe land surveying

6. Name methods of legal land description and apply the method used in your state

Land Surveyor Reference
http://www.lsrp.com/

TERMS

aerial photograph
area measurement
base lines
best land use
boundary
capability factors
compass
course
cropland
deed
direction measurement
elevation measurement
geodetic survey
geographic information
    system (GIS)
global positioning system
    (GPS)
land
land capability
land capability classification
land description
land surveying
linear measurement
meridian
metes and bounds
monument
plane surveying
plat
point of reference
rectangular survey system
remote sensing
section
slope
soil depth
survey
township
warranty deed

LAND IS MORE THAN SOIL

Land is a broad concept that is somewhat difficult to define. Land is more than soil fertility, though fertility is important with cropland. *Land* is all of the natural and artificial characteristics of an area on the surface of the earth. It is sometimes known as real property or real estate. Land is also referred to as the part of Earth's surface that is not underwater (some land is underwater). People can make land better and more valuable than it is naturally. The actions of people can also degrade land and make it less valuable.

WHAT LAND INCLUDES

Land is the surface of Earth. But, some things go with it. Land includes both renewable and nonrenewable resources as well as improvements that have been made and damage that has been done. In some cases, the rights to some minerals may be owned by someone other than the owner of the land. The concept of land is not always easy to understand.

Land includes:

11-2. Land may be quite rugged yet have appealing qualities.

- soil texture, soil fertility, and soil pH

- mineral deposits on the surface and underground

- water supply, including surface and groundwater (but use is restricted and permits are often needed)

- topography, such as rolling, flat, or rugged and the presence of gullies, streams, and other features

- climate, such as tropical, temperate, or tundra

- precipitation, including amount and kind and the way runoff is conserved or drained away

- vegetative cover, such as pasture, trees, and scrub growth

11-3. Unfortunately, abandoned vehicles may be a part of land when it is sold.

■ improvements, such as ponds, fences, and buildings

■ degradation, such as junk equipment, eroded areas, dilapidated buildings, and polluted areas

■ wildlife that live on the land area

■ proximity to roads, towns, factories, landfills, and farms

■ other natural and artificial characteristics

Most of the time, land refers to the surface of the earth that is not covered with water. Crop producers often refer to their land and its condition. Sometimes, land can be temporarily or permanently covered with water. Land near a creek may be briefly flooded following a heavy rain. This may interfere with crop production. Land is also used for roads, cemeteries, athletic fields, building sites, fence rows, and other purposes. Land covered with a parking lot is still land!

Land used for aquaculture may be covered with water on a long-term basis, if not permanently. A pond used for aquaculture is land. The area of an ocean near the shore where oysters are farmed is land. The location of roads, towns, and other features also influences land and its use. For example, proximity of land to markets and consumers may influence its use.

LOCATION

Land location is important. Location influences the value of a tract of land just as its natural and artificial features are important. Land may be good for a number of uses but be used for a specific purpose based on its location.

The use of land may be based on its natural features. This includes good fertility, favorable climate, and level of moisture. The use of land can also be based on its proximity to residential, commercial, and other property. Land along major highways is more likely to be used for business activities than the land that is away from good roads.

Land value is often based on location. Land at intersections of interstate highways is often more valuable than comparable land a few miles away. Shopping malls, factories, and structures often inflate the value of land over its value for agricultural uses.

11-4. Land supporting these towering buildings in Chicago is more valuable than land elsewhere used for agriculture.

LAND QUALITY

Land used for agricultural purposes may be for pasture, crops, forests, and wildlife habitat. Many people feel that the best land should be used to grow crops. That is not always how it is used.

AGRICULTURAL LAND

Agricultural land may be used for crops, pastures, forests, and other purposes. Land used for crops is known as ***cropland***. It varies from land suited for wheat to that suited for corn, cotton, soybeans, sugar cane, and vegetables. Typically, growing crops involves tilling the land. Practices that do not require tilling are being more widely used.

Land that is productive for growing crops has certain characteristics. It provides a good environment for the crop to grow. The soil provides the nutrients that the crop needs to grow (often with a little fertilizer added). Land that is less well suited to tilled crops may be placed in pasture. Land that is less well suited to pasture may be put in forests. Some land is so rugged and inaccessible that it is left in a natural condition. Understanding cropland will help in assessing how land can be used.

The major characteristics of cropland include:

- Soil—Soil texture, nutrients, and internal structure are major factors that influence its productivity.

- Climate—The crops that can be grown on land are related to the climate. Some locations have tropical climates, where the weather is always warm. Other locations have temperate climates, where the weather varies between warm and cool. Arctic climates have cool or cold weather conditions that may severely limit the crops that can be grown.

- Topography—The form or outline of the earth's surface influences its use as cropland. Some land may have a nearly level or gently rolling topography. Other land may have steep hills and mountains. Row crops cannot be planted on steep mountains.

- Water supply—Available moisture determines if crops can be grown and the kinds of crops to plant. Water may be from precipitation, moisture within the soil, or from irrigation. Land in dry areas may have water rights that allow the owner to use water from a canal or well. Without water, the land is of little value for crops.

- Subsurface conditions—Conditions found below the surface are important in crop production. Soil texture may influence internal drainage. Some areas

11-5. This land on Maui is well suited to papaya production.

may have shallow rock or hardpans. Cultural practices can be used to help alleviate subsurface problems.

- ■ Pollution—Land may be polluted and unsuited for crop production. The pollution is in the soil and results from materials dumped on the land. At other times, the pollution may be in the air or water.

BEST LAND USE

Some land has many potential uses. Other land has few uses. People are frequently faced with determining the best use of land.

Best land use is the use of land that produces the most benefits to society. Some view land from the standpoint of cropping that will result in the highest returns. Land varies in the kinds of crops to which it is best suited. Some land is suited to row crops, while other land is suited to pasture and forests.

The best use may be for factories, homes, shopping malls, or other purposes. Land near major highways and cities may have a higher value for uses other than crops. Economic return to the owner may be more if the land is not used for crops. Some land is too valuable for cropping. The land cannot be bought and paid for with the returns from crops. This is the case around sprawling cities.

When should cropland not be used to grow crops? The earth's population is rapidly increasing and is predicted to double in about 30 years. What will happen if too much productive cropland is used for non-crop purposes?

11-6. Land has been improved to produce an attractive golf course. (Courtesy, Vernie Thomas, Illinois)

LAND CAPABILITY

Land capability is the suitability of land for agricultural uses. The uses should not result in damage to the land, though nutrients may be removed from the soil. Practices should be used that sustain the productivity of land.

Capability factors are the characteristics that determine the best use of land for crops. These factors include both surface and subsurface characteristics. Six common factors are:

■ Surface texture—Surface texture is assessed to the typical depth of plowing— about 7 inches (17.8 cm). Soil can be classified into three major groups: sandy, loamy, and clayey soils. Each of these textures is further divided into more specific texture groups.

■ Internal drainage—Internal drainage is the movement of air and water through the soil. It is also known as permeability.

Resource Connection

CHANGING LAND

People attempt to improve land. They try to change the quality of land and improve what is growing. Their goal is to make the land more productive and increase its value. This photo shows special cutting equipment being used to clear scrub timber from land. (Courtesy, U.S. Fish and Wildlife Service)

Opinions differ on how land should be changed. What do you think? Should the surface be altered from what is naturally growing on land? As you have learned in this book, some natural land features may need to be protected. Where do you draw the line?

Of course, people are to be stewards of the land. They are to use it, care for it, and sustain it.

■ Soil depth—*Soil depth* is the thickness of the soil layers that are important in crop production. Both topsoil and subsoil are included. Four soil depths are used: very shallow soil (less than 10 inches [25 cm] deep), shallow soil (10 to 20 inches [25 to 61 cm] deep), moderately deep soil (20 to 36 inches [61 to 91 cm] deep), and deep soil (over 36 inches [91 cm] deep).

■ Erosion—Erosion destroys the productivity of land. Four categories of erosion are used: very severe erosion—75 percent or more of the surface soil has eroded, and large gullies are present; severe erosion—75 percent of the surface soil has eroded, but no large gullies are present; moderate erosion—25 to 75 percent of the surface soil has been lost with small gullies present; and none to slight erosion—less than 25 percent of the topsoil has been lost and no gullies are present.

■ Slope—*Slope* is the rise and fall in the elevation of land. It is commonly measured in percent or the number of feet of rise and fall in 100 feet (metric conversions can also be used). For example, a hill that drops 5 feet in 100 feet has a 5 percent slope. Six land slope classes are used: very steep—more than 12 percent, steep—8 to 12 percent, strongly sloping—5 to 8 percent, moderately sloping—3 to 5 percent, gently sloping—1 to 3 percent, and nearly level—less than 1 percent slope.

■ Surface runoff—Surface runoff is the water that does not soak into the ground and instead runs off. As runoff is reduced, infiltration (soaking in) increases. This helps restore groundwater levels and provide moisture for crop growth. Four categories of surface runoff are used: very slow—deep sandy soils with low areas and little slope present, slow—clayey soils with little slope, moderate—non-clay soils with 1 to 3 percent slope, and rapid—usually on land with over 3 percent slope with surface water that flows rapidly causing some erosion.

CAPABILITY CLASSIFICATION

Land capability classification is a system for classifying land based on its highest potential use. The system includes the land capability factors (see the previous section of the chapter).

Eight land capability classes are used:

■ Class I: Very Good Land—This is the best agricultural land. It has deep, fertile topsoil, is nearly level, and does not erode easily. Some people feel that homes, businesses, and factories should not be built on this land because of its high crop productivity.

11-7. This Class I Land is well suited to parsley production.

■ Class II: Good Land—This is good agricultural land. The soil is very productive, but may have some limitations. Practices need to be used to maintain the soil.

■ Class III: Moderately Good Land—This is fair agricultural land. Some limitations on the use of the land may be severe depending on the amount of slope. It can be cultivated if important conservation practices are followed.

■ Class IV: Fairly Good Land—This is poor land for tillage, but can be good in pastures or forests. Severe erosion may result if Class IV Land is plowed or

11-8. This Class III land planted to soybeans has some limitations caused by poor surface and internal drainage.

11-9. This Class VIII Land is limited to forestry and recreational use.

excavated. This is the highest class where plowing should be attempted in agriculture. Residential and commercial uses may be very good.

- Class V: Land Unsuited for Cultivation—This class is unfit for field crops. The land may be subject to overflow from streams, poor drainage, and rocks or other objects that deter use.

- Class VI: Land Not Suited for Row Crops—This class has land restricted to use as pastures, woodlands, or wildlife refuges. The limitations are more severe than Class V Land.

- Class VII: Land Highly Unsuited for Cultivation—This land has very limited use. The limitations are more severe than Class VI Land.

- Class VIII: Land Unsuited for Plant Production—The land in Class VIII is steep mountain sides, sandy beaches, and river washes that have little productive use. The land is rugged and often difficult to develop as residential and business areas.

Applying a land capability classification system helps consider the best use of land. Land should be used for its best purpose without degrading it.

LAND SURVEYING

Land surveying is the process of measuring and marking real property. Maps and field notes may be prepared along with the written description.

The survey serves as the basis for preparing a legal description. Surveying is also used to install structures on land, such as ponds, terraces, and ditches.

MAKING MEASUREMENTS

Accurate measurements are essential. A first step is to decide on the unit of measurement that is being used. Land is measured in inches, feet, rods, chains, links, miles, etc. Most land in the United States is measured in the English system rather than the metric system. Some use is made of metric measurements in natural resources work, such as forestry. A few areas of the southwestern United States have used the Spanish vara, which equals 33½ inches.

How is the curvature of the earth handled in surveying? With small areas, curvature is not considered. *Plane surveying* is used in making flat measurements that do not consider curvature. With larger areas, the curvature must be considered. This involves a geodetic survey. *Geodetic surveying* requires equipment that considers the curvature of Earth. Precise mathematical calculations are essential with both types of surveying. Counties, states, nations, and continents are measured with geodetic survey methods. Electronic total station equipment may account for curvature in all measurements.

11-10. Total station surveying instruments electronically sense elevations and horizontal distances. (The small LCD screen reports vertical and horizontal distances from the instrument to the prism pole.)

Linear Measurements

Linear measurement is determining the distance between two points. The chain has been

Table 11-1.
Common Linear Land Measurements

1 mile = 8 furlongs; 80 chains; 320 rods; 5,280 feet
1 furlong = ⅛ mile; 10 chains; 40 rods; 660 feet
1 chain = 4 rods; 66 feet; 100 links
1 rod = 25 links; 16½ feet
1 link = 1/100 chain; 7.92 inches

the common unit of land linear measurement. It is 66 feet long. Chains are divided into 100 links. Each link is 7.92 inches long. A surveyor's steel tape is typically two chains long—132 feet. Ten square chains equals one acre. A distance of 80 chains is one mile.

In measuring, keep the chain or tape horizontal, straight, and free of obstacles. A chain should be held on-the-level when measuring a hill. The measurement should not be made by allowing the chain to lie on the ground and go around trees or rocks. Abney levels are used on steep land to measure the angle of a slope.

Electronic total station equipment is replacing chains and levels. This equipment automatically gives horizontal distance from the instrument station to the prism range pole. It also provides changes in elevation (vertical distance) between the instrument and range pole.

Direction Measurements

Direction measurement is used to reference a line in terms of true north. A

11-11. Signaling by the surveyor from the instrument communicates to the person with the prism range pole.

compass is the instrument used to make direction measurements. Accuracy is very important. Compasses mounted on a tripod are more accurate than those that are hand-held.

Compasses point to the magnetic north. This is not the same as the true north. The true north is where the North Pole is located. True north is about 1,300 miles from the magnetic north. Also, the distance varies a small amount from one year to the next. The angle of difference between true north and magnetic north is known as declination. Declination is determined using observations of the Sun. Compasses used in surveying land should correct for declination. If not, calculations will need to be made that make the adjustment. The assistance of a certified surveyor or civil engineer may be needed.

11-12. Using an automatic level to measure the angle of the slope on a hill and determine elevation.

Elevation Measurements

Elevation measurement is determining the altitude of a point on land above (or below) sea level. Most land is above sea level. Some land is below sea level, such as areas in the Death Valley region of California.

Altimeters are sometimes used to measure elevations. Some types of levels or transits will provide accurate elevation measurement. The Abney and Dumpy levels are used to measure the angle from a horizontal plane to an elevated point on a slope or hill. They are being replaced by automatic and electronic total station instruments.

Area Measurements

Area measurement is determining the amount of land within set boundaries. It is based on horizontal surface area. Slope is often not considered.

Area measurement gives the square units within boundaries. One approach is to make linear measurements of land boundaries and use mathematical formulas to calculate area. For example, if a rectangular residential lot is 100 feet by 300 feet, the lot contains 30,000 square feet. This is equal to .69 acre (30,000 divided by 43,560–square feet in an acre).

REMOTE SENSING

Remote sensing may be used to determine land area. **Remote sensing** is collecting information about something (land, in this case) from a distance. A person gets information about land without actually going to it. Aerial photographs, thermal scanners, and satellite images may be used.

Aerial photographs can be used to determine area. The scale of the photographs must be known. This process is known as photogrammetry. Aerial

Career Profile

SURVEYOR

A surveyor uses instruments to locate, measure, and describe land. The work is outside in fields, forests, swamps, meadows, and subdivisions. A surveyor usually has one or two assistants that carry equipment, hold targets, drive stakes, and otherwise mark boundaries. Surveyors read land descriptions, use and prepare maps, and record information about land.

Surveyors typically have college degrees in civil engineering or a closely related area. In addition, they must also meet certification requirements for the state, county, or other area in which they work. Most have considerable experience as an assistant to a surveyor. Surveyors need to be able to precisely measure and record information.

Jobs for surveyors are found in all areas of the nation. Some are hired by contractors and government agencies. Many surveyors are self-employed or have a surveying business. This photo shows a surveyor setting up a total station instrument.

photographs are available from the local office of the Natural Resources Conservation Service (NRCS) of the U.S. Department of Agriculture. Each local office has a complete set of aerial photographs for the county or parish it serves. Most provide detailed information on land. Changes in fences, fields, and other features will not be shown if the photographs were made prior to the changes.

GLOBAL POSITIONING SYSTEMS

A *global positioning system* (GPS) is a method of locating geographical positions using ground units that receive information from satellites. Accuracy of location varies from 1.0 cm to several meters (less that one-half inch to several yards). The system must be used properly and in good working condition. Some GPS units are hand-held; others are mounted on equipment or as backpacks. The unit must be able to receive signals from orbiting satellites. A system of triangulation establishes an exact location.

GPS is becoming a highly useful tool in locating natural resource features on land. Surveyors can use GPS to identify property lines. Foresters can use GPS to identify timber resources. Wildlife conservationists can use it to establish the locations of nesting boxes, habitat for wildlife, and sources of pollution.

11-13. Using a global positioning system in surveying.

GEOGRAPHIC INFORMATION SYSTEMS

A *geographic information system* (GIS) uses a computer to integrate information with geographical data. Application of GIS is useful in studying natural resources and planning how resources can be used and improved. GIS is often used in conjunction with GPS.

LAND DESCRIPTIONS

Land must often be described in writing. A ***land description*** is a written statement that describes the boundaries of land and its location in relation to other land. A description becomes legal when it is written in a legal document prepared to sell, buy, or otherwise convey information about land. Accurate descriptions are needed for changing ownership, taxation, using land (such as where to locate a fence), and borrowing money in which the land is put up to guarantee a loan.

DEEDS

Land descriptions are used in property deeds. A ***deed*** is an executed and delivered contract about land, usually the sale of land. A deed defines the location of the land. It also specifies who has title or ownership to the land. A ***warranty deed*** is used when land is sold. It conveys the title to land from the seller to the buyer. A warranty deed is a means for the seller to guarantee the buyer a clear title. Deeds are legal documents and are usually prepared by attorneys. An official and notarized copy is filed or recorded with a government office that keeps copies of official records, such as a chancery clerk. Deed preparation usually involves a survey of the land.

Surveying is used to get information to prepare land descriptions and locate land from descriptions. A ***survey*** is the exact dimensions and locating of land. Accurate measurements are made. Mathematical formulas are used. Digital survey instruments, compasses, measuring chains, and other devices are used. Surveyors use land description systems in their work.

DESCRIPTION SYSTEMS

Land descriptions are important in surveying and establishing land boundaries. A ***boundary*** is the limit or line of land. Boundaries help landowners know the exact location of the property they own.

In general, two survey systems are used in describing land—metes and bounds system and rectangular system.

11-14. An iron rod has been driven in the ground to serve as a property point of reference. (The temporary wooden stake makes it easy to find the rod.)

Metes and Bounds

Metes and bounds is a system of describing land in which a known starting point is used to establish and describe lines forming the boundaries of property. The property is not referenced to a map or a lot on a map. The known starting point is the ***point of reference***. Lines run a certain direction for a number of feet and then another direction for a number of feet. This is repeated until the property is described in entirety.

Monuments are used as points of reference. A ***monument*** is a permanent marker placed on or near the land. Natural monuments or artificial monuments may be used. Whatever is used should be permanent. A wooden stake will decay and is easily moved. A tree may die or be cut. Large stones or iron rods driven into the ground may be used. The point of reference should be a permanent feature not easily moved.

11-15. A circle with sample angular courses showing divisions into quarters.

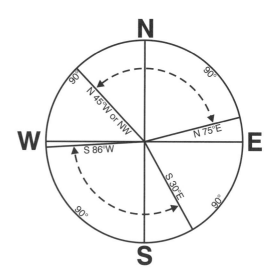

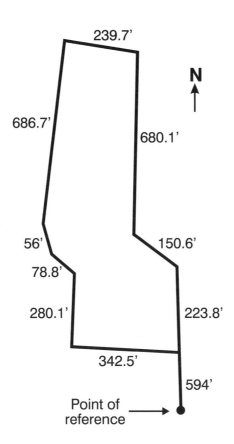

11-16. How this irregular-shaped piece of land containing 7.03 acres would be described using the metes and bounds system: "Beginning at a point 594 feet north of the point of reference; thence north 223.8 feet; thence north 50°58' west 150.6 feet; thence north 680.1 feet; then north 73°36' west 239.7 feet; thence, south 8°24' west 686.7 feet; then south 15°36' east 56 feet; thence south 52°02' east 78.8 feet; thence south 7° west 280.1 feet; thence east 342.5 feet to the place of beginning." (Note: In an area where rectangular survey system is used, reference would be included to townships and ranges.)

From the point of reference, lines of direction or courses are set. Directional lines are given in the number of degrees each varies east or west from the north or south starting points. A **course** is set at an angle to the point of reference. Angles are based on a circle, which has 360 degrees (designated °). Each degree is further divided into 60 minutes (designated '). For example, a course might be described as "starting at the iron pipe, thence north, 13° and 53' east, a distance of 330 feet." Rather than feet, land distance may be measured in chains. Precision linear measurements and compass directions are essential for accurate surveys. Boundaries that are not straight or that have irregularities require special skill.

The metes and bounds system was the first system of land description used in the United States. It is used today in twenty eastern states from Maine to Georgia and westward to Tennessee and Kentucky. Texas is included. Florida is not included.

Rectangular Survey System

The **rectangular survey system** is a method of describing land based on two fixed lines that are at right angles to each other. One line goes in a north-south direction; the other east-west. Accurate use of a compass is essential with the rectangular survey system. The rectangular survey system evolved through engineering and government laws as settlers moved westward in the midwest and west. Today, thirty states use the rectangular system, including Alaska and Hawaii.

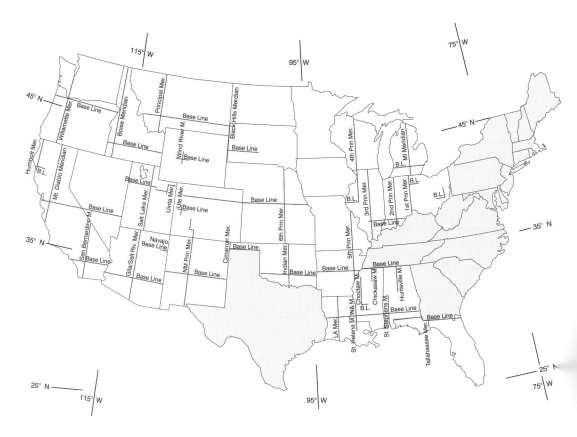

11-17. Land description system by state. (The shaded states use the metes and bounds system. Other states use the rectangular system. Meridians and base lines are shown.)

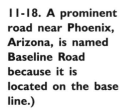

11-18. A prominent road near Phoenix, Arizona, is named Baseline Road because it is located on the base line.)

The two kinds of lines are the meridian and base line. A **meridian** is a true north-south line. Meridians were set by surveyors from identifiable points and are not in agreement with geographic longitude lines.

Two kinds of meridians are used: principal and guide. Principal meridians were set first based on a substantial landmark. The locations of the meridians are set based on degrees, minutes, and seconds west of the Greenwich Meridian.

The east-west or horizontal lines are known as **base lines**. They are sometimes known as latitude lines, but they do not follow latitude lines on the globe. Since Earth is round, correction lines are used every 24 miles to account for the curvature.

Land is divided into squares and rectangles within the principal meridians and base lines. Guide meridians are set at intervals of 24 miles between the principal meridians. These 24-mile squares are divided into 16 smaller tracts that are six-miles square. The six-mile square forms a **township**. There are 36 square miles in a township. Township lines and range lines are used to make the tracts. Township lines run east and west parallel to the base line at 6-mile intervals. Range lines run north and south at 6-mile intervals. This is why land descriptions use township numbers and range numbers. (Note: In describing land, it is important to know the distinction between "miles square" and "square miles.")

The first meridian forms the line between the states of Ohio and Indiana. All land descriptions in areas of the United States where this system is used

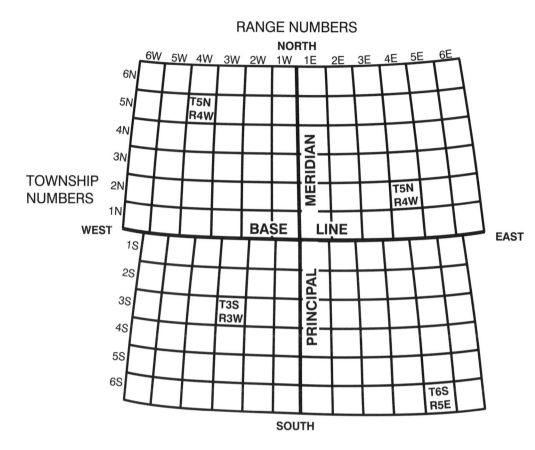

11-19. Sample township and range lines.

is based on only 35 meridians. A few of the meridians were established based on Native American treaties.

Using townships and ranges simplifies land descriptions. Dividing large areas into squares makes it easy to locate land within range and township lines. Both range and township lines are needed.

The 1-mile squares in townships are known as sections. A *section* is a block of land that contains 640 (because of Earth's curvature the six northernmost sections have fewer than 640 acres). To locate and describe land, the section must also be known. Each section in a township has a number ranging between 1 and 36. The numbering begins with section 1 in the northeast corner of a township and ends in the southeast corner with section 36.

Sections are further divided into quarters containing 160 acres. The quarters are known by location within the section, such as "the southeast ¼ of section 31" (which often appears as SE¼ of section 31). Quarters can be further divided, as needed, to describe land. Quarters can also be combined to form halves, such as "the W½ of section 31."(See Figure 11-20 for details on how sections are divided.)

Land boundaries may not follow a township or range line. As land is subdivided into smaller parcels for residential lots and other uses, a plat system is used. Curved lines formed by streams and roads require special care by trained surveyors. Accurate land measurement is very important.

Measuring land with chains and rods works well with the

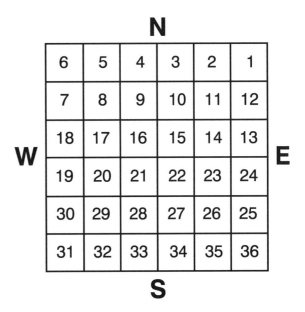

11-20. How a township is divided into sections.

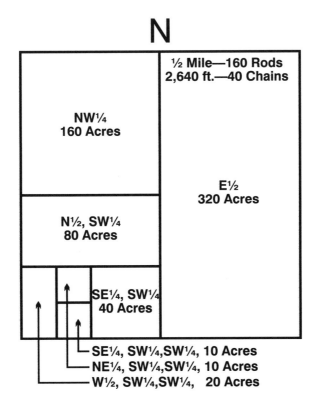

11-21. Divisions within a section.

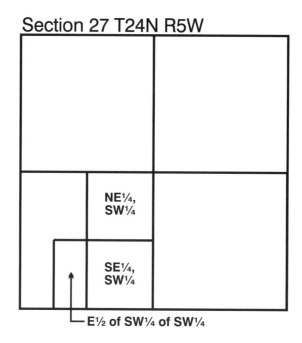

Section 27 T24N R5W

NE¼,
SW¼

SE¼,
SW¼

E½ of SW¼ of SW¼

11-22. How the land shown here is described: "the southeast ¼ of the southwest ¼ of section 27, plus the east half of the southwest ¼ of section 27, plus the northeast ¼ of the southwest ¼ of section 27, Township 24, north, Range 5 west."

rectangular system. Refer to Table 11-1 for the measures that are used and their equivalents.

PLAT PREPARATION

A *plat* is a map that shows land boundaries. Most plats do not show topographic features, such as creeks and streams. They do not include land elevations. Plats are more often used with smaller parcels of land, such as lots in residential areas. Plats may show the location of roads, utility lines, and the position of major structures on the property. The items included are those needed to satisfy the use being made of the plat.

Plats can begin with any corner of the property that is found to be original. The corner may be set in relationship to a monument located on other property. Individual residential lots may be part of a larger subdivision plat. The lots are surveyed (measured and marked) when the subdivision is surveyed. Lot buyers want individual plats for their property. Accuracy is very important. Written descriptions may have plats attached. Builders want accurate plats so structures can be placed properly on the land. Incorrectly

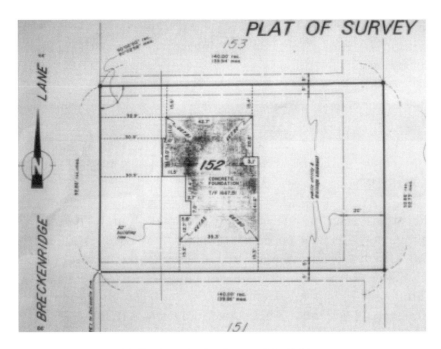

11-23. Sample plat for a residential lot.

building a home across property lines creates big problems for all who are involved.

AERIAL PHOTOGRAPHS

Aerial photographs may be used in locating and describing property. An *aerial photograph* is made downward from an airplane to show features of land. Roads, buildings, fences, fields, ponds, forests, and other features are easily seen on an aerial photograph. At the proper scale, a device known as a planimeter can be used to determine the acreage within fields, pastures, or other areas distinguishable on the aerial photograph.

Images are also made from satellites. Satellites operate at higher alti-

11-24. Aerial photograph showing a section of the Shenandoah Valley in Virginia. (Courtesy, U.S. Department of Agriculture)

tudes than airplanes. Satellite images tend to cover larger areas of land with less attention to detail. Global positioning can be used with satellites to precisely locate points on the earth.

REVIEWING

MAIN IDEAS

Land is the surface of the earth. This includes all of the natural resources and improvements as well as degradations that have been made to it. Land is usually an area of the surface measured in acres, square miles, or hectares.

Land quality is the characteristics of land for a particular use. The best land is cropland. This is followed by pasture, forests, and land that is left in its natural state. Best land use is a concept to explain that the best use of land is one that produces the most benefits for society.

Land capability is the suitability of land for agricultural uses. Surface texture, internal drainage, soil depth, erosion, slope, and surface runoff are factors in capability. Land is classified into capability classes based on the capability factors. Eight capability classes are used, with Class I being the best land and Class VIII being the land least capable of agricultural use.

Land surveying is used to measure and mark real property. Written descriptions as well as maps are used. Land measurements include linear, direction, elevation, and area. Most surveying has involved personal presence on the land. New methods of remote sensing are making it possible to collect information from a distance.

Land descriptions are written statements of boundaries and location of a parcel of land. Systems of surveying land include metes and bounds and rectangular survey system. Careful measurement and recording are essential with either method. The information becomes part of legal documents known as deeds.

QUESTIONS

Answer the following questions using complete sentences and correct spelling.

1. What is land?

2. What does land include?

3. How is the location of land important?

4. What is land quality? Relate land quality to cropland.

5. What are the major characteristics of cropland that determine its quality?

6. What does the concept of "best land use" mean?

7. What are the major land capability factors?

8. What is land capability classification?

9. What kinds of land measurements are made in surveying?

10. What is a land description?

11. What are the two major methods of surveying land? Briefly distinguish between the two.

12. Select the system of surveying used in your state. Explain how it is used.

EVALUATING

Match the term with the correct definition. Write the letter by the term in the blank provided.

a. plat
b. point of reference
c. monument
d. boundary
e. geodetic survey
f. meridian
g. section
h. township
i. land capability
j. compass

_____ 1. Linear land measurement that considers the curvature of Earth's surface.

_____ 2. An instrument used to make directional measurements.

_____ 3. The suitability of land for agricultural uses.

_____ 4. A permanent marker that serves as a starting point for surveying.

_____ 5. The known starting point in making a survey.

_____ 6. A map prepared during a survey that reports land boundaries.

_____ 7. A north-south line used in the rectangular survey system.

_____ 8. A block of land 1 mile square containing 640 acres.

_____ 9. A measure containing 36 square miles based on guide meridians.

_____ 10. The limit or line of a partial of land.

EXPLORING

1. Visit the local government office that records deeds and land transactions. Have a person in the office give a tour of the facility and explain how deeds are recorded and what recording means. Read one or more recorded deeds. Note the information that is included in a deed. Note: If the office for recording documents is not convenient, a local attorney that prepares deeds and closes real property sales would be a good resource person in class.

2. Arrange to survey a small partial of land. Work with a surveyor. Study the written description and identify the monument of the land that marks the point of reference. Prepare a plat of the property. Give a report in class on your experiences.

3. Invite a representative of the local Natural Resources and Conservation Service office to visit class and bring aerial photographs of the area. Have the person describe how aerial photographs are used. Locate the school, your home, and other features on the photographs. Determine the scale of the photographs.

12

RANGELAND

Vast areas of the United States are covered with rangeland. Grasses, yucca, cactus, and other plants are on it. In some areas, low rainfall often means these plants grow very little each year. In other areas, adequate rainfall promotes fairly lush plant growth.

People have different ideas about what rangeland is and how it is used. Some view it as land that is dry and cannot be used for much of anything. Other people view it as a valuable natural resource that provides food for animals.

Rangeland typically grows plants with little value other than for forage, such as for cattle and sheep. These animals have digestive systems that can handle large amounts of roughage. Animals eat the leaves, stems, and twigs of the plants. They convert low-grade plant materials into meat and other products.

12-1. Sheep have the unique ability to live on rangeland. (This shows a range scientist recording the kinds of plants that sheep eat.) (Courtesy, Agricultural Research Service, USDA)

OBJECTIVES

This chapter explains the meaning, types, and importance of rangeland. It also includes important practices in rangeland management. The following objectives are listed:

1. Define rangelands and identify their uses

2. List and explain the types of rangelands

3. Describe the plant materials on rangeland

4. Select and implement appropriate rangeland management practices

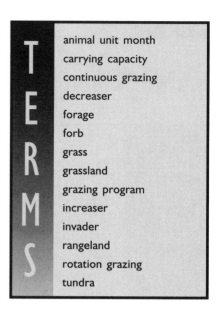

TERMS

animal unit month
carrying capacity
continuous grazing
decreaser
forage
forb
grass
grassland
grazing program
increaser
invader
rangeland
rotation grazing
tundra

Bureau of Land Management
http://www.blm.gov/

RANGELAND AND ITS USES

Rangeland is land that grows native forage plants. The kinds and extent of plant growth vary with moisture, soil fertility, and other conditions. Rangeland often has vast areas of open space. Some rangeland may have limited forest areas and other natural resources.

WHERE IT IS FOUND

Rangeland is found on most continents. Vast land areas in Africa and Asia are rangeland. Australia is 70 percent rangeland. In some countries, nomadic tribes tend livestock that roam the rangelands.

Rangelands occupy 29 percent of the land area in the United States. Most of this is in prairies where low-growing grasses predominate. Some is in desert-type conditions where forage production is very low. Arizona, New Mexico, Nevada, and Wyoming have the highest percentage of rangeland.

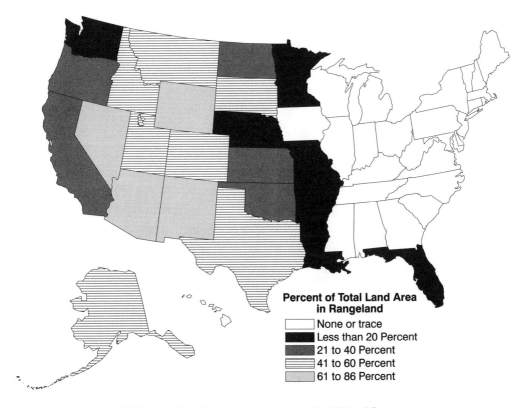

Percent of Total Land Area in Rangeland

- None or trace
- Less than 20 Percent
- 21 to 40 Percent
- 41 to 60 Percent
- 61 to 86 Percent

12-2. Location of rangeland areas in the United States.

Slightly over half of the rangelands in the United States are owned privately. Some 43 percent is owned by the federal government. The Bureau of Land Management (BLM) and U.S. Forest Service oversee rangelands owned by the federal government. The BLM oversees 270 million acres of public land, primarily in the western states and Alaska. Ranchers can obtain permits to graze livestock on some of the federally owned lands. The Natural Resources Conservation Service of the USDA is also involved with protecting privately owned rangelands.

USES OF RANGELAND

Rangeland is used in many ways:

■ Forage for Animals—***Forage*** is the leaves and stems of plants that are eaten by animals. Rangeland has native plants that are forage. The land is typically not seeded to improved grasses and legumes. The land often receives little care. Millions of cattle, sheep, goats, and other species graze on native rangelands in the United States. The stocking rate may be quite low because of limited forage growth. Plants on some rangelands grow quite slowly due to hot and/or dry weather. In some cases, 200 acres or more may be needed for each animal grazing on rangeland. This is quite different from the carrying capacity of improved pastures, where one cow may need only a couple of acres.

12-3. Cattle often graze rangeland. (Courtesy, Texas Department of Agriculture)

■ Wildlife Habitat and Conservation—Rangeland often serves as the habitat for wildlife. Deer, antelope, rabbits, birds, and other species are found in rangeland areas. Wildlife is protected on government-owned rangelands.

Range managers also realize that wildlife competes with domestic animals for resources. Wildlife uses food and water, space, and, sometimes, preys on domestic animals. Ranchers occasionally set about to destroy some wildlife populations, such as wolves, because of the damage they cause by killing livestock.

12-4. Jack rabbits compete with domestic animals for food.

■ Mineral and Fossil Fuel Deposits—Some rangeland areas have reserves of minerals and fossil fuels. Oil wells are often found in rangeland areas.

■ Wood Products—Rangeland areas may have limited forests, especially smaller trees with special-purpose uses. For example, mesquite is a small tree often used for special purposes, such as charcoal. Overall, rangelands are limited in wood production.

■ Recreation—Rangelands are used as recreation, such as hunting, birding, and hiking. Areas owned by the federal government are available for citizens to use. Of course, they may need to obtain the necessary permits and pay the required fees. Private rangelands are posted and not available to the public unless permission is granted. National forests that are made up of rangelands are open to the public for recreational uses.

■ Aesthetics—Rangeland is often attractive and appealing. People enjoy viewing the beauty and life forms that are found on it. Some areas are used to attract tourists, such as the Tonto National Forest area of Arizona. Individuals who own rangeland should keep it free of junk, such as old cars and dilapidated buildings.

TYPES OF RANGELAND

Rangeland is classified by the type of vegetation that grows on the land. Vegetation growth is often related to the amount of precipitation and overall climate of the area. Grassland and desert shrubland are by far the largest rangeland areas in the United States.

■ Grasslands—*Grassland* is an area that grows grasses and forbs. It is usually in a temperate climate. The annual precipitation is 10 to 30 inches (25 to 75 cm).

12-5. Shortgrass is ideal for sheep production. (Courtesy, American Sheep Industry Association and National Lamb and Wool Grower Magazine, Englewood, Colorado)

A *grass* is a plant with flat leaves that have parallel veins. Grasses usually grow no more than a yard (meter) in height though some are much shorter and others are taller. Some 1,400 different species of grasses have been identified. Common grasses on rangelands include blue grama and green needlegrass.

A *forb* is a small broad-leaf plant that does not develop a woody stem, such as clover. A mix of forbs with grasses is often best.

The grassland of the plains area in the United States reaches from Canada to Mexico and forms the largest area of grassland in the world. Large herds of wild animals, such as bison, once roamed this area. The plains grassland is often known as prairie. Much of this area has been plowed; consequently, the native grasses have been destroyed. Originally, the prairie had three vegetation regions: tallgrass, shortgrass, and transition. Tallgrass was in the eastern part of the prairie and covered the states of Indiana and Illinois northward through Wisconsin and Minnesota to the Canadian border. The shortgrass stretched southward from the Canadian border across North Da-

12-6. Much of the native rangeland has been converted to crop production. (Courtesy, AGCO Corporation, Georgia)

kota into Texas. The transition region, with a mix of grasses, was between the tallgrass and shortgrass regions.

■ Desert Shrublands—Desert shrublands take up the largest area of rangelands in the world. The annual precipitation is less than 10 inches (25 cm). The soil is often not fertile, but the major limiting factor is moisture. Vegetation growth is sparse.

A shrub is a low-growing woody plant that often has several stems. Shrubs are usually more appealing to deer than to cattle. Cactus and other plants that need little moisture offer limited grazing.

■ Temperate Forests—The temperate forest rangelands may provide considerable grazing if covered with grasses. These areas may be natural or artificial.

12-7. This horse finds limited forage in desert shrubland.

12-8. A temperate forest rangeland.

Artificial temperate areas have resulted from clear-cutting trees for timber. Some temperate forests are covered with dense shrubs that provide little grazing for cattle.

■ Tundra—*Tundra* is an area with permafrost subsoil. Tundra in the United States is in Alaska or high elevations of mountains. Mountain tundra is known as Alpine tundra. Limited vegetation grows in the tundra area.

■ Savannas—A savanna is an area without trees and has relatively flat topography. Though not found except in isolated areas in the southeastern United States, large areas of tropical grassland savannas are in Africa and South America.

■ Shrub Woodlands—These areas are found in the same general areas as grasslands but are covered with shrubs. These areas are small and limited in the United States.

■ Tropical Forests—Tropical forests usually have dense canopies and allow little vegetation to grow on the forest floor. Few areas of tropical forest are found in the United States except for isolated areas in Hawaii.

RANGELAND ECOLOGY

Rangeland ecology deals with the vegetation that grows on rangelands and interactions of the vegetation with animal life. Some animals, such as deer, eat leaves, twigs, and shoots. Others, such as cattle, prefer grass. The rate of grazing influences the growth and condition of vegetation on rangeland.

PLANT DYNAMICS

The vegetation on some rangelands is sparse and fragile. Animals prefer to feed on some species over other species. Important relationships exist among plant species as related to animal feeding. This is known as plant dynamics.

Based on dynamics, plants that grow on rangeland are classified into three groups: decreasers, increasers, and invaders.

A *decreaser* is a plant species that is easily damaged by grazing. The plants are highly nutritious and palatable to animals. Because animals prefer to eat the decreasers, these species are eaten first. They may be damaged so they die and are no longer found on the rangeland. Rangeland management uses practices to prevent overconsumption of decreasers.

An *increaser* is a plant species that tends to do well in areas where animals are grazing. This is because increaser species are less palatable to animals. They tend to avoid eating the increasers. After long periods of heavier

Career Profile

RANGE SCIENTIST

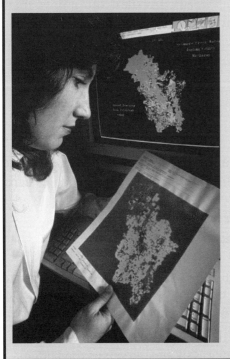

A range scientist studies and recommends practices to sustain rangeland. The work may be indoors or outside in range areas collecting information. They also study wildlife and various ecological relationships. This photograph shows a range scientist reviewing land use data for a watershed to determine the impact of nitrate nitrogen on leaching into underground aquifers. (Courtesy, Agricultural Research Service, USDA)

Range scientists need college degrees in range management, turf management, wildlife management, or a closely related area. Many have masters degrees; a few have doctors degrees. Practical experience with range, including livestock production on rangeland is beneficial.

Jobs for range scientists are found with government agencies, colleges and universities, and some private agribusinesses in areas where rangeland is important.

12-9. Rangeland in Hawaii shows the effects of overgrazing and the emergence of invaders–cactus.

than desired grazing, the increasers begin to decline. Decline may be due to damage by hooves as well as grazing.

An *invader* is a plant species that is not appealing as food to animals. These species move into areas that have been overgrazed. Animals do not like to eat the invader species. Examples of invaders include ragweed, cactus, and thistle. These are sometimes known as weeds. Invaders often have massive root systems that allow them to survive where grasses could not. A good range should have almost no invaders and a high percentage of decreasers. As the percentage of invaders increases, the quality of rangeland for forage declines.

CARRYING CAPACITY

Carrying capacity is the number of animals that an area of rangeland will support. It is usually stated on a per unit area of land basis, such as acre, section, or hectare. If the capacity is exceeded, the quality of the range goes down. Carrying capacity is also known as stocking rate.

Several factors that affect carrying capacity are:

■ Animal Species—The species of animal affects carrying capacity as related to the vegetation on the range. Sheep, for example, graze differently from cattle. Five sheep or goats are equal to one steer in terms of forage needed. Four deer equal one steer.

■ Plant Species—Some plants are more appealing and nutritious than others.

- Climate—Climate has a major role on the growth of vegetation. Precipitation and temperature are most important.

- Soil Type—Soil fertility and texture are important in grazing rangelands. Fertile soils will produce more vegetation if moisture is adequate.

Determining carrying capacity involves animal unit months. An ***animal unit month*** (AUM) is the amount of forage needed to keep a 1,000 pound (454 kg) animal well fed for a month. Wildlife must be considered along with domestic animals. Most rangeland supports deer, elk, or other wildlife in addition to cattle, goats, sheep, or horses. Horses and bull bovines require 25 percent more than a steer.

Range scientists have developed information for use in managing local areas. The Bureau of Land Management or local office of the Cooperative Extension Service will have materials available.

12-10. How do you assess the stocking rate of this range? (The sheep are being herded to another pasture!) (Courtesy, National Lamb and Wool Grower, Englewood, Colorado)

RANGELAND MANAGEMENT PRACTICES

Proper management is needed to protect and get productivity from rangelands. Most rangelands are fragile and easily damaged. Good management helps sustain rangelands.

HOW RANGELAND IS DAMAGED

Rangeland is damaged by human activity as well as natural events. Much rangeland was destroyed and converted to other uses by the settlers that

12-11. This cow is starving on overgrazed rangeland.

moved westward. Human activity that damaged rangeland has been in two major areas: plowing up rangelands and improper grazing.

Millions of acres of rangeland have been plowed in the plains of the United States. Plowing the rangeland was called "sodbusting." This is because the land had heavy sod that required special kinds of plows. The steel moldboard plow was developed by an Illinois blacksmith named John Deere. It was designed to plow heavy soil covered with sod. Changing the use of the land was appropriate in most cases. The land was needed to produce corn, soybeans, wheat, and other crops. This converted rangeland must be given proper care to prevent erosion, conserve moisture, and maintain fertility. In some cases, irrigation is essential for the land to be productive.

Improper grazing destroys vegetation. The rate of grazing involves a careful balance. Overgrazing is stocking at a heavier rate than the carrying capacity of the rangeland. Undergrazing also results in damage. It allows too much vegetation to grow. This results in larger-size plants. Large plants have limbs well above the ground. They offer less protection of the soil and forage for animals.

Drought, fire, floods, and other natural events can damage rangeland. In some cases, insects and plant diseases may invade rangeland.

Building residential and commercial areas damages rangeland. Roads, pipelines, utility lines, and other structures cause damage. Of course, the land is needed for these purposes. People have to make choices about the use of land!

GOOD MANAGEMENT

The major goal of range management is to maximize the growth and use of vegetation without damaging the quality of the rangeland. Some things are fairly easy to do. Others may require a little more effort.

Here are several practices that promote good range management.

Grazing Programs

A **grazing program** is the schedule and sequence of allowing animals to graze an area. Several approaches are used. They are all based on removing an appropriate quantity of vegetation.

Grazing programs are implemented to adjust grazing pressure to a level that is desirable for a native species. Grazing pressure deals with the intensity and duration of grazing.

Resource Connection

APACHE TRAIL

The Apache Trail in southern Arizona passes through rugged desert rangeland. Today's tourists can begin the trail just out of Phoenix on a road that will lead through canyons and cactus. Summer temperatures reach 110° F (45°C) or more on most days. Winter nights can be below freezing. Precipitation averages less that 10 inches (25 cm) a year!

Driving through the area in an automobile is fun. It is difficult to appreciate the hard times of the early settlers walking on foot or riding pack animals. Cactus spines, rattlesnakes, and sharp rocks were ever-present to delay travel. Today, cattle glean some forage from the area. The carrying capacity is quite low.

12-12. These sheep can be rotated from one area to another.

Continuous grazing is keeping animals on an area year-round. Carrying capacity must be carefully determined. Larger areas are often grazed. Fewer fences are needed than with other approaches in grazing management. Salt block and mineral supplements may need to be moved about to keep animals from grazing too heavily in one area.

Rotation grazing is restricting animals to one area for a period and moving them to another area. Various systems of rotation are used. Fences are needed to divide the rangeland. People must be available to herd animals from one range area to another. While the animals are grazing in one area, vegetation in other areas can be growing. Rotation grazing may require additional sources of water.

12-13. Eastern gama grass is used on some rangeland for forage.

Seeding and Fertilizing

Damaged rangelands may be restored by planting adapted species. Seeds may be distributed by hand, ground seeding equipment, or airplane. Airplanes are needed in rugged terrain. The species planted are native to the area. Planting rangeland is an important practice in restoring vegetative growth.

Fertilizing is used to improve the nutrient levels in rangeland. Adding nutrients may not be profitable if water is the most deficient item for plant growth.

In some cases, rangeland may be reclaimed and made into improved pasture. This results in greater carrying capacity but may be impractical if moisture is not available to support plant growth.

Controlling Pests

Rangeland is subject to pests just as cropland and improved pastures. Pests include undesirable plants, insects, animals, and diseases.

Mesquite, sagebrush, and juniper invade some rangelands. These are woody-type plants that produce little or no forage. They have massive root systems and compete for limited soil moisture. In some cases, biological control of undesirable plants is possible. For example, goats will consume woody-type plants that cattle will not eat.

Some plants are poisonous to animals. These may need to be controlled, but control may be difficult in the widespread areas in rangeland. Some common plants can be poisonous. For example, tannins in oak leaves and acorns can cause poisoning in cattle. Halogeton is a plant accidentally introduced from Russia that now infests 10 million acres of western rangelands.

Insects, especially grasshoppers, may consume large amounts of vegetation. They typically damage the tender, most palatable leaves desired by graz-

12-14. Spanish goats are used on Texas rangeland to control woody plant pests. (Courtesy, Texas Department of Agriculture)

ing animals. More than 142 species of grasshoppers have been identified in the western rangeland area of the United States. Populations of grasshoppers may reach 180,000 or more per acre.

Jackrabbits, prairie dogs, and rats compete for vegetation. Jackrabbits feast on the same vegetation as that which is most preferred by livestock.

Predators are problems in some areas. Coyotes and wolves may cause big losses on rangeland among sheep. They also prey on rabbits and rodents, which helps keep those populations down. Most livestock producers experience losses from predators on rangelands, such as attack by a wolf on a baby calf. Some producers use guard llamas and donkeys to ward off predators.

Preventing Fires

Wildfires can burn and severely damage rangeland. Many years of growth can be destroyed with one fast-moving fire. In some cases, controlled burning is used to remove mesquite and other pest plants. Some ranchers place fire lanes around areas of rangeland to slow the movement of fire should one occur. Always be careful with fire around rangeland. It is a good idea to never have open fires in dry areas. A spark can quickly result in a fire that is out of control. Remember, fires are more likely to get out of control quickly on a hot, dry, windy day.

REVIEWING

MAIN IDEAS

Rangeland is land on which native plants grow, usually grasses and forbs. Rangeland in the United States is primarily in the midwest and west. The Bureau of Land Management oversees much of the rangeland owned by the federal government.

Rangeland is thought of primarily in agriculture as a source of forage. It also serves as wildlife habitat, a source of minerals and fossil fuels, a source of wood products, a place for recreation, and a place for enjoying nature.

There are several types of rangelands: grasslands, desert shrublands, temperate forests, tundra, savannas, shrub woodlands, and tropical forests.

Plants have important dynamics on rangelands. Plant species are classi-fied into three groups: decreasers, increasers, and invaders. Actions within the plant community influence the carrying capacity of the rangeland.

Good management can sustain and improve rangeland. Major causes of damage can be reduced. Practices can be used to improve the vegetation and overall condition of the land. Grazing programs, seeding, controlling pests, and controlling fires are important practices.

QUESTIONS

Answer the following questions using complete sentences and correct spelling.

1. Where is rangeland found in the United States? Who owns the land?
2. What are the uses of rangeland?
3. What are the types of rangeland? Which is most important in the United States?
4. What plant dynamics relationships exist on rangeland?
5. What is carrying capacity? How does this relate to animal unit month?
6. How has rangeland been damaged?
7. What is the major goal of range management?
8. What is a grazing program? Distinguish between the two general types of programs.
9. What pests damage rangeland?
10. How do fires damage rangeland?

EVALUATING

Match the term with the correct definition. Write the letter by the term in the blank provided.

a. rangeland
b. forage
c. grass

d. forb
e. shrub
f. decreaser

g. increaser
h. carrying capacity

_____ 1. A plant that tends to do well in areas where animals are grazing but is less palatable to the animals.

_____ 2. The number of head of animals that an area of rangeland will support.

_____ 3. Land that grows native forage plants.

_____ 4. Leaves and stems of plants that are eaten by animals.

_____ 5. A low-growing woody plant.

_____ 6. A plant species easily damaged by grazing.

_____ 7. A small broad-leaved plant.

_____ 8. A small plant with flat leaves having parallel veins.

EXPLORING

1. Assess your local community. Determine if rangeland areas are present. If not, select an area in a nearby community or state. List the species of grasses and forbs on the land. Prepare a report on your findings.

2. Research the foraging traits of cattle, sheep, goats, horses, and deer. Identify local forage species that these animals would prefer. Prepare a report on your findings.

3. Prepare a report on the Bureau of Land Management. Determine the mission and functions of the Bureau. Investigate the practices followed in leasing federal range lands for grazing. Determine the number of years in a lease, the rate of charge, and other regulations that relate to the use of these lands. Use the web site listed on page 260 as a major source of information. Present your report in class.

Fannette Island, Lake Tahoe, California

axter State Park, Maine

Anna Ruby Falls, Georgia

Monterey Bay, California

Prickly Pear Blossom, Tonto National Forest, Arizona

orest Park, Georgia

Rachel Carson Marshland, Maine

Having Fun With Natural Resources ...

On the Beach of Waikiki

Landing a Big Fish

Hunting Favorite Game

Mountain Climbing

Sportskiing

Kayaking in Whitewater

Surfing

Mining Copper

ng Steel

Building With Clay Brick

ng Metal

Irrigating Dry Land
(Courtesy, Agricultural Research Service, USDA)

ng With Wood

Plumbing With PVC

Having Fun With Wildlife: Birds ...

Short-eared Owl

White Pelican

Great Blue Heron

Peregrine Falcon

Wild Turkey

Trumpeter Swan With Cygnets

Blue Jay

Double-crested Cormorant Chicks

Snow Geese

Bald Eagle

Timber Wolf

ote Howling

Bull Elk

Grizzly

obcat

Badger

ccoon

Musk Ox

Enjoying Rocks and Gems ...

Azurite Malachite

Amethyst With Calcite

Brazilian Agate With Growth Rings

Fishtail Selenite

Mexican Selenite

Citrine Crystal

Phantom Quartz

Malachite Stalagmite

Pyrite Suns

Enjoying Underwater Resources ...

Diver With Octopus

Spotted Trunkfish

Diver With Short-spine Star

ay Reef Shark

Lion Fish

Blue-banded Sea Perch

Banded Butterfly Fish

Enjoying Desert Plants: Cacti …

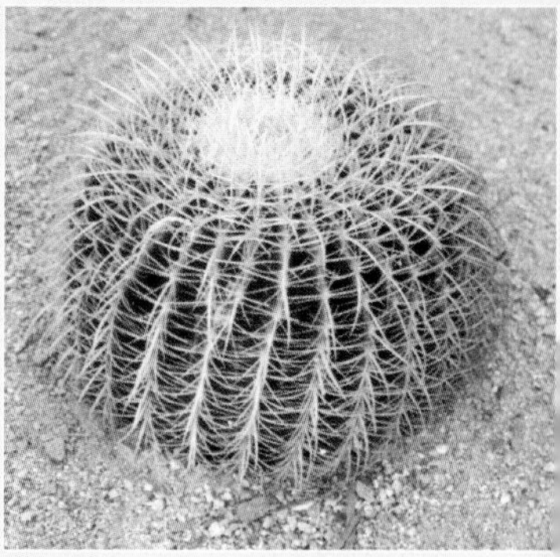

Fish-hook Barrel

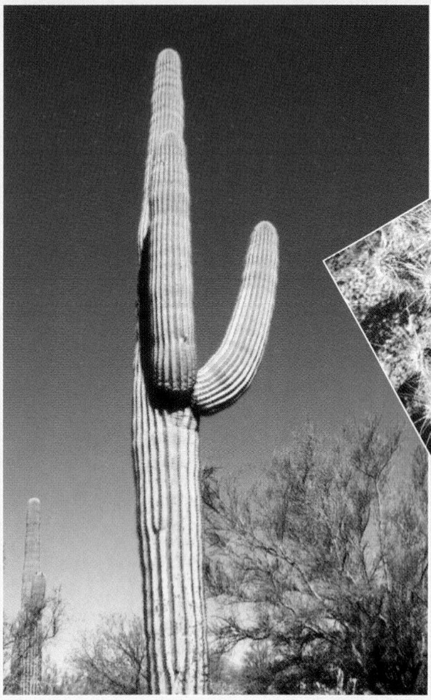

Saguaro

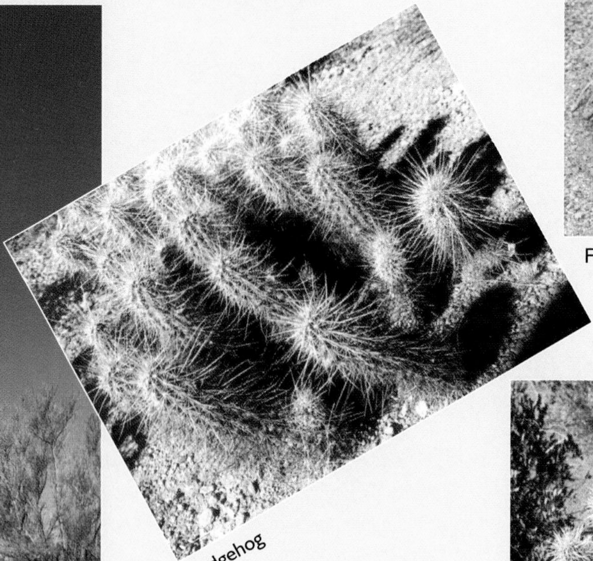

Hedgehog

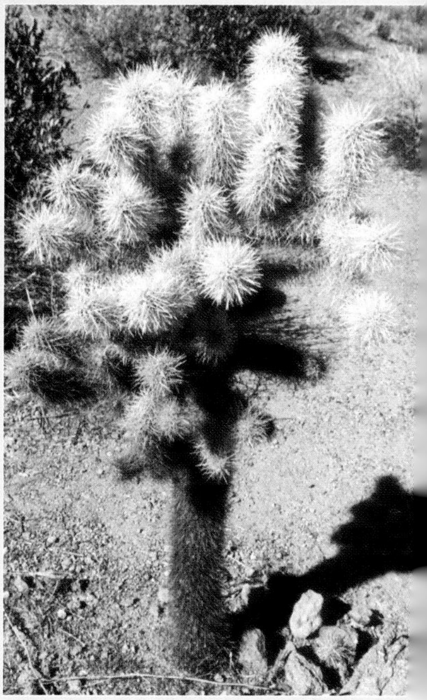

Teddy Bear Cholla

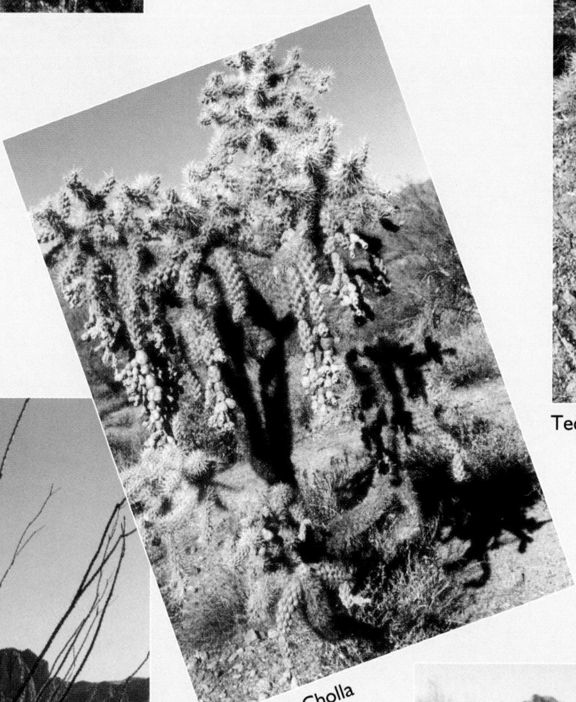

Chain Fruit Cholla

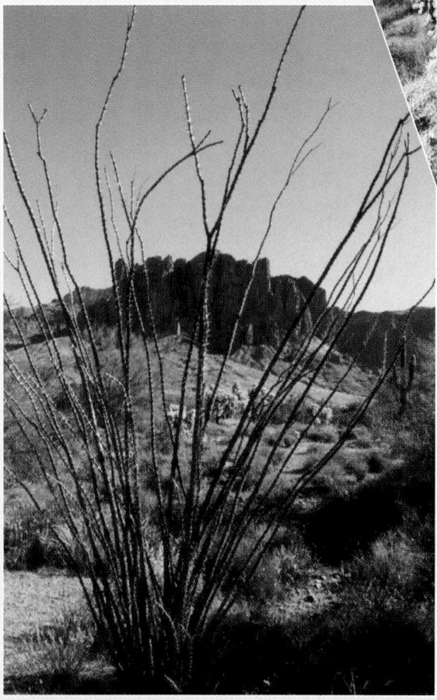

Ocotillo

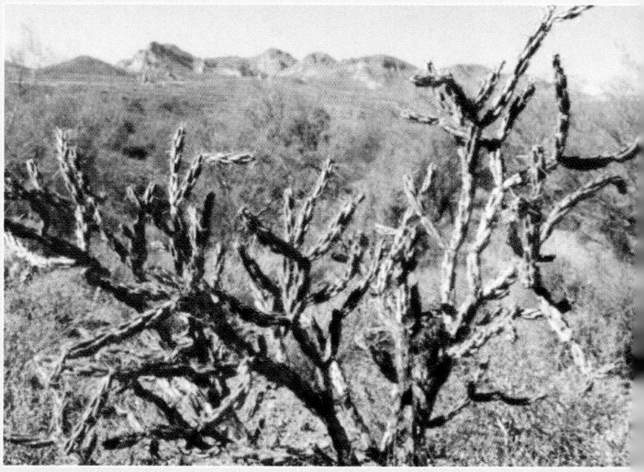

Buckhorn Cholla

13

WEATHER AND CLIMATE

Is the climate changing? If so, what is causing the change? Some people think that the climate is changing because humans are abusing the atmosphere. Others think that changes in the climate are just a part of the evolution of our world.

Scientists thought it was changing enough for steps to be taken. The first step was a Climate Change Action Plan. This was a voluntary program for industry set up in the mid-1990s by the federal government. Fifty actions were proposed. If the actions are implemented, annual carbon dioxide emissions into the air will be cut by 109 million tons! Some of the steps are quite simple, such as planting 10 million fast-growing trees to absorb carbon dioxide.

Weather and climate are natural resources tied to the atmosphere. They are important to our welfare.

13-1. Snow surfing is recreation that makes use of weather conditions.

OBJECTIVES

This chapter introduces important areas of weather and climate. Emphasis is on weather and climate as natural resources. The chapter has the following objectives:

1. Define and distinguish between weather and climate

2. Explain how the climate is a natural resource

3. Relate latitude and longitude to weather and climate

4. Assess methods used in measuring weather conditions

5. Relate weather fronts to natural resources

6. Explain relationships between weather and climate and the environment

TERMS

altitude
atmospheric pressure
atmospheric temperature
biome
climate
cloud
dew point
fog
global climate
hail
hurricane
latitude
longitude
precipitation
rain
relative humidity
sleet
snow
storm
temperate climate
temperature
thermometer
thunderstorm
tornado
tropical climate
weather
weather front
winter storm

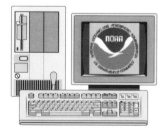

**National Oceanic and
Atmospheric Administration
http://www.noaa.gov/**

WEATHER MAKES THE CLIMATE

The weather influences how we go about each day. It helps us decide if we need to wear a raincoat or a short sleeve shirt. Climate, however, helps us plan for longer periods such as how we prepare our homes for the winter. We have a general idea what each season has in store for us.

Climate is the weather that is generally found in a location. It is the average of all weather conditions. The climate varies by season of the year and geographic location. Some places have warm, dry climates, such as the southwestern United States. Other places have cool, wet climates, such as the Puget Sound area in the northwestern United States.

What is the climate like where you live? Are the seasons quite different? Is it typically cold, hot, wet, dry, or windy? You can begin to describe the climate by keeping weather records.

13-2. Riding a horse is more fun in good weather.

WEATHER

Weather is the condition of the atmosphere at a specific time. Weather measurements are typically made at or near ground level several times a day.

Weather conditions on any one day do not have much affect on the overall climate. Each day is one small bit of information that makes our overall climate. We need information for many years to describe the climate. The climate is somewhat like an average of all weather conditions. For example, the average low temperature in the winter is often used to describe the climate.

The five major factors in weather are:

■ Temperature—***Temperature*** is a measure of the warmness or coldness of the weather. It is reported using Fahrenheit (F) or Celsius (C) scales. Keeping long-term temperature records allows us to know one of the features of the climate for a location.

■ Precipitation—***Precipitation*** is the moisture that is deposited on the earth from the atmosphere. It is often as rain, dew, or snow but may be as frost, hail, or sleet. Precipitation is measured in inches or centimeters.

■ Wind—Air movement makes wind. Wind is measured as miles per hour or kilometers per hour. Gentle winds are refreshing and help move polluted air away from where we live. Strong winds may damage our property and natural resources, such as trees.

■ Atmospheric pressure—***Atmospheric pressure*** is the pressure exerted by the weight of the atmosphere. It is sometimes known as air pressure. Pressure at sea level tends to be constant at all places on the earth except for low and high pressure weather systems. Pressure decreases with increased elevation.

■ Altitude—***Altitude*** is the distance a point on the earth's crust is above sea level. Altitude is the elevation of the land. Measurements into the depths of oceans or lakes are reported as below sea level. As altitude increases, temperature typically decreases. Atmospheric pressure also decreases with altitude.

13-3. Sea level conditions are important in weather and climate.

GLOBAL CLIMATE

Climates vary from one location to another. The climates on the earth form the ***global climate***, which is the general climate of the earth. The global climate can be compared to the climates of specific locations. If compared, we would find that some places meet our needs better than others.

The climate varies from one place to another. How does the climate in South Texas differ from Alaska? Some locations are considered warm; others are cold. Some are dry and others are wet. The climate on land (known as continental climate) is different from that over the ocean (known as maritime climate).

WEATHER AND CLIMATE AS RESOURCES

Weather and climate are important in our environment. They influence natural resources, such as the growth of forests and formation of soil. Keeping the air free of pollution helps maintain the climate we want.

INFLUENCES BIOMES

A *biome* is a community of living organisms. Many different biomes are found on the earth. Most biomes cover a fairly large region. For example, tropical rain forests tend to be similar wherever they are found.

Each biome is influenced by the climate. The kinds of plants, the amount of water, the weathering of parent material, and other characteristics of a biome are influenced by the weather.

The most important feature of a biome is the growth of vegetation. The kinds of plants determine the kinds of animals found in any location. Temperature and rainfall are important in plant growth.

WEATHERING

Weathering is a natural process of change in the materials on the earth's crust. Weather conditions cause weathering. They exert strong forces in changing the earth. Cold, freezing weather causes changes just as does warm weather with rain. All weather conditions affect natural resources one way or another.

13-4. Climate influences the biome where this mushroom is growing.

POWER

Wind is a source of power. Some of the power can be used to do useful work, such as pump water. Direction and presence of wind are important in power. Wind moves boats and turns windmills. Wind speed and direction are influenced by the weather. Long-term winds are a part of the climate.

Wind power can be destructive. Strong winds can uproot trees and destroy our homes. Storms can inflict damage on towns and cities.

AIR EXCHANGE

Wind exchanges the air and refreshes areas where the air is polluted. Prevailing winds along the seashore move stale air out and fresh air in.

TOURISM

People are attracted to areas because of the climate. Hawaii is appealing to people who live in colder climates because of its tropical climate. Nothing

Career Profile

METEOROLOGIST

A meteorologist studies the atmosphere and conditions that produce weather. A meteorologist sets up and uses equipment to measure and record conditions. The information is used to make reports and forecasts. This photo shows a rain gauge being unlocked to see the amount of precipitation.

Meteorologists have college degrees in meteorology or a closely related area. Those doing research have masters or doctors degrees. Practical experience is very beneficial. Some have additional training to prepare them as broadcasters and writers.

Job opportunities are with federal agencies that deal with the atmosphere and weather, such as the National Oceanic and Atmospheric Administration (NOAA). Some meteorologists work with colleges, research stations, and businesses. A few work with radio and television stations and news organizations.

13-5. Climate attracts tourists to Waikiki Beach in Hawaii.

beats an escape to warm weather when it is cold outside! Likewise, mountain climates are popular in hot summer weather.

LATITUDE AND LONGITUDE

Scientists use a system of lines to pinpoint locations on Earth. These lines are latitude and longitude. You may want to look at a map or globe to see the lines and how they intersect.

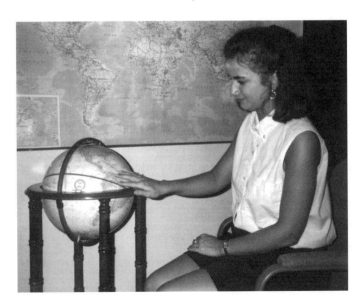

13-6. Using a globe to identify latitude and longitude.

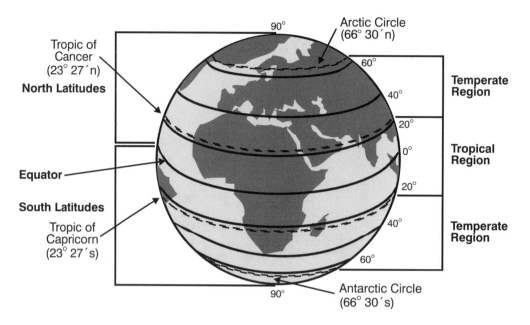

13-7. Location of major latitude lines.

LATITUDE

Latitude is an imaginary line that runs east and west that gives the distance north or south from the equator. The lines are parallel with the equator. On a map or globe, you will see the latitude lines running east and west.

Lines of latitude are given numbers known as degrees. The equator has a latitude of 0°. Degrees latitude are further divided into minutes and seconds. Minutes are designate by ′ and seconds are designated by ″. Areas north and south of the equator have an increasing latitude the greater the distance from the equator. Each pole is 90° from the equator.

Latitudes north of the equator are known as degrees north, while those south are degrees south. Every location north of the equator that is the same distance from the equator would have the same latitude. For example, Atlanta, Georgia, has a latitude of 33° north. This is similar to many other cities in the United States. Atlanta is a large city and covers a fairly big area. If we want to know specific sites in Atlanta, we would use minutes and seconds. For example, Olympic Stadium in Atlanta is 33°43′20″! These numbers, together with longitude, allow the use of global positioning to identify and mark precise locations on Earth.

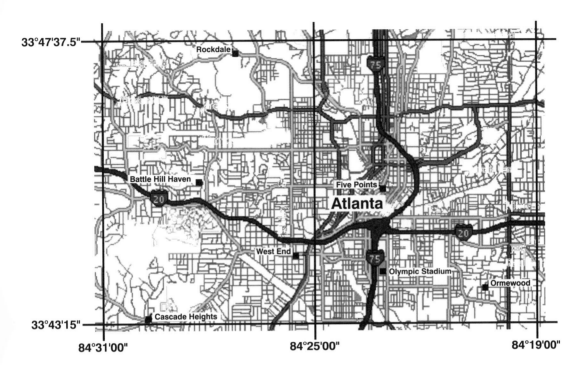

13-8. Map showing latitude and longitude degrees, minutes, and seconds.

LONGITUDE

Longitude is the east-west distance between any location on the earth. It is based on the prime meridian, which is a line that passes over Greenwich, England. Longitude lines are drawn north and south on a globe or map.

The Greenwich meridian has been given a 0° longitude. The location of other points is within 180° east or west of Greenwich. There are 360° in a circle, such as around the earth. The middle of Atlanta, Georgia, is approximately 84°24' west longitude.

Longitude in combination with latitude helps find precise locations. Using the Olympic Stadium in Atlanta as an example, the longitude is approximately 84°23'00". Combine that with latitude from the previous paragraphs and you have the precise location! No other place on Earth has the same combination of latitude and longitude.

Time is also based on longitude, with 24 hours being equal to one revolution of Earth or 360° longitude. Some clocks divide 24-hour days into two 12-hour segments. Other clocks use 24 hours.

RELATIONSHIP TO CLIMATE

Longitude has little relationship to climate. Latitude has a big relationship to climate. Latitude is often divided into low, middle, and high for the sake of studying climate.

Low Latitudes

The low latitudes are near the equator. The climate has hot, wet weather and is said to be tropical. The *tropical climate* is the climate between latitude 23½° north and 23½° south. These are the farthest north and south latitudes that the Sun is ever directly overhead. The boundaries of the tropical climate region are called the tropic of Cancer in the Northern Hemisphere and the tropic of Capricorn in the Southern Hemisphere.

Middle Latitudes

The middle latitudes have a temperate climate. The *temperate climate* is between the tropic of Cancer and the Arctic Circle and the tropic of Capricorn and the Antarctic Circle. The climate here is generally neither hot nor cold for a long time. Much of the earth's natural resources, population, and agricultural production is in the temperate region. Most of the United States has a temperate climate.

High Latitudes

The high latitudes are near the poles and have a colder climate. The Arctic Circle is the location farthest north where the Sun stays above the horizon at least one day a year. The similar location in the southern hemisphere is the Antarctic Circle. The Arctic Circle and Antarctic Circle are approximately 66° latitude north and south.

A few plants grow at high latitudes. These are cool season plants that grow in the lower latitudes of this region. Crops grown include rhubarb, cabbage, and hay crops. Some high-value crops for the fresh market, such as tomatoes, are grown in greenhouses.

Areas near the North and South Poles are covered with ice caps that have remained in place for thousands of years. The areas are very cold and virtually uninhabited.

MEASURING WEATHER

Methods have been developed for measuring weather conditions. There are four commonly measured areas: temperature, moisture, wind, and air pressure.

TEMPERATURE

Weather temperature is measured in the atmosphere and known as *atmospheric temperature*. Other temperature measurements of the environment are also used. The temperature of natural water in streams and oceans may be measured. Crop producers often decide when to plant seed based on soil temperature. Seed must have enough warmth to germinate and grow!

Temperature is measured with a *thermometer.* Thermometers are made in different ways. The glass bulb thermometer is most common. Digital, bimetallic, and thermocouple thermometers are also used.

Several temperature scales are used. As reported earlier, Celsius (C) and Fahrenheit (F) are most common. Atmospheric temperature in the United States is reported using the Fahrenheit scale. People in other nations and scientists in the United States use Celsius.

The common temperature scales are based on the freezing and boiling points of water at sea level. Water freezes at 32°F and 0°C and boils at 212°F and 100°C. Conversion from

13-9. Two kinds of thermometers: glass bulb (left) and bimetallic.

Converting Fahrenheit (F) to Celsius (C)

Formula: $C = \frac{5}{9}(F - 32)$

Steps:
1. Determine the F temperature.
2. Subtract 32 from the F temperature.
3. Multiply the difference found in step 2 by 5.
4. Divide the amount found in step 3 by 9.
(The result is the equivalent temperature in degrees C.

Example: If the temperature is 100°F, what is the C temperature?

$$100 - 32 = 68$$
$$68 \times 5 = 340$$
$$340 \div 9 = 37.7°C$$

Converting Celsius (C) to Farenheit (F)

Formula: $F = \frac{9}{5}C + 32$

Steps:
1. Determine the C temperature.
2. Multiply the C temperature by 9.
3. Divide the amount found in step 2 by 5.
4. Add 32 to the amount found in step 3.
(The result is the equivalent temperature in degrees F.

Example: If the temperature is 40°C, what is the F temperature?

$$40 \times 9 = 360$$
$$360 \div 5 = 72$$
$$72 + 32 = 104°F$$

13-10. Formulas for converting temperatures from F to C and C to F.

one scale to another uses simple formulas. Some thermometers have both scales.

HUMIDITY

Humidity is the presence of water vapor in the air. It is the amount of water in a per unit mass of air. Air with high water vapor has high humidity. Dew forms when the air is saturated with water vapor.

Relative Humidity

Relative humidity is a comparison of the amount of moisture in the air with the ability of the air to hold moisture. High relative humidity means the

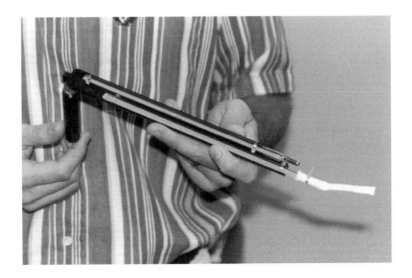

13-11. A sling psychrometer is used to measure relative humidity.

amount of water vapor the air can hold is approaching 100 percent. Low relative humidity means that the air can hold more water and that precipitation is not likely. Air temperature influences relative humidity. Cool air can hold less water than warm air.

Humidity is measured with several different devices. Hygrometers, psychrometers, and sling psychrometers are common. Humidity is more difficult to measure than temperature.

Dew Point

Dew point is the temperature of the air when dew begins to form. Dew is often seen on plants in the early morning. It forms when plants and other objects cool below the temperature of the air and moisture (humidity) collects on the surfaces. Dew is similar to the moisture that condenses on a soft drink can in warm weather. Dew freezes to form frost when the temperature approaches freezing.

PRECIPITATION

Precipitation forms in clouds when the temperature of the air cools. The tiny drops of water in the clouds combine. The drops fall when they become too heavy to stay afloat.

Rain is liquid drops of water that fall from the atmosphere. It often results from weather fronts and temperature changes. Rain changes to ice after

13-12. A simple rain gauge can be used to measure precipitation as well as irrigation water.

it falls if the surface and atmosphere are at or below the freezing point. Rain that freezes forms a glaze over surfaces and is known as freezing rain. Snow, sleet, and hail are frozen forms of precipitation.

Snow is crystals of ice known as snowflakes. Snowflakes are hexagonal in shape, with no two flakes alike. Snow forms in clouds at temperatures below freezing. If the weather is warm near the ground, the snow may melt and fall as rain.

Sleet is raindrops that freeze as they fall through the air. The surface temperature must be near or below freezing for the sleet to remain frozen as it reaches the ground. (Rain that freezes after it reaches the ground is frozen rain—not sleet.)

Hail is large lumps or balls of ice formed in cold clouds during storms in warm weather. Most hail is 1 inch (2.5 cm) or less in diameter, though it can be much larger. Hailstones form when raindrops freeze in clouds, but do not fall to the earth. Upward wind currents keep small hailstones aloft, where they grow larger as more moisture collects on them. Hail falls when it becomes too heavy for the upward wind to support. Large hail damages crops, wildlife, buildings, and other structures.

Precipitation is primarily measured as water using rain gauges. Snow may be measured by the depth of accumulation. The amount of precipitation is based on melted snow, sleet, and hail. A rain gauge is a tube that is open at one end. A graduated scale along the tube makes it easy to learn the amount of precipitation.

ATMOSPHERIC PRESSURE

Atmospheric pressure is measured with a barometer. Denser air has more pressure. Elevations, such as mountains, have less pressure than sea level. Low air pressure is the sign of warm air. High air pressure results from cool air.

At sea level, the average air pressure is 14.7 pounds per square inch (101.3 kilopascals). Air pressure goes down with elevation. There is less atmospheric pressure on a mountain than in the valley. Because of this, water boils at a lower temperature in higher elevations. This often means that food must be cooked longer and water must be heated longer to kill pathogens.

Air pressure is important in weather forecasting. Low air pressure may mean that a storm is approaching. High air pressure usually indicates fair weather. Barometers alert people to changes in air pressure.

13-13. Combination digital barometer and wind anemometer and vane. (The anemometer and vane are outside and connected to the digital control, which may be inside.) (Courtesy, Davis Instruments, Haywood, California)

WIND

Wind is caused by differences in air pressure. Wind moves from areas with high pressure to those with low pressure.

Wind is measured as to direction and speed. Direction is the direction the wind comes from and is measured with a wind vane. Speed is measured with an anemometer and reported as miles per hour in the United States. Local winds are caused by temperature differences in land and water areas and elevations in the land. Weather fronts may cause strong, dangerous wind.

WEATHER FRONTS

Weather fronts cause most of the changes in the weather. A *weather front* is a condition resulting from the meeting of a warm air mass and a cold air mass. The front is the boundary separating the air masses. Cold fronts are large masses of cold air moving near the earth that forces the warm air upward in the atmosphere. A warm front is a warm mass of air pushing a cold front back. Weather fronts become stationary when they stop moving or move very slowly.

Above the ground, the front slopes so the warm air moves above the colder air. Clashes between the two air masses may happen. As air masses bump together, some mixing of the air occurs; however, the masses tend to retain their identity.

The action of weather fronts is shaped by geographical features of the earth. Mountains and large bodies of water have the greatest influence. For example, warm air cools as it moves over mountains and, as it cools, precipitation is formed as rain or snow on the mountains.

Weather fronts in the United States appear to follow similar directions. Cold fronts move from a westerly or northwesterly direction. People in the east look at the weather west of them to see what they are likely to have the next day.

Clashes between weather fronts may cause storms.

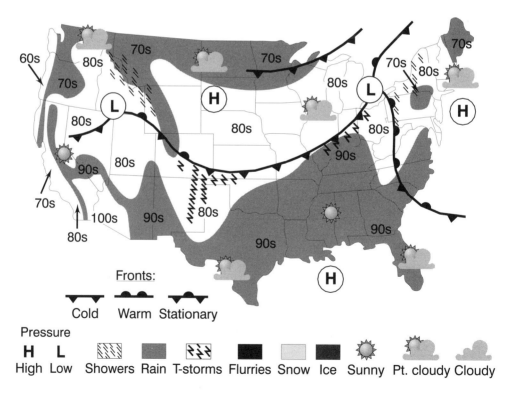

13-14. Weather front map.

STORMS

A *storm* is violent weather. Locally high winds, heavy rain, lightning, and other conditions may be a part of storms. The most common storms are thunderstorms, winter storms, hurricanes, and tornadoes.

Thunderstorms

Usually occurring in warmer weather, a **thunderstorm** is a combination of gusty wind, hail, lightning and thunder, and rain. The winds may gust up to speeds that can destroy buildings and damage trees. The lightning can strike structures and natural objects and electrocute organisms. Strong thunderstorms can spawn tornadoes. Heavy rains may cause flash flooding.

Winter Storms

A **winter storm** is a cold weather storm and typically involves snow, freezing rain, and sleet. Winter storms are typically at the higher latitudes.

Resource Connection

HOW FAST A CACTUS GROWS

The desert of southern Arizona is quite dry. Plants and other living things form a biome that accommodates the climate. Within the biome, plants have different conditions for growth. One of these plants with unique microclimate needs is the saguaro cactus.

The saguaro may grow 40 to 50 feet (12 to 17 m) tall. Many years are needed to reach this size. As tiny plants, saguaros need protection from the hottest weather and typically grow in the shade of other plants. Saguaros cannot survive more that a few hours of frost.

Annual growth of this saguaro is being tracked at the Lost Dutchman State Park near Phoenix. Why did it grow more some years than others? Growth rate is probably associated with moisture, temperature, and other conditions that made its environment more or less favorable.

13-15. A remote weather station powered by solar energy near Donner Pass, California.

Winter storms damage plants, animals, and structures. Travel can be treacherous. Large amounts of snow can fall rapidly, especially in higher elevations.

Hurricanes

A *hurricane* is a large, whirling storm that typically develops over water in the tropical region near the equator. Hurricanes usually weaken when they reach land. High wind and heavy rain may cause damage and flooding. Tornadoes may form near the edge of a hurricane.

Tornadoes

A *tornado* is a powerful, violent storm with wind that moves in a circular direction. Wind speeds may reach 200 miles per hour (320 km/hr). Tornadoes can destroy everything in their paths— trees, houses, and even lift pavement from a highway. Tornadoes form during thunderstorms and low air pressure. Most tornadoes are in the southern and midwestern parts of the United States. Tornadoes on water are known as water spouts.

CLOUDS

A *cloud* is a mass of tiny water droplets or ice crystals in the atmosphere. Clouds are classified by appearance and height, or distance from the ground. High clouds are made of ice crystals and are white. Low clouds are dark, have more water vapor than high clouds, and are likely to cause rain. Clouds in layers generally indicate that the atmosphere is stable.

Cloud Formation

Clouds form when water vapor changes to a liquid droplet or crystal form. The liquid forms because the air is saturated with water vapor.

Droplets form by condensing on tiny particles of dust, smoke, or salt. The process is similar to the way dew forms on plant leaves.

Clouds are made of tiny droplets of water. The droplets are much smaller than the diameter of a human hair. If these tiny droplets start falling, they would never make it to the ground before evaporating. The droplets have to join to produce raindrops. It takes about a million droplets to form a raindrop!

Fog

Clouds are sometimes close to the ground. This kind of cloud is known as fog. *Fog* is a cloud at or very near the ground. There is no difference in a fog and a cloud other than where they are located and how they are formed.

Fog usually forms when warmer air moves over cooler ground. This is often at night when the sky is clear and the humidity is high. Driving an automobile in fog can be very dangerous. Thick fog makes it hard to see the road and other vehicles.

RELATIONSHIPS TO THE ENVIRONMENT

Weather and climate have a big influence on our environment. It affects what we do and how we do it. It affects the organisms that live on Earth.

Weather and climate influence agriculture. Crop growth and failures result from weather conditions. Lightning strikes can kill livestock, plants, and humans. Extremely cold or hot weather can injure plants and animals.

Some organisms, including people, cannot adapt to certain weather extremes. Fortunately, people were smart enough to learn how to make clothes and build housing.

CONTINUAL CHANGE

Weather conditions are continually changing but tend to be consistent from one year to the next. Weather repeats itself in specific locations though never in exactly the same way. This creates the climate and environment that are associated with a location.

Changes promote the weathering process as well as natural life cycles and seasons. For example, southern Arizona is a warm, dry climate known for winter vacations and crop production. People plan vacations and crops years

13-16. Weathering is a continuous process that shapes mountains, forms soil, and makes our environment appealing.

ahead because weather repeats itself. The climate creates a reasonably consistent environment. Likewise, snow sports enthusiasts know that the skiing will be good in the winter on slopes in Vermont or Colorado.

POWERFUL FORCE

Weather is a powerful force in changing the environment and altering or producing natural resources. Cold, freezing weather causes changes just as does warm weather with rain.

All weather conditions affect the environment. Extremes can cause considerable damage to crops, livestock, and other property. Food shortages can develop if crops are destroyed by hurricanes, floods, lack of rain, or freezing. Extremes result in more energy being used to heat or cool our homes.

REVIEWING

MAIN IDEAS

The climate is the weather that is generally found in a geographic location. It includes temperature, precipitation, wind, atmospheric pressure, and altitude. The global climate is the general climate that is found in all regions of the planet Earth.

Weather and climate are natural resources. They often interact with other resources to form the environment we enjoy. Even tourism is associated with weather!

Weather and climate vary from one location to another. Latitude and longitude are used to locate precise geographic points on Earth. Latitude is distance north and south of the equator. It is represented by imaginary lines that run east and west. Longitude is distance east and west from the Greenwich meridian that runs north and south over Greenwich, England. Only latitudes have a relationship to the climate, with low latitudes having warmer climates and higher latitudes having cool or cold climates.

Weather is measured with various devices to convert observations to numbers. Thermometers are used to measure temperature. Humidity is measured with hygrometers and psychrometers. Precipitation is measured with a rain gauge or linear scale. Atmospheric pressure is measured with a barometer. Wind direction is measured with a vane and speed with an anemometer.

Weather fronts bring changes in atmospheric conditions. Storms and clouds are indications of weather fronts. Weather and climate are closely related to the environment and natural resources.

QUESTIONS

Answer the following questions using complete sentences and correct spelling.

1. How does the weather relate to the climate?

2. What are five major factors in weather?

3. What is global climate?

4. How does the climate influence biomes?

5. How is tourism related to a climate?

6. What are latitude and longitude? How are these indicated on a map or globe?

7. How is latitude related to a climate?

8. How is weather temperature measured?

9. What are the major kinds of precipitation?

10. What are weather fronts? How are storms and clouds related to fronts?

EVALUATING

Match the term with the correct definition. Write the letter by the term in the blank provided.

a. storm
b. thunderstorm
c. thermometer
d. dew point

e. tropical climate
f. climate
g. atmospheric pressure
h. biome

i. latitude
j. longitude

_____ 1. The climate between latitude 23½° north and 23½° south.

_____ 2. Distance east and west of the Greenwich meridian.

_____ 3. A community of living organisms influenced by climate.

_____ 4. The weather generally found in a geographic location.

_____ 5. The pressure exerted by the air on the surface of the earth.

_____ 6. An imaginary line parallel with the equator that goes east and west around Earth.

_____ 7. Violent weather.

_____ 8. A device that measures temperature.

_____ 9. Type of storm that may involve wind, hail, lightning and thunder, and rain.

_____ 10. Temperature at which dew forms on surfaces.

EXPLORING

1. Set up a weather station to collect data for a week about your local weather. Determine the instruments you need in your weather station. Select a place for accurate readings. Collect data two or three times each day. Use a log to record your observations. Prepare a report that presents your findings.

2. Read the weather forecast in a daily newspaper each day for a week (a month would be better). Prepare a narrative that describes reported weather information and general trends that you observe in weather conditions.

3. Use a map or globe to identify the exact location of your home or school using latitude and longitude. Use a global positioning system to assess your accuracy in reading the map. Prepare a report on your observations.

14

ENERGY

Your life depends on energy! The energy you use has traveled 93 million miles or more to reach you. It is not that far to the nearest gasoline station, so how could the energy have traveled so far?

The energy we use originated with the Sun. That is why it had to travel such a great distance to reach you. All life depends on energy from the Sun. Plants use sunlight in making food. Then the plants become food and other products that meet our needs. Wind, waterfalls, and fossil fuels all have energy that originated with the Sun.

People are getting smarter about using the Sun's energy. They are installing solar collectors and insulating buildings. They are also protecting themselves from the harmful rays of the Sun. The human body should definitely be protected from anything with as much energy as the Sun! Use hats, long sleeves, sun screen, and other products when outside in sunlight.

14-1. Assuring good fit and secure joints helps conserve energy in a building.

OBJECTIVES

This chapter provides background information on the meaning and importance of energy and fuels. It has the following objectives:

1. Explain the meaning and importance of energy

2. Identify sources of energy

3. Classify energy as fuel and nonfuel forms

4. Describe the conservation of energy use

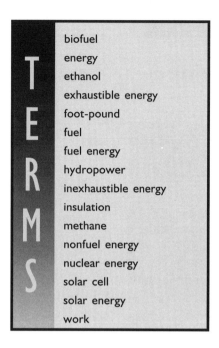

TERMS

biofuel
energy
ethanol
exhaustible energy
foot-pound
fuel
fuel energy
hydropower
inexhaustible energy
insulation
methane
nonfuel energy
nuclear energy
solar cell
solar energy
work

U.S. Department of Energy
http://198.124.130.244/

ENERGY AS A RESOURCE

Energy is the ability to do work. To scientists, **work** is moving objects vertical distances. Determining the amount of work done requires measuring the weight of the object that is moved and the distance it is moved.

Since distances are often measured in feet in the United States, energy is measured in foot-pounds. A *foot-pound* is the amount of work done in lifting one pound a distance of one foot. If a stone weighing 20 pounds is lifted 2 feet, 40 (20x2) foot-pounds of work would be done. The joule is the metric measurement of work. It is moving an object one meter against a force of one Newton. If converted, a joule equals approximately ¾ foot-pound.

ENERGY CHANGES FORMS

Energy has two forms: movement and potential movement. Energy that is involved in moving objects is kinetic energy. It fits the definition of energy as foot-pounds—the ability to move an object a vertical distance.

Potential energy is due to the place or position of something. It is not moving but could do so under the right conditions. A rock resting on a cliff has potential energy in that it could suddenly fall. Materials used as fuel have potential energy until it is released. At that time, it becomes kinetic energy.

Energy is constantly changing from potential energy to kinetic and back to potential. Every change on Earth represents the transformation of energy or, as it is also known, energy conversion.

14-2. The potential energy in water behind a dam is converted to kinetic energy as it is carried in the pipes down to the powerhouse containing turbines.

Using the example of an automobile, here is how the transformation of energy takes place: A car may use potential energy stored in fuel to go up a mountain. At the top of the mountain, the fuel tank contains less fuel. However, the automobile has the potential of coasting down the mountain without using fuel as it moves.

Energy may change to heat. In an internal combustion engine, burning fuel creates heat. Heat causes gases to expand forcing the piston to move inside the cylinder. When this happens, energy is converted to mechanical power.

CLASSES OF ENERGY

There are two classes of energy—inexhaustible and exhaustible. The distinctions between them are based on exhaustibility.

Inexhaustible Energy

Inexhaustible energy occurs repeatedly even as it is used. It is continuous and occurs whether or not it is harnessed and used. Examples include wind, flowing water, and sunlight (solar energy).

Solar energy is an inexhaustible energy source. The Sun repeats itself every 24 hours. Solar energy passes through the environment and, in some cases, is intercepted and used. Plants capture and use it in photosynthesis. Solar energy provides warmth and shapes the climate. Most solar energy goes unharnessed.

14-3. Energy put into a lawnmower as gasoline is exhaustible.

Career Profile

HYDROPOWER PLANT ENGINEER

A hydropower plant engineer oversees the operation of an electrical generating plant powered by water. The work involves monitoring computer reports, gauges, and other information on the plant. Rates of electricity generation are monitored. Turbine and other problems in the plant are identified. Assuring safety of the plant, the people who work in it, and in the surrounding area are important in the work.

Hydropower plant engineers may have college degrees in areas of engineering, such as electrical and mechanical engineering. Years of practical on-the-job experience as an assistant is very important. Workshops and training to learn the specific workings of system are needed.

Jobs for hydropower plant engineers are found wherever plants are located. Most of the jobs are with power generating plants at reservoirs on rivers. This photo shows an engineer operating a hydropower facility with four plants from a central location on the Tugaloo River on the state line between South Carolina and Georgia.

Inexhaustible energy causes little or no pollution, except for wood. It is safe to use in moderation. Large collectors or users may disrupt the environment, such as hydropower dams and reservoirs.

Exhaustible Energy

Exhaustible energy is energy that is used up by human activity. It is from sources that are unused unless they are released. This energy naturally occurs in the environment. It is stored as potential energy and is released only when we use or waste it. Exhaustible energy is limited. There is only so much on Earth. Once used, it is gone!

Some people are concerned about running out of energy. All of us should share the concern about exhaustible energy. Supplies of coal, oil, and natural gas are limited. When used, all forms of exhaustible energy release pollution. Efforts are being made to reduce pollution by using energy wisely and installing devices that clean emissions.

Wastes from nuclear energy are most hazardous. Careful and detailed disposal of these wastes is essential. Some wastes can remain dangerous for many years.

SOURCES OF ENERGY

Sources of energy are in two groups based on combustion: fuel and nonfuel. People are giving more attention to new kinds and uses of energy from nonfuel sources.

FUEL ENERGY

A *fuel* is a substance that is burned to make a fire. The fire produces heat. The heat is converted to power with a mechanical device, such as an internal combustion engine. The form of the fuel is changed. Most fuels give off smoke—a combination of visible gases, vapor, and particulate.

Fuel energy is from fuels that are consumed while releasing energy. They are nonrenewable. Fuels produce heat by either combustion or nuclear activity. The major fuels are the fossil fuels and nuclear power.

Fossil Fuel

A fossil fuel is a naturally occurring fuel formed by the decomposition of organic matter. Thousands of years were needed for the fuel to form in the

14-4. Coal is being loaded on a ship for export near Port Angeles, Washington.

14-5. An oil producing area with pumps and storage tanks.

earth. The original source of the energy in fossil fuel is the Sun. Examples include coal, natural gas, oil, peat, and oil shale.

Fossil fuels are decomposed plant and animal remains. Most people think they are only from plant remains. The plants took energy from the Sun and used it in the photosynthesis process. Animals come into the picture by consuming the plants and, therefore, also had energy from the Sun.

Different ways are used to get the fuel. Coal is a solid material mined from the earth. Oil, or petroleum, is a thick liquid taken from the earth with wells. Some wells must be pumped; in other wells, the oil flows out under pressure. Natural gas is a gaseous fuel from wells drilled into the earth or as a by-product of oil refining. Large coal mines and oil and gas fields may be used to extract fuel needed for energy. Most all fossil fuels need some preparation for use. Coal is broken into pieces that can be easily used. Oil is refined into gasoline, diesel fuel, and lubricants.

Fossil fuels are sometimes known as commercial energy. The fuels are produced to be sold for a profit. Oil accounts for about 40 percent of the energy used on the earth. Coal accounts for 28 percent and natural gas 21 percent of all commercial energy.

Nuclear Energy

Nuclear energy is produced by fission (splitting or breaking up) of the atomic nuclei of uranium or a similar heavy element. Only three fission fuels

14-6. A nuclear power plant exterior and the process of loading fuel in a reactor.

are used: uranium-235, uranium-233, and plutonium-239. Nuclear electric power plants use nuclear energy.

Fission produces heat energy. The heat is used to power electric generators, nuclear submarines, and other machinery. Fission produces more energy than burning fossil fuels.

Nuclear reactors are specially-designed plants that release nuclear energy. For example, in an electric power plant, the fission releases tremendous heat that causes turbines to rotate and produce electricity. The electricity made by a nuclear power plant is no different from that of a coal- or oil-fired plant.

Nuclear energy provides about 7 percent of the commercial energy used.

Biofuels

With occasional shortages of fossil fuels, people have looked for other fuels. One group of fuels getting more attention is biofuel. A *biofuel* is any plant or animal material that burns to release heat or produces methane or other gases during decomposition. Wood is the most common biofuel. Other biofuels include any type of vegetation or animal life cell.

Wood was once the most important fuel used. It was burned for heating, cooking, and other purposes. Today, wood has declined in use. Wood pro-

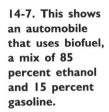

14-7. This shows an automobile that uses biofuel, a mix of 85 percent ethanol and 15 percent gasoline.

duces smoke and ash that pollute the air. In some regions, wood supplies have been exhausted because of overuse.

Biofuels are sometimes known as alternative fuels. These include methane and ethanol. *Methane* is a colorless, odorless, and combustible gas. It is naturally found near marshes and coal mines. It is also produced by animal digestive processes. *Ethanol* is a colorless, liquid kind of alcohol that can be made from corn and other grain crops. In some cases, ethanol is mixed with gasoline to reduce the amount of petroleum fuel used. Mixing the two makes the product more acceptable and assures the fuel can be used by an engine.

Some biofuel can be taken from landfills where garbage has been dumped. The decomposition of garbage releases methane. Crop residues, forestry product wastes, and other sources of wood are used in making biofuels. Using agricultural wastes to produce methane has received more interest in recent years.

Fuels made from grain products are largely inexhaustible. More can be made from the harvested crops. Grain producers are promoting the use of ethanol. It is a new market for grain.

NONFUEL ENERGY

A *nonfuel energy* is a source of energy that is not consumed when it is used. Several sources are free and readily available on the earth. Finding efficient and economical ways of capturing nonfuel energy is a challenge. Most of the nonfuel energy sources are inexhaustible fuels, such as solar, wind, and water power. Solar energy is the most important because it makes wind and water power possible.

Solar Energy

Solar energy is energy from the Sun. It arrives on Earth as solar radiation. This radiation has useful purposes, but it can also damage plants and people.

Some plants and animals are damaged by solar radiation. Plants may get sun scald, especially those not adapted to full sunlight. Animals may need shade so they can escape from the rays of the Sun. Those with light or white hair and skin are more likely to be injured than those with darker colors. White hair and skin around the eyes results in some animals being more likely to develop eye cancer. Animals with dark pigments are less likely to have cancer.

14-8. A small solar system used to generate electricity in Illinois.

A *solar cell* is a collector that converts energy from the Sun into electrical energy. Small solar cells are used as power for equipment with low electrical power needs. Good potential exists for producing electricity with large solar cells. More solar energy will be used as the fossil fuels are depleted. Solar-powered vehicles may be used in the future.

Solar radiation can be used to heat water. Flat collectors are used to absorb heat from solar energy. The water can be used to heat buildings much as a coal-fired boiler. Solar systems work best on clear days with bright sunlight. Shade reduces the ability of collectors to absorb radiation.

Wind Power

As the large-scale movement of air, wind can be harnessed for its power. Turbines or wind mills are used to gather power from the air. The power can be used to generate electricity, pump water, or for other purposes.

Wind is free of cost except for the equipment to harness it. Wind power produces no pollution. A drawback is that wind is unpredictable. Its direction and velocity may change. In some places, prevailing winds make it a better source of power.

14-9. A large installation of wind turbines used to generate electricity. (Courtesy, Vernie Thomas, Danville, IL)

Water Power

Water can be harnessed for power. The power produced by water is known as **hydropower**. Hydropower captures the energy of falling water. The water is used to turn turbines or other equipment.

In the past, streams have been dammed to provide hydropower. The dams create large reservoirs of water. The water flows downward over turbines causing them to rotate. The rotation turns a shaft connected to an electric generator.

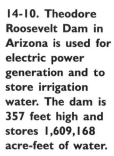

14-10. Theodore Roosevelt Dam in Arizona is used for electric power generation and to store irrigation water. The dam is 357 feet high and stores 1,609,168 acre-feet of water.

14-11. A hydroelectric turbine as used in a power plant.

Water wheels may be used to harness water power. The flow of water turns a wheel that is attached to a shaft. Belts and pulleys are used to move the power to equipment that does work. Waterwheels are now kept more for novelty than practical use.

Water is an inexpensive source of power. The major cost is for constructing reservoirs and turbines. Using water also does not create environmental pollution. Creating reservoirs, however, does create major environmental issues. No dams are now being built on streams to capture water for power.

Other Nonfuel Power

Other sources of nonfuel power may be useful. These depend on features of the local area.

Geothermal power is from naturally-heated water deep within the earth. The water is heated by contact with hot rocks in the earth. Geothermal water and steam are used to produce electricity, warm buildings, and, when properly cooled and conditioned, grow fish that require warm water (80° F or so).

Natural water movements in oceans and waves can be used for energy. These movements are as tides and waves. The energy is captured at high tide and released when the tide is low. The flowing water rotates turbines. A disadvantage is that it is available only following high tides and waves.

ENERGY CONSERVATION

14-12. Reviewing the plans for a building to determine energy efficiency design features.

Energy should be used wisely, especially exhaustible energy. Everyone has a role in conserving energy. How we go about our daily lives can help conserve energy. Four areas to consider are buildings, transportation, work, and recreation.

BUILDINGS

Many of the buildings we use have heating and air conditioning. These are known as climate control systems. A climate control system is designed to keep the temperature at the desired level year round. The system provides heat in the winter and cooling in the summer. Some buildings may have only heating systems. Natural gas, heating oil, coal, or electricity are often used by climate control systems. Some use is made of wood and solar heat.

A building should be constructed to use energy efficiently. This requires good insulation, tight-fitting doors, storm doors and windows, and other

14-13. "House wrap" is being installed on a home under construction to assure good insulation.

construction features. Exterior walls need to be made of materials that seal tightly and thick enough for insulation to be used.

Here are a few things people can do:

■ Use Insulation—***Insulation*** is material that restricts the exchange of heat. It is a barrier to air movement. Use windows and doors, wood, and other materials that have good insulation ratings. Using insulation materials in walls and attic areas helps reduce energy use. Select all materials on the basis of energy efficiency.

■ Set Thermostat Properly—Energy is saved by setting the thermostat at the right temperature. People can be comfortable without having a building too warm or too cold. In the winter, set the heating thermostat at 66° F (18.8° C). In the summer, set the thermostat for the air-cooling system at 72 to 76° F (22.2 to 23.9° C). Remember to lower the setting in the winter or raise it in the summer when people are gone.

■ Close Doors and Windows—An open door or window allows heated or cooled air to escape. Doors and windows should fit tightly. Storm doors and windows may be needed.

■ Use Lights and Equipment as Needed—Turn off lights, equipment, appliances, and other devices when they are not being used. These use energy and create the need for additional cooling in the summer.

■ Keep Systems in Good Order—Heating and air-conditioning systems should be kept in good condition. Inefficient older systems may need to be replaced. Ducts and insulation should fit tightly and be kept in good condition.

Resource Connection

EQUIPMENT EFFICIENCY

Use equipment to do the job it was intended to do. Using equipment otherwise results in increased wear and inefficient work. Keeping tractors and implements in good condition makes them more efficient.

Here are a few suggestions:

- Read and follow the owner's/operator's manual.
- Operate the equipment properly.
- Adjust the equipment to meet needs.
- Lubricate and provide service as needed.
- Follow all safety rules.

This shows an efficient operation. Hay is being cut and conditioned properly. The swath is the proper width. All hay is cut and placed in uniform windrows. The tractor and implement are clean and in good condition. (Courtesy, New Holland North America, Inc.)

TRANSPORTATION

Transportation is an important part of living and working. Much energy is used in transportation. Most means of transportation, such as airplanes and automobiles, are powered with engines that use fossil fuels, such as gasoline, propane, diesel fuel, and jet fuel.

Energy use in transportation can be conserved. Here are a few suggestions:

- Use Public Transportation—Many places have buses, subways, ferries, and commuter trains. Energy is saved when people ride these rather than drive their own vehicle. One loaded bus uses far less fuel than would the number of cars required to transport the people.

- Walk or Ride a Bicycle—For short distances, people can walk or ride a bicycle rather than use a vehicle that uses fuel. The exercise is good because it im-

14-14. Using the right oil in an engine improves performance. (This shows a demonstration of the specific gravity of 10W30 oil.)

proves our health. Starting an engine that is cold for a short trip increases engine wear.

■ Share Rides—Sharing rides is also known as car-pooling. Most sport utility vehicles and automobiles will seat at least four people. It is fun to talk with friends while traveling together. Many large cities promote car pooling to reduce fuel use, decrease air pollution, and keep down the number of vehicles on the streets. Some highways have HOV lanes. These are "high occupancy vehicle" lanes that give preference to vehicles with more than one person. Note: In sharing rides, be safe. Never give a ride to a stranger. Only accept a ride with someone you know is a safe driver.

■ Maintain the Engine—An engine that is properly maintained uses fuel more efficiently. A worn engine may burn lubricating oil and pollute the air. An engine that burns oil also needs to have more oil added. The engine oil and transmission fluid should be changed as recommended by the manufacturer. Used oil should be disposed of properly and never be run into streams or on land.

■ Be a Good Driver—How a person drives a vehicle is related to fuel use. Engines are designed to be more efficient at reasonable speeds. Driving fast uses more fuel than driving at a reasonable speed to reach the same destination. Avoid quick takeoffs at traffic lights and begin slowing down well before a stop. (These will also make you a safer driver!)

■ Get the Right Vehicle—Some vehicles use more fuel than others. Get a vehicle that will do what you want and gets good fuel economy—more miles to the gallon! Smaller vehicles typically have better fuel economy. Sport utility

14-15. A conveniently located fuel center on a research farm helps save energy.

vehicles and pickup trucks are popular. These often use more fuel than auto-mobiles.

■ Do "Fuel-Free" Things—Do things that do not use fuel. Rather than "cruis-ing," play games, read a book, or use a computer to explore the Internet. It is also a good idea to study your lessons for school! Cruising is dangerous, uses fuel, and adds wear to the vehicle.

WORK

The places where people work often use much energy. With planning, these places can be more efficient. Ways of conserving fuel with buildings and transportation also apply in the work place.

Several suggestions are:

■ Use Machinery Only When Needed—Running motors and engines when not needed wastes fuel and wears out the engine. It also adds to air pollution and wears out the motors and engines. These add up to more costs to the owner.

■ Load Properly—Organize freight shipments so one vehicle can make several stops rather than using different vehicles. Use the right vehicle for the job. Use a small truck for a small job and a big truck for a big job. Fuel is used more efficiently if vehicles are loaded properly. Proper loading makes a vehi-cle safer to drive.

■ Select the Right Equipment—Select equipment that is suited to a job. Equip-ment that is too large or inappropriate wastes energy. A good example can be found on a farm. Using a big tractor to do the job of a small one is wasteful. Big tractors use more fuel and cost more to buy and repair.

■ Use Machinery Properly—Adjust machinery properly. Operate it as it was intended to be used. Avoid horseplay and taking joy rides. A simple example is a riding lawnmower. Cut a swath of turf the full length of the blade. Mowing with only half the blade wastes fuel, adds wear to the mower, and increases the time to do the job. Follow all safety rules.

■ Do the Job Right—Pay attention to the work. Do it right the first time. Energy is wasted when work has to be repeated or repaired. Doing a job right also saves labor and money.

RECREATION

Energy is used with some recreational activities. Here are a few suggestions on how to conserve energy with recreation:

■ Choose Carefully—Choose recreational activities that do not require energy. If travel is involved, go in groups or use public transportation. Select activities that use little fuel, such as hiking or rowing instead of car racing and high-speed boating. In some cases, you can stay at home and listen to an event on the radio or watch it on television.

■ Be Efficient—Operate the engine or motor only as it is needed. Be sure to use the equipment properly. Keep it in good operating condition. For example, a snowmobile or four-wheeler that is in good condition saves fuel.

■ Stay Near Home—Recreation that requires traveling long distances takes more fuel. Do things near home. It is also safer than traveling long distances in heavy traffic. An example is birding in a park or vacant area near your home rather than driving a long distance.

REVIEWING

MAIN IDEAS

Energy is the ability to do work. Work is energy measured in foot-pounds (joules in the metric system). A knowledge of physics helps in understanding energy and work. Energy is in one of two forms: potential or kinetic. The forms may change back and forth.

Energy sources are of two classes: exhaustible and inexhaustible. Exhaustible energy is gone once it is used. Petroleum is an example. Inexhaustible energy, such as energy from the sun, occurs repeatedly.

Energy is from fuel and nonfuel sources. Fuel sources include fossil fuel, nuclear power, and biofuels. Nonfuel sources include solar energy, wind, and water.

Steps can be taken to conserve energy. Energy can be conserved in buildings, transportation, work, and recreation. Going to school actually includes all of these! You can help your school to be a more efficient user of energy.

QUESTIONS

Answer the following questions using complete sentences and correct spelling.

1. What is energy?
2. What is work?
3. How is work measured?
4. How much work is done if a box weighing 17 pounds is lifted 2 feet?
5. Distinguish between kinetic and potential energy?
6. What are the two classes of energy based on exhaustibility? Explain each class.
7. What are the major sources of fuel energy? Nonfuel energy?
8. What biofuels are used? Why are producers of grain crops promoting biofuels?
9. What steps can be taken to conserve energy in buildings?
10. How is energy use related to the driving habits of an automobile operator?

EVALUATING

Match the term with the correct definition. Write the letter by the term in the blank provided.

a. foot-pound
b. work
c. fuel
d. biofuel

e. nuclear energy
f. ethanol
g. solar energy
h. hydropower

i. insulation
j. exhaustible energy

_____ 1. A substance used for make a fire.

_____ 2. A plant or animal that produces heat or fuel gases during decomposition.

_____ 3. Energy produced by fission.

_____ 4. Energy produced by water power.

_____ 5. A measure of work.

_____ 6. Moving objects vertical distances.

_____ 7. Energy from the Sun.

_____ 8. Material used to prevent the exchange of heat.

_____ 9. Energy that is used up and in a limited supply.

_____ 10. Alcohol fuel produced from grains and other vegetative materials.

EXPLORING

1. Prepare a report on fuel efficiency of motor vehicles. Visit an automobile dealer and note the fuel ratings posted on the windows of new vehicles. Compare the highway and city ratings of a full-size car, intermediate, compact, sport utility vehicle, and a small pickup truck. Also, compare engine size with fuel use, such as four-cylinder, six-cylinder, and eight-cylinder engines. Prepare a report on your findings.

2. Make a survey of your home to identify strengths and weakness of the structure from the standpoint of energy use. List the items you find. Propose action steps to overcome problems where energy is lost.

3. Investigate the use of electricity at your school. Identify steps that can be taken to reduce energy use. Prepare a report on your observations.

15

MINERALS

Minerals have been useful for a long time. Some minerals have been valued for their beauty. Other minerals have been valued for the things that could be made from them. Most of the things we use each day are made of minerals!

We could not live the way we do without minerals. They are used to make tools, containers, wheels, engines, and many other things we use each day. A problem appears to be developing with some minerals: The supply is running out!

How do we use minerals to assure a supply in the future? We begin by learning what minerals are and how they are produced. We can recycle and find better methods of mining. We can be smart consumers and use only what we need.

15-1. A wheel is being used to make a bowl out of clay. (Pottery has been used for thousands of years. Most pottery is made from the mineral known as kaolinite [$Al_4Si_4O_{10}(OH)_8$] formed by decomposed feldspar.)

OBJECTIVES

This chapter provides background on the meaning and importance of minerals. It has the following objectives:

1. Explain the meaning of minerals

2. Identify important minerals

3. Describe how minerals are located and extracted

4. Describe the role of conservation with minerals

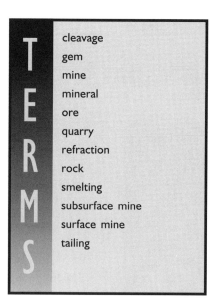

T
E
R
M
S

cleavage
gem
mine
mineral
ore
quarry
refraction
rock
smelting
subsurface mine
surface mine
tailing

Minerals Management Service of the
U.S. Department of the Interior
http://www.mms.gov/

THE MINERAL TEST

The crust of Earth contains many important minerals. A ***mineral*** is an element or a compound that naturally occurs on Earth's surface. Minerals may be metals or nonmetals. Each mineral has specific characteristics that distinguish it from other minerals.

How do we know if something is a mineral? Here are three characteristics of minerals:

1. Minerals are inorganic materials that naturally occur in the earth's crust. (This means that they do not contain carbon.)

2. Minerals are solid materials with a definite chemical composition.

3. Minerals are materials with atoms arranged in specific patterns.

Use these three criteria as the test to see if something is a mineral.

Here is an example: Azurite is a mineral that is mined for the copper ore it contains. Azurite naturally occurs in the earth's crust, it has a definite chemical composition, and has atoms arranged in specific patterns. All three criteria are met; therefore, azurite is a mineral.

Some people confuse minerals and fossil fuels. Fossil fuels, such as coal and petroleum, contain carbon and do not meet the three criteria listed above.

15-2. Three minerals from which copper is obtained are (from the left) azurite, chalcopyrite, and malachite.

IMPORTANT MINERALS

Most minerals are not found in a pure form. Many are in rocks. Valuable minerals are usually found mixed with less valuable materials. Methods are used to separate and refine the materials of high value.

ROCK

Rock is the hard, solid, and natural part of the earth's crust. Rock is often covered with a layer of soil. In some places, rock extends above the surface of the soil. Large mountains may be almost exclusively solid rock.

Areas with rock are usually large and rise above the landscape. Some rock is common and contains only one mineral. An example is limestone. Limestone is made of calcium carbonate ($CaCO_3$). Other rocks contain two or more minerals.

15-3. Many tons of rock are broken and moved to obtain ore in this mine.

Ore

Some rock is ore. *Ore* is rock that contains desired minerals. Ore is separated from the rock by mining and processing. High-grade ore contains relatively large amounts of the mineral. Low-grade ore contains lesser amounts and is usually more costly to process. The valued mineral is removed from the ore and manufactured into different products.

Granite rock is a common example. Granite is made of feldspar, quartz, and biotite. Each of these contains minerals. Feldspar and biotite contain silicon. Feldspar contains calcium, potassium, or sodium. Iron and magnesium are found in biotite. Iron is obtained by refining the biotite to separate the iron from the other materials.

Deposits

The location and concentration of minerals vary. Some places have few minerals. Other places have a great amount. Minerals with copper have been mined in several areas of the United States. Utah, New Mexico, and Arizona are now the leading producers of copper ore. The leading states in iron ore production are Minnesota and Michigan. Aluminum ore is found in a number of areas of the United States. However, no aluminum is found in Canada. The ore containing chromium is often found in conjunction with iron ore. The leading states for gold mining are Nevada, California, Utah, South Dakota, Montana, and Washington.

The most abundant metals are aluminum, iron, and magnesium. They are of lower value. Gold and platinum are very scarce and of higher value. Copper is important in many ways and is becoming increasingly scarce. Mineral value is related to the amount available and the usefulness of the mineral.

GEMS

A *gem* is a mineral valued for its beauty and rarity. Gems are natural materials found in the crust of Earth. They are made into gemstones that are used in rings and other jewelry. Common gems include diamonds, opals, rubies, and emeralds. Gems are also known as precious or semiprecious stones.

15-4. Searching for gems and minerals in rock is an interesting tourist activity in some areas.

Most gems are rough and irregular when mined. They are polished and cut to add appeal and value as well as bring out the beauty in the gem.

The major characteristics of gems are:

1. Gems have crystal shapes. The shapes vary with the type of gem.

2. Gems have colors that give them beauty, value, and appeal. Colors of gems may vary. In some cases, color is not a reliable method of distinguishing between gems.

3. Gems refract light. *Refraction* is bending light rays as they pass through a gem or other material. Gems also disperse light. Dispersion is how a gem separates light into rays of different colors. That is why diamonds reflect bright flashes of light.

4. Gems split in directions often forming flat surfaces. This smooth surface is known as *cleavage*. An uneven surface is a fracture, which is different from cleavage.

5. Gems are hard. Hardness is measured using the Mohs scale, which has a numbering system of 1 to 10—with 1 being soft and 10 being hard. Gems with a Mohs scale rating above 7 are considered hard.

6. Gems of the same kind have the same specific gravity. This relates to the amount of water a gem will displace.

15-5. Hundreds of amethyst gems are found inside this large geode. (A geode is a hollow stone lined with crystals that remained when water containing silica evaporated.)

COMMON MINERALS

Some minerals are common. Others are rare. More than 2,000 minerals have been identified. Only a few are valuable and widely used. Some minerals are of low value but are used in many ways.

Examples of minerals and the metals made from them are: bauxite—aluminum; chromite—chromium; azurite—copper; malachite—copper; chalcopyrite—copper, silver, and gold; magnetite—iron; galena—lead; molyb—molybdenum; carnalite—potassium; agentite—silver, and wolframite—tungsten.

Sand and gravel are used in making concrete, mortar mix, and other materials. These are important in roads, building construction, and sidewalks. Note that sand and gravel are not minerals. They are terms that refer to sizes of mineral pieces, which are sometimes known as aggregate. Sand may be of quartz, feldspar, calcite, or lava.

Minerals vary in the amount of refining needed to use them. Minerals mined as sand and gravel need little refining before use. Other minerals require considerable refining. Iron is smelted and removed from the ore to manufacture products. It is mixed at a high temperature with other metals, such as chromium in making stainless steel. Stainless steel is about 12 percent chromium. Stainless steel is a very useful, nonrusting steel product.

USING MINERALS

Minerals often require considerable processing to get the desired metals from them. This involves locating a supply of mineral, mining, and processing the mineral to get the desired products.

LOCATING MINERALS

Most people are familiar with stories about prospectors in the 1800s. They were bold people who moved into the western states and Alaska searching for gold and copper. In many cases, they endured big hardships and found little in the way of valuable minerals. Some prospectors found minerals and gained wealth from their mining.

Minerals are in many places. Sometimes, they are below the surface of Earth's crust. They may be mixed with other materials that have little value. Careful study is needed to locate mineral sources.

15-6. The Bingham Canyon Copper Mine in Utah is the world's largest human-made excavation.

Geologists study the surface of the earth and prepare maps showing mineral deposits. On-site inspections are made to see if rock containing minerals are present. Samples may be taken and additional exploration made to locate minerals in new locations. Aerial photography, remote sensing, and global positioning are used. Drilling may be used to collect samples below the surface.

Some minerals are at the bottom of the ocean and others are in seawater. Those on the ocean bottom are difficult to remove and are in low concentrations. Much seawater is needed to yield many minerals. Examples of minerals that can be extracted from seawater include table salt (NaCl), bromine, and magnesium.

MINING

Once a mineral has been located, it must be extracted or mined. A *mine* is an excavation for removing minerals from the earth. Methods of mining vary with the location of the deposit and the nature of the mineral.

Surface Mining

A *surface mine* is an excavation to get minerals that are on or near the earth's surface. It is the most common method of mining and is the least expensive method. Examples of minerals removed by surface mining include ores for copper and iron, granite, and limestone. Sand and gravel are also mined from the surface.

15-7. Large trucks haul ore out of the Bingham Canyon Copper Mine.

Two methods of surface mining are used: open-pit and strip mining. Open-pit surface mining is digging a large hole in the earth to get the minerals. The large pit is a *quarry*. Granite, iron and copper ore, and sand are often mined with open pits.

Strip mining is digging a long trench to get the minerals. A series of strips is dug. The strips are parallel to each other. The soil and rock that are not extracted are put into the previous strip. Rows of dug-out materials, known as spoil banks, are created on the surface.

Subsurface Mining

A *subsurface mine* is deep inside the earth to remove minerals. The surface of the earth may be disturbed very little. A mass of tunnels may be used to go into the deposits of minerals. This type of mining is more expensive and complex than surface mining. The people who work in the mine are exposed to additional hazards. Shafts may be dug straight down to the mineral ore or they may slope downward. Special equipment is needed to bring minerals out of subsurface mines.

PROCESSING

Ore must often be separated from material that does not contain the desired metal. The processing needed varies with the mineral and its use. Common processing procedures include:

■ Grinding and crushing—Grinding and crushing are used to get materials into the desired sizes. Grading may be used to separate the materials based on size.

■ Sorting—Various ways may be used to separate valuable metals from the ore. Water may be used to "float" metal materials from the ore. One function of smelting is to separate metal from ore.

15-8. Ore crushed into small pieces is separated into mineral and rock in a concentrator plant. (These large "tumblers" sift minerals from the rock pieces.)

■ Smelting—*Smelting* is heating ore so the metal separates from the undesirable material. The process may also be used to cast the metal into the desired products. Large furnaces are used in smelting. Most smelting produces several products that can be used. Iron smelting usually produces silicon and phosphorus. Copper smelting may produce sulfur and other materials. Both iron and copper smelting produce slag. Since iron melts at 2,795° F or 1,535° C, iron ore may be heated to 3,000° F (1,600° C). The iron is molten or liquid-like. The melting points of other metals vary. In liquid form, the metal separates from the gases and solid materials. The metals with the lowest melting points become liquid earlier and can be removed.

■ Purification—Various methods are used to purify the metal from the ore. Smelting often involves some purification.

Some minerals require little processing, such as limestone, sand, gravel, and kaolin. Limestone may be crushed or ground into small particle sizes. No smelting or purification is needed. Sand and gravel may require no processing; however, they are sometimes washed and graded to uniform size.

Washing removes clay, particles of decaying plant and animal remains, and other materials in the sand and gravel. Kaolin and other clays may be extracted and used with little purification.

Tailing is the solid waste material that remains from ore. Large amounts may result from processing depending on the yield by the ore. For example, copper ore produces only about 1 percent copper. This means that a ton of copper ore will result in nearly a ton of tailings.

ENVIRONMENTAL IMPACT OF MINERAL USE

Locating minerals, mining, and processing minerals affects the environment. There is no way to get and use minerals without some intrusion into the environment. Using good practices helps keep damage to the environment small.

MINING DAMAGE

Mining can disrupt the earth's natural landscape. Excavation makes the surface unsightly. The top soil may be removed and large areas excavated to expose minerals. These areas may collect water and create polluted runoff. Large piles of tailing can be left. Excavated land can erode and damage water quality. Mined areas may have substances that react with water to form acid.

15-9. This abandoned mine has left the earth's surface severely degraded.

Resource Connection

THE GOLD STANDARD

Money developed around gold and silver. The first coins were made in 600 B.C. in Turkey. The coins were useful currency because they were uniform in size and were made of silver and gold. In 1652, Massachusetts was the first colony to make coins using silver. The United States used a bimetallic standard: 16 ounces of silver was equal to one ounce of gold.

In 1900, Congress adopted the gold standard for money. A unit of money was worth a specific amount in gold. Paper money and coins of other metals were compared to gold. Paper money could be exchanged for gold until 1933. That year the minting of gold coins as currency ended. Gold coins are now for collectors. In 1970, any relationship between gold and dollars ended.

Just think what it would be like to use gold coins to buy something, such as an automobile. A new car would require about 60 ounces of gold!

Today, the value of money has little relation to gold and silver. In this photo, $20 and $5 gold pieces are compared to a dime. Do a little calculation: A $20 gold piece weighs 1.2 ounces. Based on the price of gold in today's paper, how much is the gold worth?

Water that seeps or runs out of a mine may contain acid. For example, iron ore often has sulfur mixed with it. Runoff from the mine will have a high acid content. Streams and lakes may be damaged by the acid runoff. With other minerals, toxic materials enter the runoff. A good example is lead. The runoff from a lead mine will contain some lead.

The land areas damaged by mining can be filled and graded to a natural contour. Grasses and trees may be planted on the land. Often, little top soil is available for the plants. Some mine sites may contain toxic substances that kill common vegetation. Special kinds of plants may be needed to grow in these places.

Mine sites can be restored, but time is required. Good planning can help prevent and reduce damage.

WASTE DISPOSAL

Tremendous amounts of solid waste materials may result from processing minerals. Often, 80 percent or more of the ore may be waste after processing. The amount of tailing produced is greater with low-grade ore. Large piles of tailings may be seen at smelting plants. The tailings are sometimes used as fill for low land areas.

Some solid waste products from smelting are put to good use. Slag is used as a source of phosphorus and calcium in fertilizer. Slag is also used in road paving and making lighter-weight concrete.

15-10. This large pile of tailing has been formed over many years of mining.

EMISSIONS CONTROL

Smoke, steam, particulate, and other materials may be released by mining. Some of these cause serious pollution problems.

Burning coal to heat minerals in smelting releases substances into the air. The minerals themselves also give off gases in smelting. Sulfur, nitrogen, and carbon are commonly released causing air pollution. These materials also find their way into the water and soil. Acid rain, unproductive soil, and water without living organisms may result.

The Clean Air Act and Clean Water Act regulate air and water pollution. Mining and processing are covered in these Acts from the standpoint of what can be released into the air and water.

USE AND SUPPLY

The supplies of some minerals are being depleted. The rate of use and natural supply of the mineral is important in sustainability.

Scientists have estimated the number of years the known supply of some minerals will last. Less than a 50-year supply of copper, lead, mercury, and zinc remain. The supply of iron ore will last up to 200 years. No depletion is likely of magnesium and sodium chloride. How long they last depends on efforts to conserve their use. In some cases, alternatives can be developed. An example is using plastics to replace metals. Since petroleum is used in manufacturing plastics, we must also be careful in the use of plastics.

Using minerals so supplies are available for a long time is important. This does not mean that the mineral is not used at all. It means that the mineral is used wisely. Here are some ways to make mineral supplies last longer:

■ Mineral Alternatives—Substitute materials can sometimes be used in place of scarce minerals. Plastic can be used to substitute for many metals. Glass,

Career Profile

CONCENTRATION PLANT ENGINEER

A concentration plant engineer oversees the operation of mining facilities that extract ore materials from raw materials. The work varies with the size of the plant and extent of technology used. This engineer uses elaborate computer systems to operate large machines that separate copper from ore (see Figure 15-8).

Concentration plant engineers need a college degree in mining engineering or related area. Some have masters degrees. Practical on-the-job experience is essential.

Jobs are found where mines that operate concentration plants are located. The number of jobs is small; however, people begin in lower level positions and advance to that of engineer. This photo shows an engineer overseeing the concentration facilities of a copper mine.

15-11. Recycled iron is being smelted in this steel facility.

paper, and aluminum are also substitutes. However, some of these also deplete mineral resources. Tree farms can grow new pulp and lumber wood. The pulp can be used to make paper. Plywood, lumber, and particle board can be used in building construction rather than metal. Further, growing trees has a good impact on the environment. Trees do not produce pollution as do mining and processing ore!

■ Recycling—Many metal products can be recycled. Using a product or the materials used in making a product another time reduces demands on natural resources.Recycling aluminum and tin cans, glass bottles, and old automobiles saves mining and processing minerals. In some cases, processing is needed to prepare an item that is being recycled into another product. Recycling helps conserve mineral resources that are scarce.

■ Reduce Waste—People create waste in their daily living. Some of the wastes can be reduced. Use no more than is needed of a product.

■ Avoid Throwaways—Use products that can be cleaned and used again. For example, rather than using a plastic throwaway soft drink bottle, use a glass one that can be returned for reuse. This suggestion is becoming more difficult. Bottlers are using fewer reusable bottles for beverages.

■ Use Wastes to Make Products—Byproducts from manufacturing are now used to make other products. An example is using slag from iron smelting for fertilizer. The wastes from most manufacturing have good alternative uses.

■ Take Care of What You Have—Products that are properly used and cared for will last longer. This will require fewer minerals to manufacture another product. For example, properly caring for a sport utility vehicle will extend its useful life. Drive it in a reasonable manner. Do the proper preventive maintenance so it will last longer.

■ Choose the Right Product—When selecting a product, get one that is best for your use. There is no need to buy a large, heavy item when a smaller, lighter item will be adequate. A good example is a farm tractor. Why buy a large tractor for a small farm when a small tractor will do the job just as well?

REVIEWING

MAIN IDEAS

A mineral is an element or a compound that naturally occurs on Earth's surface. Three criteria can be used with any substance to see if it is a mineral: Minerals are inorganic, minerals have definite chemical composition, and minerals have atoms arranged in specific patterns.

Rocks are important sources of minerals. Rocks that contain minerals are known as ore. An example is granite, which contains feldspar, quartz, and biotite. Each of these contains specific minerals.

A gem is a mineral valued for beauty and rarity. Diamonds, rubies, opals, and emeralds are examples. Shapes, colors, refraction, splits or cleavage, hardness, and specific gravity can be used to identify gems.

Mining is the process of obtaining minerals from raw materials in the earth. A surface mine is an excavation on or near the earth's surface. A subsurface mine is deep inside the earth and may use a network of tunnels to connect deposits of minerals with the surface of the earth.

Mining often creates environmental damage. The impacts can be reduced by following good practices and working to restore mined areas that are no longer needed. Mineral supplies can be made to last longer with good attitudes toward their use.

QUESTIONS

Answer the following questions using complete sentences and correct spelling.

1. What three characteristics can be used to determine if a substance is a mineral?

2. What is ore? Distinguish between high-grade and low-grade ore.

3. What are the forms in which minerals are found?

4. What is a gem? What are the six characteristics of gems?

5. What are the most abundant minerals? What metals are obtained from each?

6. How are mineral deposits located?

7. What are the two major types of mines? Distinguish between the two.

8. What activities may be needed in processing minerals?

9. How does mining damage the earth?

10. What can be done to sustain mineral supply? Name at least three practices and explain one.

EVALUATING

Match the term with the correct definition. Write the letter by the term in the blank provided.

a. quarry   e. mineral   i. mine
b. tailing   f. rock   j. cleavage
c. smelting   g. gem
d. ore   h. refraction

_____ 1. The smooth, flat surface created on a gem.

_____ 2. A mineral valued for its beauty and appeal.

_____ 3. A large open mine.

_____ 4. The bending of light rays by a gem.

_____ 5. An element or compound that naturally occurs on the surface of Earth.

_____ 6. The hard, solid portion of the earth's crust.

_____ 7. Rock that contains desired minerals.

_____ 8. An excavation for removing minerals from the earth.

_____ 9. The solid waste material that remains when ore is processed.

_____ 10. Heating ore in the purification process.

EXPLORING

1. Look up the market value of gold in the business section of the local newspaper. Keep a record of the stated value of gold for one or two weeks. Prepare a graph that demonstrates short-term changes in its value. Give an oral report on the value of gold in class. (An additional activity is to study the use of gold as currency and why that practice was discontinued.)

2. Survey your community to determine the minerals that are produced in the area. Determine how the minerals are extracted and the processing needed to use them. Remember to include sand and gravel in your investigation. Prepare a report on your findings. (Note: You may wish to organize your class into small cooperative groups for this investigation.)

3. Investigate the home in which you live. Determine the minerals used to manufacture the building materials used in its construction. For example, if your home has brick, clay was used in making the brick. Prepare a written report on your findings.

16

SUSTAINABLE AGRICULTURE

Agriculturists are concerned about our natural resources. They take care of the land, water, and air–all areas of the environment. They follow practices that prevent the loss of soil and damage to the streams, atmosphere, and wildlife habitat.

A great deal of emphasis has been given to using practices that protect natural resources. These practices are good for land owners as well as citizens who use the products of land. In recent years, more attention has turned to the practices used on golf courses, home and business lawns, and public lands. Abuse in using these areas can be just as damaging to the environment as abuse on farms and ranches.

Practices that assure future productivity are essential. All people need to get involved. The failure of one person can result in problems for many people.

16-1. A global positioning system is being used by scientists to study areas of soil salinity. (Courtesy, Agricultural Research Service, USDA)

OBJECTIVES

This chapter introduces the concept of sustainable agriculture. The following objectives are included:

1. Explain the meaning and importance of sustainable agriculture

2. List and explain four major areas of a sustainable crop production system

3. Identify and describe important sustainable agriculture practices

4. Explain the role of precision technologies in sustainable agriculture

5. Identify issues associated with animal agriculture and sustainability

TERMS

agricultural industry
cover crop
cultural practices
economic threshold
incineration
injury threshold
integrated pest management
legume
pest
planting date
plant population
precision farming
prescriptive agriculture
sustainable agriculture
sustainable agriculture system
symbiotic bacteria
tillage
variable rate technology

Sustainable Agriculture Research and Education (SARE) Program
http://www.sare.org/san/

THE MEANING OF
SUSTAINABLE AGRICULTURE

Sustainable agriculture is using practices that maintain the ability to produce food, fiber, and forestry products. Resources are used so they last a long time. Plants and animals will have good environments for growth. Humans will have quality air, water, and other resources.

Farmers have often been blamed for environmental problems. Research at the Mississippi Agricultural and Forestry Experiment Station by scientist Jonathan Pote has found that farmers are leading the effort to sustain the environment. New practices are being used. Protecting and sustaining the environment are now important to farmers.

Most agricultural producers use some sustainable practices. Plants and animals are grown in such a way that the ability to produce them is not destroyed. Crops may be grown with little or no plowing. Animal wastes may be placed on pastures and cropland to promote soil fertility. Irrigation water is managed to avoid waste. Chemicals are used only as needed through integrated pest management. More and more producers are using sustainable practices.

16-2. Planting without tilling the soil helps sustain moisture and fertility. (Courtesy, New Holland North America, Inc.)

CHARACTERISTICS OF SUSTAINABLE AGRICULTURE

People often want to know the characteristics of sustainable agriculture. Here are some:

■ Meets human food needs now and far into the future

16-3. A special stream crossing has been constructed for cattle. (Fences are used along the stream bank to keep cattle out. Keeping cattle out of the stream protects the water and keeps it clear.)

- Integrates plant and animal production
- Relies on natural processes and cycles to the extent possible (rather than sole reliance on chemicals, etc.)
- Specific to the particular site or geographic location where used
- Provides sufficient income to agricultural producers
- Protects natural resources
- Enhances quality of life for agricultural producers and all of society

AGRICULTURE IS MORE THAN FARMING

The meaning of agriculture has changed. Thinking of it as living on a farm in a rural area and producing crops is incomplete. Agriculture is a commercial venture. Products are produced for specific uses and markets. Science and technology are used to promote plant and animal production.

Agriculture is more than traditional work on a farm. Large factory-type production may be used with both plants and animals. These approaches typically produce high-quality food products. Modern production and marketing systems form the agricultural industry.

The *agricultural industry* is all of the processes in producing food, clothing, and forest products and getting them to the consumer in the desired forms. Horticulture is often included as a part of the agricultural industry. The agribusinesses that provide fertilizer, pesticides, machinery, and similar products are in the agricultural industry. It also includes food processing enterprises, such as canneries, creameries, and frozen food companies.

RESEARCH REVEALS ANSWERS

Research helps find ways of sustaining agricultural production. Research is the process of scientifically seeking answers to questions. Carefully designed experiments are used. These may be as plots in fields, laboratories, or other places. Without the findings of research, we would not have most of the practices that are used today in producing food, fiber, and forestry products.

Research is carried out by private companies, government agencies, and colleges and universities. Each state has a land-grant university that does research. Branch research stations are often located in different geographical areas of the states.

This photo shows research on grain sorghum. The bags are used to cover the forming heads on the plants. The heads contain the seed. Covering the heads with bags prevents unwanted pollination. The bags also prevent damage to the heads by insects and other pests. (Courtesy, Agricultural Research Service, USDA)

Some people refer to agriculture as a food production system. This notion is incomplete. Agriculture is more than just food production. It includes fiber and forestry, horticulture, and environmental areas.

SUSTAINABLE AGRICULTURE SYSTEMS

Sustainable agriculture uses a number of practices. A single practice does not stand alone. Using multiple practices in combination creates a ***sustainable agriculture system***. For example, growing crops with less plowing and reduced chemical use forms a system.

Practices are used to assure long-term ability to produce crops. The four major areas in sustainable crop production systems are:

- Diversification—This is planting different crops on land rather than planting the same crop year after year. An example is planting corn one year and soybeans the next. Legumes are part of the diversification because they return nitrogen to the soil. Planting different crops in successive growing seasons is known as crop rotation.

16-4. This pirate bug is feeding on whitefly nymphs on a leaf. (A pirate bug is a beneficial insect. It eliminates the need for insecticides and is killed when they are used.) (Courtesy, Agricultural Research Service, USDA)

■ Biological pest control—Biological pest control is using biological means rather than pesticides to control insects, weeds, and diseases. A good example is using predatory insects to control insects that damage crops. Lady bugs are among the best known predators on other insects.

■ Disease prevention—Keeping animals healthy improves their resistance to disease. This reduces the use of antibiotics to treat disease. Observing good nutrition habits and following quarantine and sanitation recommendations help prevent disease. An example is with poultry where the farms are quarantined and strict sanitation practices are followed.

■ Improved varieties—Planting genetically improved crops may reduce the need to use pesticides. New crop plants have been and are being developed that resist drought, pests, and disease. This eliminates the need to use pesticides and enables crops to grow during mild periods of drought. Crop varieties have been improved for a number of reasons. Most improvements focus on only one or two characteristics, such as resistance to certain disease or their ability to be stored longer after harvest. An example is the tomato. At least one variety has been genetically altered to increase the length of time the fruit can be stored.

CROP CULTURAL PRACTICES

Crops need certain conditions to grow and produce. Careful study has identified these conditions. On a farm, these form the cultural practices.

Cultural practices are the procedures followed in growing a crop. A number of decisions are made about cultural practices. Those used should promote sustainability. Cultural practices should use a minimum of energy, nutrients, water, chemicals, and other inputs.

Several cultural practices are presented here.

- Adaptation—Select adapted crops. Crops that are adapted to the climate, soil, and other conditions in an area promote sustainability. Some crops require warm weather; others require cool weather. Sugar cane, for example, grows best in a tropical climate. Cabbage grows best in a cool climate or at cool times of the year. Plant breeders have developed varieties that are better suited in some locations than others. A good example is corn. Some corn varieties mature in 90 days or less; other corn varieties may need 120 days or more. A variety is selected based on the length of growing season.

- Planting date—***Planting date*** is the period in the year that is best for planting a crop. Crops sensitive to frost are planted after the danger of frost in the spring. Planting dates depend on the nature of the crop, as well as the climate where it will be grown. Producers need to know the date that will produce maximum yield with the lowest investment. Planting too early or too late will result in a lower yield.

- Plant population—***Plant population*** is the density of the plants in a field. It is usually stated on a per-acre basis, such as 40,000 plants per acre. Too many plants results in over-crowding. Over-crowded plants do not grow well. Plants compete for light, moisture, and nutrients. Too few plants results in open spaces in the field. The open spaces expose the soil to damage and allow weeds to grow. Get information on seeding rates from a seed dealer or the land-grant university in your state.

- Spacing—Spacing is the distance between plants and how the space is organized. Some crops are in rows; others are planted "broadcast" without regard to rows. Crops that are broadcast cannot be cultivated (plowed) to control weeds. Broadcast crops do have

16-5. An agronomist is studying soybeans for maturity. (Courtesy, Agricultural Research Service, USDA)

16-6. A scientist is studying new technology for crop production. (Courtesy, George Bostick, North Carolina State University)

the advantage of reducing soil loss to erosion. Row spacing is the distance between rows. Increasingly, crops are being grown on narrower rows.

- Tillage—Some crops are tilled. *Tillage* is plowing the soil. It may be plowed to prepare the seedbed or to cultivate the growing crop. Tillage exposes the soil to erosion and water evaporation. Alternatives to tillage have become widely used. No-till cropping involves planting seed into soil that has not been plowed. No-till often involves using pesticides to kill weeds before or at planting time. Minimum-till involves some tillage, but not a complete plowing of the soil into a loose seedbed.

- Harvesting—Harvesting is the process of picking, cutting, or otherwise taking a crop at the proper time. This varies with the kind of crop. Broccoli is harvested while green and rapidly growing. Wheat is harvested after the heads are dry. A crop in which pests have been controlled is easier to harvest and requires less energy. Harvesting in dry weather protects the land from damage by machines forming deep ruts in the soil. Harvesting involves residue management. Crop residue is stalks, leaves, pods, and other materials. Most residue is left on the field to protect the land. In a few cases, the residue is burned. Burning leaves the soil unprotected and pollutes the air.

SUSTAINABLE AGRICULTURE PRACTICES

Sustainable agriculture involves a number of practices, with two or more often combined. The major areas are managing soil, water, and pests.

SOIL MAINTENANCE

Crops need nutrients to grow. Crop plants grow slowly and produce low yields or fail to grow if nutrients are deficient. The presence of nutrients determines the fertility of the soil. Practices can be used to maintain and im-

16-7. A laser-guided system is being used to prepare land to prevent erosion and sustain productivity. (Courtesy, Spectra-Physics, Dayton, Ohio)

prove soil fertility. These tend to be the same practices as those used in soil conservation.

- Controlling erosion—Soil losses can be reduced to conserve fertility. Since most losses are due to water and wind, steps can be taken to protect the soil from these elements. With water, the goal is to reduce the impact of raindrops and slow the rate of water runoff. Planting cover crops, leaving residue from harvested crops, and using artificial ground covers can reduce the impact of raindrops. Using terraces, contour plowing, and strip cropping can slow the rate of runoff and keep soil in place. Wind erosion is prevented by using cover crops, leaving stubble from harvested crops, and following other practices that prevent exposure to wind.

- Using soil and plant tissue testing—Soil and tissue tests are used to identify nutrient deficiencies. Soil tests are fairly easy to make. Tissue tests are more complicated and require laboratory methods. Tissue tests may show deficiencies in a growing plant. Such deficiencies reflect the absence of nutrients in the soil. These tests are the basis for determining the amount and kind of fertilizer to use. Only the needed amounts should be applied. Applying fertilizer that is not needed is a waste. Excess fertilizer can get into runoff and damage streams and lakes.

- Rotating crops—Crop rotation is alternating the kinds of crops produced on land. Crops vary in nutrient requirements. Some crops are legumes. A *legume* is a plant that has the ability to convert nitrogen from the air into nitrogen in the soil. *Symbiotic bacteria* must be present in the soil. These are bacteria that form nodules on the roots of legume plants. For example, soybeans are legumes. Following a soybean crop with corn (a non-legume) provides nitrogen, which was "fixed" by the soybeans, for the corn. Other legumes include alfalfa, clover, peas, snap beans, and lima beans.

Career Profile

ENTOMOLOGIST

An entomologist studies insects–how they live, what they eat, and the damage they cause. The work involves both beneficial and harmful insects. Entomologists study ways of reducing the damage caused by the insects that are pests.

Entomologists have college degrees in entomology or closely related area of biological science. Many have masters and doctors degrees in the same areas. Taking agricultural and science classes in high school is a good beginning. Practical experience with insects, crops, and laboratory work is essential. A good background with agricultural and forestry crops is also helpful.

Jobs for entomologists are found where agricultural and forestry crops are produced. Some work as self-employed crop consultants. Others work with pesticide companies, research stations, and colleges and universities. This photo shows an entomologist applying fungi to plants in an experiment to control white flies. (Courtesy, Agricultural Research Service, USDA)

■ Planting cover crops—A **cover crop** is a crop planted to protect the soil and increase fertility. Many are planted in the fall to grow and protect the land in the winter. Cover crops are planted after the harvest of a cash crop, such as cotton, or between the rows of other crops. For example, vetch (a legume cover crop) may be planted in the fall after cotton has been harvested.

WATER MANAGEMENT

Water is essential for all living organisms. Crop and animal production depend on an adequate supply. Precipitation, usually rain, is adequate for some crops depending on the location. The soil holds some water for crops. Without sufficient water, crop yields are lower.

■ Providing quality water—Water quality is important in determining how it can be used. Animals and crops require freshwater. (A few species of plants can use saltwater. Research is underway to develop crop plants that can be grown with saltwater.) Water containing salt damages the land. Seawater cannot be used for irrigation unless the salt is removed. Some water from aquifers and streams may also contain salt. Water may contain minerals that need to be removed. Filtration systems are sometimes used to remove minerals and sediment from water. Homes and businesses may have filtration systems. These need to be maintained properly to operate efficiently.

■ Irrigating properly—Irrigation is used to assure adequate soil moisture for crops. It may be used to supplement precipitation or as the major source of water for crops. Supplemental irrigation is watering crops when there has been no recent rainfall. For example, grain sorghum may be irrigated in Texas in mid-July if there has been no recent rain or showers. Moisture meters can be used to measure soil moisture before crop plants are stressed by low water. Stress reduces the productivity of crops.

■ Managing water supply—Water supply management is using available water efficiently to meet agricultural and other needs. Precipitation should be stored for later use. For example, melting snow is stored in large reservoirs. A system of canals or irrigation ditches may be used to get water where it is needed. Water should be used only as it is needed.

■ Preventing water loss— Various methods can be used to prevent water loss. Crop residues (stems and stalks from the previous year) can be chopped or shredded and left on the land. The residues reduce the rate of precipitation runoff and encourage infiltration and percolation. Plowing the soil exposes it to the air. This allows moisture to evaporate resulting in the loss of water that may be needed later.

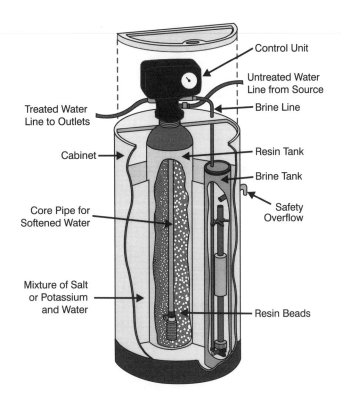

16-8. Softening water makes it possible to use water that otherwise would not be suitable for use. (This shows how a water softener is made. As the hard water passes over the resin beads in the tank, the calcium and magnesium are deposited on the beads. The resin contains salt. Salt causes the exchange to occur.)

16-9. A tensiometer can be used to determine when irrigation is needed. (The tensiometer is placed in the soil to the depth pointed on the tube. After several hours, the need for irrigation can be determined.)

■ Using buffer strips—Leaving strips of grass and trees at the edges of fields along creeks and rivers helps prevent soil from washing into the stream. These are known as buffer strips. They also help keep the stream bank in place. Unprotected banks tend to erode and wash away. In nature, the roots of plants help prevent stream bank erosion.

■ Disposing of wastewater—Properly disposing of wastewater should involve reconditioning it so it can be used again. Wastewater is sometimes applied to the land. Depending on its source and content, wastewater may be used on roads to settle dust or to irrigate golf courses and crops.

PEST MANAGEMENT

A *pest* is anything that harms, destroys, or annoys plants and animals. Pests may also annoy humans and damage property, such as the homes in which they live. In agriculture, weeds, insects, diseases, small ani-

16-10. Scouting is the process of checking for insects in a crop. (This shows a cotton field being scouted as a part of IPM.) (Courtesy, Mississippi State University)

mals, and some other species are pests. They may cause damage to crops and lower its quality or yield.

Different practices have been used to control pests. Some damaged the environment and soil. Chemical pesticides have often been blamed for problems. People do not always agree on the use of pesticides; however, all people would agree that excessive use is to be avoided.

Some change in attitudes has occurred. It is virtually impossible to completely control pests. The presence of some pests does not cause large losses. This has led to the notion of pest management. Some pests can be tolerated if damage is low.

16-11. Damage by worms to this corn plant is beyond what the plant can overcome. (Scouting and earlier application would have been useful.)

- Integrated Pest Management—*Integrated pest management* (IPM) is using a number of different techniques in a unified program of pest control. Crops are checked for pests. Control measures are used only when the level of pest infestation is great enough to cause a loss that is significant. The presence of a few insect or weed pests may not merit the use of a control. Some of these practices damage or destroy beneficial insects that are present.

- Threshold Levels—The concept of threshold levels is used to assess the need for using a pesticide. *Injury threshold* is determining if sufficient damage is being caused to a crop to merit the use of a control measure. Finding a few pests does not result in much loss or damage. One weed in a field does not justify treating an entire field! *Economic threshold* is the pest density at which control measures should be used to promote monetary returns to the producer. Good judgment is needed to determine when it is time to use control measures. A pesticide should be used only when the cost of the application is less than the increased yields due to a decrease in the number of pests.

PRECISION TECHNOLOGIES

Sustainability is being promoted with site-specific cropping practices. *Variable rate technology* (VRT) is varying the practices used based on conditions that are present. Soil varies within fields. By varying the fertilizer and other inputs used, only small areas needing the application receive it. Using VRT protects the environment and sustains natural resources.

Two approaches to VRT are being used: precision farming and prescriptive agriculture.

PRECISION FARMING

Precision farming is combining information and technology to manage crop production. Fields of crops are divided into smaller units on the basis of specific criteria. Each smaller part of the field can be treated according to its needs. In the past, an entire field received the same treatment whether all of the field needed treatment or not.

16-12. A computer and global positioning system on this tractor guide the application of fertilizer. (Courtesy, Top Soil Testing Service Company)

Precision farming uses satellites and maps to guide field work. It uses control maps of a field that include soil test and yield information from previous years. A geographic information system (GIS) plots the features of a field on a map. A global positioning system (GPS) is a satellite-based navigation system that can precisely identify points on the earth. Radio signals from three satellites are precisely timed by the GPS receiver. A GPS receiver in a field will plot with considerable accuracy. Pests, fertility, soil compaction, and other features can be considered.

Yield monitors are used on harvesters to determine yields throughout all areas of a field. This information is plotted and used for the next growing season. Practices to improve the low-yielding parts of the field are used on only the part where they are needed. The treatments can be accurate to within less than a meter of land surface. Controllers are used on the application equipment using a global positioning system to apply the recommended amounts of materials to the land.

PRESCRIPTIVE AGRICULTURE

Prescriptive agriculture uses techniques similar to precision farming. *Prescriptive agriculture* involves testing and mapping fields and the application of needed materials. Prescription fertilizers and other materials are applied using variable rate application equipment, including through irrigation water. Prescriptive agriculture does not use global positioning and is not as precise as precision farming.

ANIMAL AGRICULTURE AND SUSTAINABILITY

Animal agriculture has been attacked as a source of environmental problems. Most everyone is familiar with the odor from intensive animal production facilities. We also realize that animal wastes can pollute streams and lakes. We must have animals for the protein they provide in human nutrition. Ways can be used to reduce problems from animal wastes. Using animal wastes can promote sustainability.

Intensive production results in a greater concentration of animal wastes and dead animals. In nature, animals are scattered about the landscape. The factory approach concentrates large numbers of animals together in one facility. Such facilities should be located away from residential and business areas.

ANIMAL DISPOSAL

Appropriate methods are needed to dispose of dead animals as well as animal tissues. Animal tissues result from placentas following the birth process, broken horns or hoofs, injuries that dismember an animal, and other causes. (Note: Always follow safety precautions. Protect the human body, other animals, and the environment when disposing of animals and wastes.)

Even in the healthiest herds and flocks, some animals will die. Proper disposal of dead animals is essential to prevent disease and odors from decaying

16-13. A small incinerator is used on this poultry farm to dispose of dead birds.

flesh. If a contagious disease is suspected as the cause of death, laboratory diagnosis is needed. Get the assistance of a local veterinarian or other animal health care provider. The surviving animals may need preventive treatments to keep them from getting the disease.

Dead animals may be disposed of in several ways:

■ Burying—Dead animals can be buried. The location should be away from areas where water supplies could be contaminated. Most animals should be buried at least three feet (1 m). A greater depth is desirable. The depth depends on the size and number of animals at one site. A disadvantage is the time and effort required to properly bury animals. Be sure to follow local ordinances on animal burial.

■ Incineration—*Incineration* is burning dead animals and tissues in intense heat. This is most widely used with poultry and animals that may be hosts of dangerous disease. Special types of incinerating equipment are used.

■ Composting—Composting is most often used with poultry. The location of the bin should be screened from public view and away from residences. Some odor may occur. Well-composted material from a poultry bin can be spread with the litter from houses.

■ Pits—A few producers have pits dug into the ground. Dead animals are put into these pits. The pits may have a cover to keep out animals that eat dead flesh, flies, and other pests. A cover also keeps people and other animals from falling into a pit. Be sure to follow applicable regulations from a local health department or other agency. Pits have declined in use.

■ Rendering plants—Rendering plants are facilities that process dead animals into other useful materials. These are not widely used today. Rendering plants are best with larger animals or large numbers of smaller animals. Special trucks come to farms to pick up and haul the animals away.

16-14. Manure spreading equipment is being used to dispose of solid animal wastes on cropland. (Courtesy, New Holland North America, Inc.)

Natural disposal occurs with animals that die in the wild. Insects, vultures, rodents, microbes, and other organisms will often begin destruction of the body within a few hours of death. Some states have laws that protect vultures because of their valued role in cleaning the landscape of dead animals.

ANIMAL WASTES

Animal wastes are the urine and feces excreted by animals. The waste material may also include bedding, such as straw and wood shavings. The bedding (known as litter with poultry) absorbs moisture and promotes decomposition of the wastes.

- Tanks and lagoons—Factory-type production facilities use large tanks and lagoons for holding and partial decay of wastes. These materials may be spread over land in semi-liquid form as organic fertil-

16-15. Two types of liquid waste systems are shown here. (The bottom photo shows a large tank and the top shows a lagoon. Solid wastes are washed into these facilities for microbial activity.)

16-16. Large trucks can be used to apply liquid sludge from tanks and lagoons onto cropland.

izer. Housing facilities should be designed for easy washing to remove manure.

■ Litter removal—Poultry houses are cleaned out between batches of chickens. The litter consists of wood shavings, manure, and feathers. Litter is often spread over land that is used for hay crops or pasture. No animals should be on the land for several weeks after spreading. Hay should not be cut for several weeks after litter has been spread.

■ No removal—Waste from animals in low-intensity production may be allowed to remain on the land and naturally decompose. Such is the case with cattle on the range. Their manure serves to maintain and increase the fertility of the pasture. Microbes and scarabs (dung beetles) aid the decomposition process. Decomposition releases nutrients in the manure back to the soil.

16-17. These chicks are being raised in a modern poultry house with clean litter. (Litter is made of wood shavings that absorb moisture.)

REVIEWING

MAIN IDEAS

Sustainable agriculture is using agricultural practices that maintain the ability to produce food, fiber, and forest products for an indefinite time. These promote quality water, air, soil, and other natural resources as well as conserve fossil fuels. The goal is to care for human needs far into the future.

Four major characteristics of sustainable agriculture are practicing diversification, using biological controls, preventing disease, and using improved varieties of crops. Cultural practices can be used to promote sustainability.

Major areas of sustainable practices include soil maintenance, water maintenance, and pest management. Precision technologies have useful roles. They allow inputs to be used only where and when needed.

Animal agriculture often has issues associated with waste management. Wastes are from dead animals and the urine and feces of animals. Problems arise when animals are held in high populations in a small amount of space, which is sometimes known as factory animal production. Proper facility design helps manage waste problems. Disposal of dead animals and wastes should be in line with local health department and environmental regulations.

QUESTIONS

Answer the following questions using complete sentences and correct spelling.

1. What are the seven characteristics of sustainable agriculture?
2. How has agriculture changed?
3. What is a sustainable agriculture system?
4. What are the four major areas in a sustainable crop production system?
5. What are the cultural practices in producing crops? Select one and describe how it relates to sustainable agriculture.
6. What practices can be followed in soil maintenance?
7. What practices can be followed in water management?
8. What practices can be followed in pest management?

9. What variable rate technologies may be used?

10. How does animal agriculture relate to sustainability?

EVALUATING

Match the term with the correct definition. Write the letter by the term in the blank provided.

a. cultural practices
b. integrated pest management
c. planting date
d. sustainable agriculture

e. pest
f. precision farming
g. injury threshold
h. plant population

_____ 1. The density of plants in a field.

_____ 2. Anything that harms, destroys, or annoys living organisms and property.

_____ 3. Using agricultural practices that maintain the ability to produce.

_____ 4. Combining information and technology to manage crop production.

_____ 5. Using a number of different techniques in a unified program of pest control.

_____ 6. The procedures followed in growing a crop.

_____ 7. The period in the year that is best for planting seed.

_____ 8. The level of damage in a crop that merits the use of pest control measures.

EXPLORING

1. Interview an entomologist or crop consultant about integrated pest management. Determine the IPM practices used with crops grown in the local area. Ask about the effectiveness of the methods. Prepare a report on your findings.

2. Select a crop grown in the local area or one that interests you. Identify the cultural practices needed to produce the crop. Prepare a report that describes the practices.

3. Investigate the use of precision farming. Visit a farm where it is used or a dealer that sells equipment for precision farming. Observe operation of the equipment. Prepare a report on your findings.

17

WASTE MANAGEMENT

Everything we do creates wastes! Each person creates more wastes than they realize. Many of our daily living activities create wastes. All of these wastes must be disposed of in some way.

Many of the things we use are in throwaway containers. Throwaway containers are wastes the moment we no longer need them. Make an assessment of your use of throwaway items. Begin with the wrap on your notebook paper and include candy wrappers, beverage cans, pizza boxes, and many more. Just think of all the throwaway stuff from a fast-food restaurant!

The wastes we create go into our environment. Many are disposed of properly. Others may be disposed of in ways that damage our environment. We know that we should not throw cans out the window of an SUV as we travel along. We know to put our garbage out on pick-up day. All waste has to go some place. We hope it is disposed of properly!

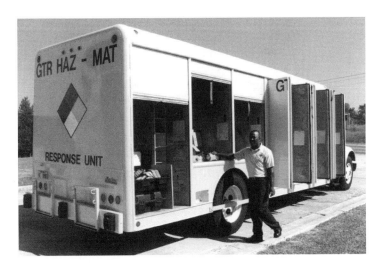

17-1. An emergency hazardous materials response truck is being made ready in case of an accident.

OBJECTIVES

This chapter covers the basic areas of waste management. The following objectives are included:

1. Name and classify the common kinds of wastes

2. Describe dangers associated with wastes

3. Identify major sources of wastes

4. Explain the disposal of common wastes

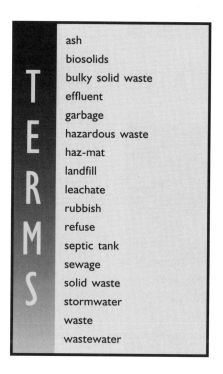

TERMS

ash
biosolids
bulky solid waste
effluent
garbage
hazardous waste
haz-mat
landfill
leachate
rubbish
refuse
septic tank
sewage
solid waste
stormwater
waste
wastewater

Garbage
http://www.learner.org/exhibits/garbage/

KINDS OF WASTES

Waste is any unused or discarded material. Human life processes create wastes. Factories, farms, and construction create wastes. Almost everything we do results in some kind of waste. Even washing the dishes at home creates wastewater!

Wastes are in three groups: solid waste, wastewater, and hazardous waste.

SOLID WASTE

It is easy to know if something is a solid waste. Just contrast solid materials with liquids! *Solid waste* is garbage, refuse, and other discarded material. Solid wastes do not dissolve in water or other solvents. *Refuse* is anything that is discarded because it is useless or worthless. Refuse includes rubbish and bulky solid wastes.

Solid wastes vary depending on how the waste was created. Wood, metal, fiber, glass, paper, plastic, animal tissues, rubber, and food scraps are solid wastes. Solid wastes that originate in the home are household wastes. Solid wastes are often grouped as garbage, rubbish, ash, and bulky solid waste.

■ Garbage—*Garbage* is the solid material discarded from a kitchen. It includes cooked and uncooked food scraps, food containers, such as cans, paper or plastic wrappers, and other items associated with cooking. Proper disposal is needed to keep down odors and pests that are attracted to garbage.

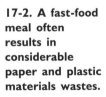

17-2. A fast-food meal often results in considerable paper and plastic materials wastes.

17-3. The liquids associated with DNA extraction are wastes that need to be disposed of properly.

■ Rubbish—**Rubbish** is paper, plastic, bottles, metals, and yard and garden wastes. Rubbish is sometimes called trash. It includes any nonfood items other than ashes and discarded household furnishings. Yard and garden wastes include grass clippings, leaves, limbs, and stalks.

■ Ash—**Ash** is the residue from the combustion process. Ashes result from burning paper, wood, or coal. The major sources of ash in the home are fireplaces and furnaces.

■ Bulky Wastes—**Bulky solid waste** is large, discarded items used in the home, business, or factory. Equipment, junk cars, old stoves, mattresses, and furniture are examples. These are not usually collected with the garbage and are disposed of differently.

WASTEWATER

Wastewater is used water that contains suspended or dissolved matter. It originates from homes, farms, offices, schools, factories, and other places. Wastewater is of three major types.

■ Domestic wastewater—Domestic wastewater is produced by humans in their daily living. It includes water used for washing dishes, taking baths, and cleaning toilets. Human urine and feces are in domestic wastewater. Domestic wastewater is also known as **sewage**. Sanitary sewers are systems of pipes that carry sewage away for treatment.

■ Spent wastewater—Spent wastewater is water that can no longer be used as it was being used because of contamination. Manufacturing plants may produce wastewater. A good example is a paper mill. Nearly 38,000 gallons (144,000 L) of water are needed to make a ton of paper. Another example is electric power generation. Water is used to power and cool equipment. After use, it is warm and needs to be reconditioned.

■ Stormwater—Though not wastewater in the sense of having been used, **stormwater** is excess precipitation that collects on streets, parking lots, and other places. It must be dealt with and conducted out of towns and cities. A storm sewer system is used. This is a separate system from the sanitary system used with domestic wastewater. Stormwater does not usually go to treatment plants but is piped directly to streams, lakes, and other outlets. It is important to keep areas where stormwater originates clean. For example, used engine oil on streets will get into storm water and be carried into streams and lakes.

HAZARDOUS WASTES

A *hazardous waste* is a waste that is potentially dangerous to the environment and human health. The materials may be solids, liquids, or gases. Radioactive wastes are also considered hazardous.

Many hazardous wastes are common materials that we use in our homes and work. Examples of hazardous wastes:

- cleaning products, such as bleach, ammonia, and detergents
- automotive products, such as brake fluid, engine oil, battery acid, and fuel
- garden products, such as fertilizer and pesticides
- building materials, such as paint, varnish, and roofing
- general items, such as matches, glue, small batteries, and nail polish

Nuclear wastes consist of fission products formed when atoms of the nuclear fuels are split and from the products resulting when uranium atoms absorb free neutrons. The materials that remain are known as spent fuel.

17-4. Common pesticides can become hazardous wastes if small quantities are unused.

17-5. Leftover paint is hazardous waste and should not be sent to a landfill. (It is acceptable to send empty paint cans or cans in which the paint has dried to landfills. Never buy more paint than you need for a job!)

The dangers posed by hazardous wastes vary. Some burn readily and will combust producing intense heat. Other hazardous wastes will react and explode, corrode other materials, or are poisonous. They pose a wide range of human health and environmental hazards.

The U.S. Department of Transportation has regulations on hauling hazardous materials. **Haz-mat** is the term applied to hazardous materials. Specially trained emergency response teams deal with accidents where hazardous materials are involved.

DANGERS FROM WASTES

Waste materials pose dangers in the environment. They can damage natural resources and threaten human well-being. Proper disposal is essential. Improperly disposing of wastes may result in hazards several years in the future. An example is building a park on the land where a hazardous waste disposal site once existed.

Several hazards from wastes are included here.

- Pollution—Wastes may pollute the air, soil, or water. Wildlife habitat can be destroyed by improperly disposing of wastes. Air pollution results as odors, smoke, and fumes. Decaying garbage can create unpleasant odors and attract pests.

    Disposing of wastes on land can degrade the soil. Discarding bulky items, such as old tires and cars, on land impairs the use of the land and lowers its

Resource Connection

HAZ-MAT: WHAT THE NUMBERS MEAN

Haz-mat information is all about us. Trucks, trailers, buildings, and other places may have special signs. This truck has 1075 prominently posted. It is helpful if we know what the sign means.

A uniform system for identifying places where hazardous materials may be present in large amounts has been developed. Diamond-shaped placards with certain colors, symbols, and numbers are used. The *Emergency Response Guidebook* from the U.S. Department of Transportation gives full details.

These two photographs will help explain how the system works. One shows the back of a truck that hauls propane. The other shows two sample pages from the Guidebook. A few common examples by number: 1005 is ammonia, 1072 is compressed oxygen, 1075 is liquified petroleum gas (propane), 1203 is gasoline, 1993 is fuel oil, 1999 is asphalt, 1831 is fuming sulfuric acid, and 2911 is radioactive instruments.

Contact a local haz-mat team through your fire department for more information. The next time a big truck passes you with one of the placards you will know what it is hauling!

value. Containers with chemicals, such as pesticides, thrown on land can damage productivity of the soil.

Both surface and ground water can be polluted by wastes. Wastes should be disposed of so the water is not polluted. Once a substance gets into water, it may be carried long distances as the water moves on the surface and as ground water in the earth. Fish kills may result from polluted water in streams and lakes.

■ Health—Wastes may pose health hazards. Humans and animals (both domestic and wild) can get disease from wastes. Air and water pollution can lead to allergies and other diseases, including cancer, depending on the kind of waste material. Pests that live and breed in the waste can transmit diseases.

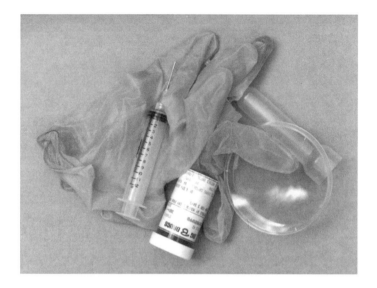

17-6. Products used in human health care should be disposed of properly.

In some cases, solid waste contains human or animal feces, which is definitely a health hazard. Broken glass, rusty nails, and chemical materials can cause injury and disease, such as tetanus. Wild animals are subject to injury. An example is a deer stepping into a can. The can slips over the deer's foot and the animal has no way of removing it!

■ Pests—Wastes often attract pests. Insects, mammals, and other pests may be associated with wastes. The kind of pest attracted depends on the nature of the waste. Food wastes attract ants, flies, rats and mice, bears, and stray dogs. Wasps or bees may live in junk and will sting you if agitated.

Proper disposal of wastes eliminates feeding and breeding areas for pests. The fly or rat you see at your home may be carrying disease from contact with garbage at another home some distance away!

■ Safety—Some wastes pose safety hazards. Broken glass can cause serious cuts. Rusty nails can puncture the skin and lead to infection. Old equipment can fall or otherwise cause injury. Junk refrigerators are dangerous if small children crawl inside and close the door (they can quickly suffocate).

Discarded appliances and equipment should be sent for recycling. Until this is possible, make these items safe by removing parts that can lead to problems. An example is to remove the door from a refrigerator. Each year small children die because they go inside refrigerators and close the door. Doors on some refrigerators are being made so they can be opened from the inside. Regulations may restrict placing appliances with freon and parts with heavy metals, such as mercury, in landfills.

■ Radiation—Radioactive materials pose health hazards to humans and other living organisms. These should be disposed of properly to prevent injury.

■ Reproductive Failure—
Some materials may disrupt the reproductive processes of organisms. Fertility may be impaired. Birth defects may be present in offspring. Exposure to chemicals, heavy metals, and radioactive materials may lead to reproductive failure.

SOURCES OF WASTE

Human life and economic activity create solid wastes, wastewater, and hazardous wastes. The sources are due to how people live and earn their income. The major sources of waste are listed here.

17-7. Could this calf born with two heads on a Nevada ranch be the result of hazardous materials in the environment of the cattle herd?

■ Domestic—Domestic waste is from homes and apartments. It is sometimes known as residential waste. A typical family in the suburbs creates about 40 pounds (18 kg) of solid waste a week! That same family would create some 2,500 gallons of wastewater a week.

■ Commercial—Commercial waste is from offices, retail stores, restaurants, and schools. Occasionally, hazardous wastes may be involved, such as animal tissues from school laboratories.

■ Medical—Medical waste is from human and veterinary medical health care. It includes body fluids and tissues, syringes, hypodermic needles, removed sutures, and other materials.

■ Municipal—Municipal waste includes solid materials from the activities of a town or city. Dead animals, materials cleaned from streets, abandoned cars, and residues from wastewater treatment.

■ Industrial—Industrial waste is waste from manufacturing. Its nature depends on the kinds of materials used in the manufacturing processes at the plant—a sawmill has sawdust and other wood materials.

17-8. Dead animals, such as this cat, on streets must be disposed of by municipalities.

■ Construction and demolition—Construction and demolition wastes are various building materials. The materials may be scraps from new construction or old materials from taking down a structure. Lumber, electrical wire, brick, roofing material, and other items are included.

■ Agricultural—Agricultural wastes are the materials created in producing plants and animals. With plants, it includes leaves, stems, fruit, and other remains. With animals, it includes animal tissues, dead animals, wastewater, and solid wastes, such as dried manure. Junk tractors and equipment as well as farm building materials are often included. Horticultural

17-9. Lumber and scraps from remodeling are construction wastes that require disposal. (Burning creates too much damage to the air!)

17-10. Junk cars and household furnishings degrade this area.

wastes from home lawns, golf courses, and other areas are quite similar to agricultural wastes and may be included here.

■ Nuclear—Nuclear wastes are generated by electrical power plants, military nuclear-powered submarines, and any other activity that uses nuclear power.

WASTE DISPOSAL

Properly disposing of solid wastes is essential. Disposal involves taking action that removes the waste from the environment. This should reduce the likelihood that the waste will cause damage to humans, other living organisms, air, water, and soil.

SOLID WASTE

Disposing of solid wastes varies with the kinds and sources of the wastes. Residential garbage and trash collection removes wastes. The garbage and other wastes should be placed in bags, cans, or other containers. The bags are picked up or the containers are emptied into the specially designed haul truck. The waste is carried to an approved disposal site.

Solid wastes from factories, businesses, and farms may be disposed of in various ways. Some dispose of their own wastes. Others contract with private firms to dispose of their wastes. Some wastes may be stored for a while before disposal. A good example is the school lab that stores dissected specimens in a freezer until pickup by a disposal service. Other wastes may be stored for pickup by a reclamation service.

17-11. Residential garbage pickup is available for a small fee in most communities.

The method used to dispose of wastes depends on the nature of the waste material and government approval. Open burning is illegal.

Several methods of solid waste disposal are listed here.

Landfill

A *landfill* is a place where wastes are placed for permanent disposal. Large holes are dug into the land. Many landfills have plastic-type liners that prevent water in the material from seeping into the ground water below. Landfills are designed for the kinds of wastes placed in them. Sanitary landfills are designed for wastes, such as garbage and sludge, from wastewater plants. Other landfills are designed to dispose of chemical wastes and solid materials, such as materials from torn-down buildings.

Landfills must comply with local, state, and federal government regulations. In most communities, the local health department can provide information on landfills. Many states have agencies on environmental quality that must approve landfills.

17-12. Entrance to a landfill for disposing of rubbish, such as building materials wastes (no garbage is permitted here).

17-13. Landfills are often divided into sections known as cells. (This shows one cell of a landfill that is partially full.)

Wastes in a landfill should not be burned. The wastes are covered each day with layers of soil. Natural decay processes destroy the waste over a long period. Pipes may be installed in landfills to collect methane gas for fuel.

Landfills may give off leachate. *Leachate* is the liquid that has passed through solid waste and contains suspended or dissolved materials from solid waste. Leachate typically drains from the bottom of a landfill. The contents and color of leachate depend on the materials in the landfill. Leachate from wastes containing lead or mercury will contain traces of these heavy metals. These are dangerous to wildlife and humans. The leachate from decaying organic matter does not pose the same level of threat. The activity of microbes in solid wastes influences leachate contents.

17-14. A system for releasing methane and collecting leachate has been installed on this filled, soil-covered landfill that is beginning to grow grass.

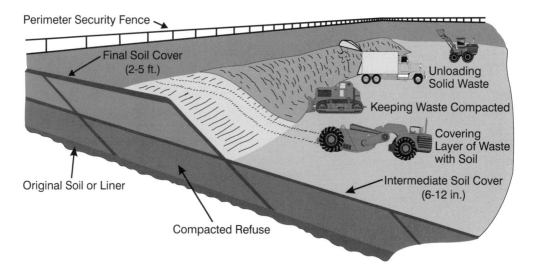

17-15. Major parts of a sanitary landfill and how it works.

The amount of leachate from a landfill depends on the volume of water that passes through the decaying wastes. Some solid wastes are disposed of so little leachate results. Landfills may have leachate treatment systems.

Microbe action in a landfill is slow. Excavations of landfills have found bananas that were recognizable after five years and newspapers that could be read after 10 years.

Incineration

Some wastes are readily destroyed by high temperatures in an incinerator. The waste material is converted to ash. Ash is nonburnable and can be safely disposed of on land or buried in some underground locations after it has cooled.

When wastes are burned, careful consideration must be given to the contents of the waste. Combustion is not always easy with some wastes. Wastes may not burn completely, leaving large amounts of ash. The ash from incineration of domestic wastes may contain heavy metals and other chemicals. If these are present, the ash is a hazardous waste.

Recycling and Reclamation

Recycling is reusing a product or the materials used to make the product. Reclamation is rendering useful materials from wastes. For example, the lead plates in an old battery may be separated from the battery and reused.

17-16. A place for visitors to deposit wastes for recycling at a park.

Paper, aluminum, plastics, glass, iron, and many other materials can be recycled. Even the asphalt in a blacktop road can be recycled! Special machines take up old asphalt and grind it into small pieces for reuse.

About 20 percent of the solid waste in the United States is recycled. Some countries recycle more. Japan, for example, recycles nearly 40 percent of the solid wastes.

WASTEWATER

How wastewater is disposed of depends on its contents and other characteristics, such as temperature. Wastewater is typically reconditioned fully or partially for future use. Disease organisms should be killed. Nutrients in the water should be removed. Toxic and other materials should be separated from the wastewater before it is released.

The treatment system used depends on the volume of wastewater produced. Systems for farms were covered in a previous chapter. Systems for homes, businesses, and factories vary.

Home Septic Systems

Homes and small businesses in rural or isolated areas may use septic tank systems. A *septic tank* is a steel or concrete container buried in the

ground that receives wastewater for action by microbes. After microbial action, the remaining solid materials settle to the bottom of the tank. Liquids flow from one end near the top of the tank into a leaching field. A leaching field is a system of pipes with small holes that disperse the liquid at a depth of two feet (0.6 m) or more underground.

Tanks typically hold 500 or 1,000 gallons of wastewater. After several years, the solids (sludge) at the bottom may need to be pumped out. Only an approved septic tank cleaning service should be used. The sludge from a septic tank should be disposed of at a sewage treatment plant.

Water containing a high amount of bleach or other toxic substance can destroy the microbes in a septic tank. This results in the solids not undergoing decay. Avoid using chlorine and other materials that kill microbes.

Municipal Systems

Towns and cities have systems to dispose of wastewater. These are known as municipal systems.

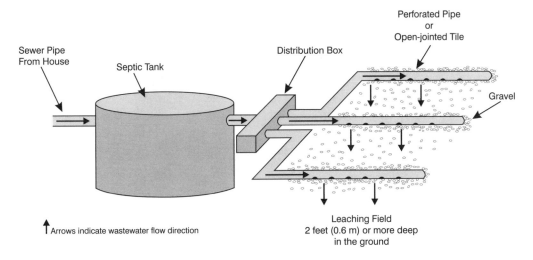

Sewer Pipe
From House

Septic Tank

Distribution Box

Perforated Pipe
or
Open-jointed Tile

Gravel

↑Arrows indicate wastewater flow direction

Leaching Field
2 feet (0.6 m) or more deep
in the ground

17-17. Design of a home septic system.

Systems of pipes take wastewater from homes and businesses and carry it to treatment facilities. The facilities are often large plants that can receive and treat many gallons (liters) of wastewater each day. A process of several steps is used to remove the solid materials and convert them to sludge. Sludge may be dried or composted. Some sludge is placed in sanitary landfills.

Wastewater treatment plants may produce biosolids. *Biosolids* are the dried remains of the wastewater treatment process. They may be used as organic fertilizer. Biosolids are typically relatively high in the nutrients, nitrogen, phosphorus, and potassium, needed by plants.

17-18. The primary settling facility of a municipal wastewater treatment system.

17-19. A pile of biosolids at a wastewater treatment facility.

The water from a wastewater treatment plant is *effluent*. It is disposed of in streams, lakes, or other natural bodies of water. Effluent can be released only if it does not alter the natural water in the stream or lake. In some cases, effluent is reused, such as in irrigation.

Commercial Systems

Factories that produce large amounts of wastewater usually have facilities for treating the water. These may be lagoons, ponds, or tanks. Many food processing plants have lagoons. This is because large amounts of water are needed to process food. The water is used to wash the products and keep them clean. In doing so, the wastewater picks up particles of food as well as dirt. Water containing these materials must be treated before it is released.

HAZARDOUS WASTE

How hazardous waste is disposed of depends on the nature of the waste materials. In some cases, specially designed landfills are used. In other cases, the wastes are placed in drums and stored. Incineration is used to dispose of some hazardous wastes, such as fuels that have been contaminated. Hazardous wastes containing toxins may undergo a process that removes the toxic substances.

Hazardous wastes should not be disposed of with garbage. For example, unused paint should not be put into garbage. Pesticide containers and small batteries should not be put in garbage. Check with the health department in your local area on the disposal of hazardous materials from the home.

REVIEWING

MAIN IDEAS

Waste is unused or discarded material. Many activities in human life create wastes.

Wastes are of three groups: solid, wastewater, and hazardous. Solid waste is garbage, refuse, and other material. Wastewater is used water that contains suspended solid matter or other substances that have altered its state. Hazardous waste is waste that is potentially dangerous to the environment and human health. The hazards include pollution, health dangers, pests, and safety hazards.

Waste is classified by sources as domestic, commercial, medical, municipal, industrial, construction, agricultural, and nuclear. Wastes from these sources must be disposed of properly.

Most solid wastes are disposed of in landfills. Some are incinerated and others may be recycled or reclaimed. Proper procedures must be followed with each of these.

Wastewater is treated in home septic tank systems, municipal systems, or commercial systems. The goal is to prepare the water for release by fully or partially reconditioning it.

Hazardous waste is disposed of following procedures appropriate for the material. Follow health and environmental regulations. Never put hazardous materials into garbage.

QUESTIONS

Answer the following questions using complete sentences and correct spelling.

1. What are the major kinds of solid waste? Briefly explain each and give examples.
2. What are the three major types of wastewater?
3. What are hazardous wastes?
4. What hazards do wastes pose? List five and briefly explain each.
5. What are the sources of wastes? What are the major components of each source?
6. What are the ways of disposing of solid waste?
7. What is a landfill? How does a landfill work?

8. What are the ways of disposing of wastewater?

9. What are biosolids? How are they useful?

10. What major criterion determines the way to dispose of hazardous wastes?

EVALUATING

Match the term with the correct definition. Write the letter by the term in the blank provided.

a. effluent
b. solid waste
c. refuse
d. garbage

e. wastewater
f. hazardous waste
g. landfill
h. leachate

i. septic tank
j. waste

_____ 1. Solid material discarded from a kitchen.

_____ 2. Unused or discarded materials.

_____ 3. Water from a treatment plant.

_____ 4. Wastes that do not dissolve in water.

_____ 5. Used water that contains suspended solid materials or dissolved matter.

_____ 6. A container in the ground that receives wastewater.

_____ 7. Anything that is discarded because it is useless or worthless.

_____ 8. The liquid from a landfill.

_____ 9. A waste that is potentially dangerous to the environment and human health.

_____ 10. A place dug into the ground for permanently disposing of wastes.

EXPLORING

1. Make a field trip to a sanitary landfill or wastewater treatment plant. Have the manager explain how the facility operates and the roles that citizens should assume to help the facility function properly. Prepare a written report on your findings.

2. Invite a representative of the local health department to serve as a resource person and discuss the design of a home septic tank system.

3. Make a study of the wastes produced by your school. Classify the wastes as solid waste, wastewater, and hazardous waste. Determine how the wastes are now disposed of and recommend improvements in the practices that are used. Prepare an oral report for the class on your findings. Also, share a summary of your findings with the school administrator. (This activity is best carried out by a team of three to five students.)

18

OUTDOOR RECREATION

Many people enjoy using natural resources for recreation. The fresh air, exercise, and appeal of the outdoors makes being outside enjoyable. The beauty of nature is appealing to many people!

There are so many wonderful things to see and do in the outdoors. With a little effort, we can enjoy our time outdoors much more. We can enjoy the outdoors but not damage it. We can look, experience, and enjoy and leave it in unused condition for the next person. You will be glad the person before you left the area unspoiled.

Understanding the outdoors helps us enjoy being outside more. We know what to expect and how to be prepared. We can also enjoy it even if we cannot walk long distances or be active in hunting or hiking.

18-1. Safety is important in outdoor recreation. (Life jackets are being put on before a water activity.)

OBJECTIVES

This chapter introduces outdoor recreation. It describes the opportunities and responsibilities in using outdoor resources. The following objectives are included:

1. Explain the meaning and kinds of outdoor recreation

2. Distinguish between consumptive and nonconsumptive recreational uses of natural resources

3. Describe how to be a good user of natural resources for outdoor recreation

4. Explain the meaning of nature study

5. Identify places where various outdoor recreation is possible

6. Describe natural cycles in outdoor recreation

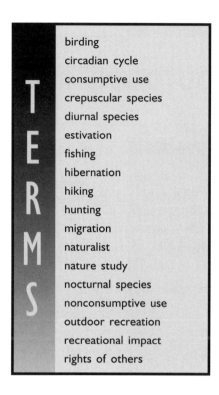

**T
E
R
M
S**

birding
circadian cycle
consumptive use
crepuscular species
diurnal species
estivation
fishing
hibernation
hiking
hunting
migration
naturalist
nature study
nocturnal species
nonconsumptive use
outdoor recreation
recreational impact
rights of others

**National Recreation
and Parks Association
http://www.nrpa.org/**

KINDS OF OUTDOOR RECREATION

Outdoor recreation is any activity that a person voluntarily does in the outdoors for enjoyment and satisfaction. The nature of the activities varies widely. Some activities are passive, meaning that people who do them do not exert much physical effort. Other outdoor recreation is quite active physically. This requires good physical condition and strength.

All outdoor recreation involves contact with and using natural resources. That is the part that people find most enjoyable. The fresh air, appealing scenery, and natural changes create excitement and help people relax and renew themselves.

Several kinds of outdoor recreation are listed here.

- Water recreation—Water recreation is using water for fun. It may involve swimming, using paddle boats, operating powered boats, skiing, and many other activities. Some are done in nonflowing water, such as lakes. Other activities require swiftly flowing water, such as white water rafting. Safety is important. Know the proper way to go about water sports. The ability to swim is essential for safety. Most water recreation is on public lakes, reservoirs, and streams.

- Winter recreation—Winter recreation includes snow skiing, snowmobiling, sledding, ice skating, and similar activities. Some of these are done in improved areas. Others are carried out in rustic settings. Those that involve motor vehicles, such as snowmobiling, require skill in operating the vehicle. Always follow the appropriate safety practices with the winter recreation that you are doing. Be sure the ice is strong before going on a frozen surface.

18-2. Tubing behind a pontoon boat is exciting to some people. (What safety precautions should be followed?)

18-3. Playing hockey on the frozen Truckee River is fun.

■ Birding—***Birding*** is the identification and study of birds as a hobby. It is also known as bird watching. Birding may involve spending many hours observing the movement and life habits of a specific bird species or a wide range of species. Birding can be in city parks as well as isolated rural areas. Binoculars may be used to observe birds some distance away. Cameras may be used to photograph the beauty and activity of birds.

■ Camping—Camping is living in close contact with nature. Tents, camper vehicles, and similar temporary housing may be used. Some camping is in improved campgrounds with running water, picnic tables, and electricity. Other camping may be in unimproved areas. National parks, national forests, state forests, private camp grounds, and others may be used. Some camping facili-

18-4. Tent camping is popular in the Blue Ridge Mountains.

Resource Connection

THE BAG LIMIT

Two duck hunters are standing in shallow water with decoys in the foreground. Do they appear to have enjoyed the hunt? Do you suppose they followed the rules on bag limit?

Bag limit is the number of animals that one person can take in a day or season. The limits are set to protect wildlife and allow more people to be able to hunt ducks. Bag limits are set by law. People who violate them can be arrested and fined. Always follow hunting regulations!

Following the rules on bag limits and other areas of hunting is part of being a "good hunting citizen." It is part of being a good user and respecting the rights of other people. How do you feel about bag limits and hunting? Opinions differ. (Courtesy, Ed Holder, Texas)

ties have nature trails, tour guides, and lectures on various topics of local interest.

- Hiking—**Hiking** is walking in natural areas for pleasure and exercise. It may be on improved trails or in areas without trails. Improved trails may have signs that mark the route of the trail and provide information about the wild plants and animals and the geology of the area. Always stay on trails and avoid snakes, insects, and other hazards.

- Horseback riding—Many people enjoy the interaction with a horse as part of their outdoor recreation. Some people own horses; others rent horses at riding stables. Riding trails are available in many public parks and at private stables. Always choose a horse that is well trained. Know the proper practices in riding. Never abuse a horse. Proper care of the horse is essential.

- Fishing—**Fishing** is capturing wild fish using hooks, nets, or other means. People sometimes differentiate between commercial fishing and sport fishing. Sport fishing is relaxing and enjoyable. Commercial fishing is a large-scale operation that provides fish for canneries, restaurants, and other uses. Sport fishing may be in streams, lakes, oceans, and other bodies of water. In some cases, artificial ponds are opened as fee lakes for fishing. In most areas, a license is needed to sport fish for game species.

18-5. This sport fisher has a nice catch—a 14-pound coho salmon!

18-6. Training in using guns is essential for hunting. (This shows learning how to shoot using a virtual reality system.)

■ Hunting—***Hunting*** is taking animals for recreation and/or food. A gun, rifle, or primitive device, such as a bow and arrow, may be used. Most hunting is on private land made available for hunting. National forests and other government lands may be open for hunting at certain times of the year. Common species hunted include rabbits, deer, geese, squirrels, and quail. Safety is essential. Most hunters use equipment that can injure and kill people and domestic animals.

USES OF NATURAL RESOURCES BASED ON CONSUMPTION

Natural resource use for recreation involves some kind of consumption of the resource. In this case, consuming means that the resource is used in some way. Based on consumption, uses can be classified into two major groups: consumptive and nonconsumptive.

Consumptive use is taking or harvesting natural resources. This includes hunting, fishing, and other activities that remove the natural resource. Some natural resources will reproduce themselves if consumed. For example, hunting should always involve leaving sufficient members of a species for reproduction. For example, squirrels that remain after hunting will reproduce themselves. It is essential to avoid taking too many so a population to reproduce remains. Other resources, such as minerals and gems, will not reproduce. A consumptive use, which has altered the natural streams of our nation, is building dams to harness water power. The nature of the stream is destroyed by this practice.

Nonconsumptive use is using natural resources so they are not used up. Watching, photographing, skiing, hiking, camping, and similar activities do not take natural resources. What a person found is left for the next person to enjoy. Many people use parks for nonconsumptive use of natural resources. An example is a weekend camping trip to a park. The camping area is left in the same condition as it was when you arrived.

18-7. Birding is nonconsumptive outdoor recreation. (Courtesy, U.S. Fish and Wildlife Service)

Parks and national forests have regulations that prohibit the taking of wildflowers, rocks, and other natural materials. Just think: If everyone who visited a park took a rock or wildflower, none would remain after a while for future visitors.

BEING A GOOD USER

Using natural resources for recreation is a meaningful and fun experience to most people. We can be better users if we know what is expected and how we prepare for the experience. We also want to find an appealing place when we arrive or participate. We do not want a place that the previous user damaged!

YOUR IMPACT

Recreational impact is the effect that using natural resources for recreation has upon the resources and the surrounding area. Many things are involved here.

The kind of outdoor recreation determines how impact can occur. Always leave an area in good condition for the next person. Follow the rules for using an area. A few examples: In hiking or riding, stay on trails. (Getting off trails packs the soil and damages plant growth.) With water, travel in areas approved for your use and be sure your equipment is in good condition. (An engine that is not operating properly may produce increased pollution in the water.)

In general, go about outdoor recreation so you leave little or no evidence that you have been there. Avoid damaging natural resources and polluting the environment.

18-8. Cross-country skiing is a winter outdoor activity.

RIGHTS OF OTHERS

Rights of others is a concept to assure opportunity for other people to enjoy a natural resource in a responsible manner. It guides how people go about using natural resources for recreation. "Rights of others" refers to doing outdoor recreation in a reasonable and proper manner. The freedoms of other people should not be trampled on. Likewise, other people should not interfere with your freedom to properly use natural resources for recreation. All users should do the proper thing!

People in outdoor recreation should respect the rights of others. Be courteous to other people. Do not damage the resources. Leave outdoor areas in the same or a better condition than you found them. Follow all rules. Keep an area clean. Do not pollute the environment.

Here are a few principles to follow in using outdoor areas:

■ Know the regulations on using an area.

Career Profile

OUTDOOR EDUCATOR

An outdoor educator teaches about wildlife, geology, and ecology. The work involves planning programs, organizing groups, setting up facilities, and speaking to groups. Visual aids and real things may be used. The teaching may be inside or on trails, in outdoor theaters, and along streambanks.

Outdoor educators may have college degrees in wildlife, environmental science, or a closely related area. Some may have masters degrees. Those involved with research and universities may have doctoral degrees in a related area of education. Practical experience working in the outdoors and a strong appreciation of nature are beneficial.

Jobs are found throughout the United States. Some are with parks while others are with local conservation groups, schools systems, and state agencies. This shows an outdoor educator teaching children about the forest floor. (Courtesy, U.S. Fish and Wildlife Service)

18-9. This sign indicates that a trail is for hiking. (No bicycles, horse riding, fires, nor camping are allowed.)

■ Respect the rights of landowners. (Stay off of private property unless you have permission to be there.)

■ If required, pay the proper user fees.

■ Do not play loud music in wilderness areas.

■ Place all trash in the proper containers.

■ Stay on trails and in designated areas.

■ Operate boats, snowmobiles, and other equipment properly.

■ Practice safety rules, including wearing hunter orange when hunting.

■ Do not carve in trees or write on rocks.

■ Always be considerate of other people.

PREPARE FOR YOUR ACTIVITY

Preparing for outdoor recreation can be fun. Get all of the information, equipment, and supplies ahead of time. In some cases, a reservation is needed well in advance of a planned activity. Planning depends on the kind of outdoor recreation.

Here are a few of the things to do ahead of time:

■ Educate yourself about the activity. (For example, know the laws on hunting and fishing.)

■ Make reservations and plans well ahead of time. (With some activities, a detailed trail plan may be needed.)

■ Leave an itinerary (schedule) with a responsible person who is not going along.

■ With some activities, physical condition is important. (An example is mountain hiking—be sure to develop stamina and strength ahead of time.)

■ Check the weather forecast. (Bad weather may mean that the activity should be postponed.)

■ Get the needed permits and/or licenses.

■ Be sure the equipment is in good condition and that you have the needed supplies. (Many things are included here such as making sure that the lights on the boat trailer work properly.)

■ Dress appropriately and use the proper footwear for the activity.

■ Carry first-aid supplies and, with some activities, maps and compasses. (Sun screen and insect repellant should be included.)

■ Have needed food and water.

LEAVE IN GOOD ORDER

Always leave the area you have been using in good condition. Many things are involved depending on the kind of outdoor recreation. Here are a few examples:

■ Put trash in the proper place.

18-10. All of the supplies and equipment needed for fishing are being loaded.

■ Use fires only as approved and be sure to extinguish a campfire before leaving. (All evidence of fire should be gone. Put water on the burning material. Any heat is a sign that something may still be burning that could set a huge forest fire.)

■ Do not dig in the ground.

■ Do not cut trees and shrubs.

■ Do not leave picnic tables and other equipment out of place.

■ Set up camping equipment at least 200 feet (65m) from streambanks or lake shores.

■ Follow the established schedule for leaving.

You want to find an area in good condition when you use it. You should leave it that way for the next person. Be responsible for what you do!

18-11. Canoeing is popular outdoor recreation in some areas.

NATURE STUDY

Nature study is learning about things in nature. It deals with the world around us. Nature study can be carried out in cities as well as remote areas. Cities have gardens, parks, museums, and nature areas. The countryside has wooded areas, streams, swamps, and forests. Sometimes, people go into remote areas far removed from city life. They may hike into valleys or up mountains to get the opportunity to see nature in unique ways.

Some people especially enjoy watching animal wildlife as part of nature study. Others enjoy wildflowers and geological formations. Regardless, never take flowers, rocks, or other living or nonliving things from a nature study area.

18-12. Sun screen is needed for many outdoor activities.

NATURALISTS

A *naturalist* is a person who studies nature. Naturalists learn about living and nonliving things and the relationships between them. Naturalists often have education and experience with nature. They know what to look for and how to do so in a safe manner. Many naturalists keep records of their observations. Some even prepare sketches or paintings of what they see.

Many people have had important roles as naturalists. Some helped influence government policies. Other naturalists helped portray the beauty of nature.

A naturalist who had a major impact on preserving many areas of the western United States is John Muir (1838-1914). He promoted the protection of land areas. His leadership led to the formation of Yosemite and Sequoia National Parks.

Another naturalist is John James Audubon (1785-1851). Audubon was especially interested in birds. He made numerous paintings of birds in their natural settings. Many of the paintings were made in Louisiana. Today, the Audubon Society promotes the conservation of natural resources.

PARTICIPATION

Many people enjoy observing nature, including wildlife. The U.S. Fish and Wildlife Service estimates that 74 million people over age 16 participate in some form of wildlife observation activity each year. The number is increasing each year.

Nature study is relatively simple and inexpensive. No special licenses or permits are needed except to enter parks. People of all ages can enjoy and participate in nature study.

18-13. Wading along the beach can be entertaining.

Information about nature is endless. Get brochures and books about the natural resources in the area you plan to visit. People who are informed have a better appreciation of what they are seeing. Enjoying nature is easy to do.

WHERE OUTDOOR RECREATION IS FOUND

Interests in outdoor recreation vary widely. Once people know their interests, they are ready to use the outdoors. Select a location that has what is desired. Some people want to see streams and waterfalls. Others want to see wild animals, wildflowers, or rock formations. Travel is sometimes needed to get to good places, but it is not always necessary. For example, a local wooded area or park is a good place to see birds.

People who want activities involving water will need to be near streams, lakes, or oceans. Those who want recreation on land will need to locate where their interests can be met.

18-14. With luck, it might be possible to see a river otter with a captured fish. (Courtesy, U.S. Fish and Wildlife Service)

TERRESTRIAL AREAS

Places for land-based recreation vary with the climate, geography, and topography. These areas can be classified by the kinds of vegetation that naturally grows in an area. The kind of vegetation is influenced by water, elevation, and temperature of the area. Vegetative growth attracts animals and creates appealing surroundings.

■ Deciduous Forests—Deciduous forests have special appeal during seasons of the year. Trees shed their leaves in the fall. Brilliant colors make this a popular time for "leaf looking." Some animal species prefer deciduous forests. The dominant tree species are oaks, maples, hickories, poplars, and gums. These trees produce acorns and other seeds and fruits that wildlife uses as food. Common mammal species in deciduous forests include white-tail deer, rac-

18-15. Black trumpet mushrooms were found in a deciduous forest. (Courtesy, Stephen J. Lee)

coons, black bear, turkeys, and opossums. Common bird species include owls, hawks, woodpeckers, vultures, bobwhite, and numerous songbirds. Reptiles include snakes, and lizards. Wildflowers include magnolias, dogwoods, redbuds, rhododendrons, jasmine, mountain laurel, and numerous annuals. Spring is a popular time for observing wildflowers.

■ Coniferous Forests—Coniferous forests have trees that are evergreen. The trees typically have needles and produce cones. Species include hemlock, pines, and firs. A few of the animals in the deciduous areas are also found in coniferous areas, such as white-tail deer. This is especially true when pockets of deciduous forests are among the conifers. Common mammals include moose, lynx, timber wolves, and flying squirrels. Mountain areas have bighorn sheep, mountain goats, and cougars. Birds include blue grouse, mountain chickadees, northern goshawks, bald ea-

18-16. A barn owl is resting in a pine tree in a coniferous forest. (Courtesy, U.S. Fish and Wildlife Service)

gles, ospreys, and some 200 other species. Reptiles include snakes, lizards, and turtles, though some are not seen that frequently.

- Tundra—In the United States, tundra is found at high elevations on mountains and in Alaska. An Alpine habitat (mountain tundra) may have musk oxen, caribou, tundra wolves, snowy owls, and arctic fox. Migratory ducks and geese are found in some areas in the summer. Bighorn sheep and mountain goats are found at high elevations in the Rocky Mountains. Small animals and tender vegetation are found in tundra.

- Pacific Coast—The Pacific Coast area includes many species of wildlife. It extends along the Pacific Coast from San Francisco to Alaska, including the Puget Sound along the Washington coast. High rainfall and moderate climate support wildlife. Trees include firs, redwoods, western hemlocks, red cedars, and spruce. Black-tail deer, black bear, cougars, and flying squirrels are in the area. Birds include red-breasted nuthatches, brown creepers, common crows, blue grouses, and others. Timber wolves and grizzly bears are found in a few locations along the Pacific Coast.

- Deserts—Deserts are areas with little moisture. Deserts may be cool climate or hot and warm climate. Cool climate deserts have many kinds of shrubs while cactus grows in the warmer areas. The shrub areas have junipers, cottonwoods, and ponderosa and lodgepole pines. Willows and aspen are found in canyons with moisture. Hot desert areas have mesquite, creosote bush, cacti, yucca, and native bunch grasses. Common mammals in the shrub-covered desert include mule deer, jackrabbits, badgers, coyotes, pronghorn antelope, and white-tail deer. Mammals in the hot desert are coyotes, jackrabbits, kit foxes, and badgers. Birds in cooler areas include golden eagles, prairie falcons, and hawks. Migratory birds may spend part of the year in areas of the shrub-covered desert. Birds in the hot desert include burrow-

18-17. The desert tortoise is found in some desert areas. (Courtesy, Ross Haley, U.S. Fish and Wildlife Service)

ing owls, prairie falcons, and roadrunners. Common desert reptiles are Gila monsters, sidewinders, and rattlesnakes.

■ Grasslands—Much of the grassland area, or prairie, is in the midwestern United States. Many native grasses have been destroyed, though some remain. Animal wildlife may be found in areas bordering desert and wooded land. Mammals in the prairie include mule deer, white-tail deer, coyotes, prairie dogs, and black-footed ferret. Common birds include prairie chickens, hawks, sharp-tailed grouse, and migratory birds, such as ducks, geese, and swans.

■ Tropical—The United States has limited tropical areas. Southern Florida and small areas of other southern states and Hawaii have tropical areas. Hawaiian wildlife differs markedly from that of North America. Most of the tropical areas have hardwood trees, including oaks and cypress. Tropical areas also have palmetto and mangrove trees. Some of the land area may be covered with water part or all of the year. Reptiles include alligators, diamondback rattlesnakes, and lizards. Mammals include white-tail deer, black bear, bobcats, and cougars. Birds include those with long legs for wading in water, such as egrets, ibises, and storks.

AQUATIC AREAS

Activities with water-based recreation are in places where the appropriate water is found. Streams, lakes, rivers, oceans, and other natural bodies of water offer recreational opportunities. Some water-based recreation is found in the terrestrial areas. A good example is trout fishing. Streams with good trout fishing have rapidly flowing cold water. Large trees along the stream bank shade the water.

18-18. The great blue heron is an aquatic bird that is interesting to watch. (Courtesy, Lynn Starnes, U.S. Fish and Wildlife Service)

■ Freshwater—Freshwater streams and lakes have little or no salt. They are popular for fishing, boating, and related recreation. In some cases, artificial reservoirs are good sources for recreation. Climate and water quality are important. Some activities require warm water; others require cool water. Some activities require clear water and others can be done in muddy water.

■ Saltwater—Saltwater is in the oceans, seas, and a few lakes, such as the Great Salt Lake in Utah. Most saltwater is in the oceans. People in coastal areas have access to saltwater. Some recreation is along the shallow shoreline and other activities are in deep water.

NATURAL CYCLES IN OUTDOOR RECREATION

The time of day and the season of the year are important in some outdoor recreation activities. For example, snow-based activities must be done in the winter. In some places the season may begin in the late fall and last into early spring.

People who "watch," hunt, fish, and do other activities involving seasons and cycles need to be aware of what the cycles are and how they can be used. Animals, for example, follow daily and seasonal cycles.

DAILY CYCLES

Daily cycles are known as circadian cycles. A *circadian cycle* is the daily living cycle that is repeated every 24 hours. Cycles tend to be reasonably predictable. For example, an animal may feed at a certain time during the day. It will follow a similar schedule each day. These cycles are referred to as the "daily biological clock."

18-19. Mule deer are crepuscular animals. (Courtesy, U.S. Fish and Wildlife Service)

The times of the day when species are active varies. Those active during the day are *diurnal species.* They may be out just about any time during daylight hours, such as songbirds. A *nocturnal species* is one that is active at night or when it is dark, such as the owl. A *crepuscular species* is one that is active at dusk and dawn, such as deer.

Here are a few examples of daily feeding cycles:

■ Dawn (early morning) and dusk (late afternoon)—deer, squirrels, and wild turkeys

- Midday—hawks, vultures, and woodpeckers

- Night—skunks, bats, owls, fox, and some deer

- All day—most songbirds and occasionally deer

- Warm days—reptiles and amphibians (These species are active only when the air and ground temperatures are warm enough. On cooler days, they may be seen sunning on logs, rocks, or other places.)

SEASONAL CYCLES

Animal species often have seasonal cycles. These are based on the time of the year. Both temperature and number of daylight hours are important.

Hibernation

Hibernation is a time of seclusion in a safe environment when the weather is cold. Being out in the weather could pose a threat to the well-being of an animal. Hibernation keeps animals safe from bad weather.

During hibernation, animals are inactive. Examples of animals that hibernate include bear, snakes, turtles, salamanders, bats, groundhogs, and frogs. These species prepare for hibernation by storing body fat in the fall. Mammals that hibernate often grow thicker coats of fur prior to winter.

Estivation

Some animals escape from hot weather by estivation. *Estivation* is the inactivity of animals during warm weather. Animals do so to escape the high temperatures and keep their bodies cool. Lizards and other animals estivate to conserve body moisture and keep cool. Most species that estivate are found in hot desert areas.

Migration

Migration is the movement of individuals from one region or continent to another to have a suitable environment for life processes. Most bird species migrate. Large numbers of ducks, geese, and songbirds migrate. In North America, they travel south in the winter to escape cold weather and return north in the summer to nest and raise their young. Their travel is during the spring and fall.

18-20. Geese on a long migratory flight. (Courtesy, U.S. Fish and Wildlife Service)

People sometimes judge the arrival of spring by the return of migratory birds. Blue birds, cardinals, and robins are among the first birds to return in the late winter or early spring. The approach of cold weather in the fall is predicted by the flight of ducks and geese to the south. During migration, birds have stopping places for rest and feeding. People who want to "watch" can often see birds at these places.

Aquatic animals also migrate. Examples are the various species of whales. Whales may travel hundreds of miles. Whales may spend the summer off the Alaska coast and winter off the coast of southern California.

REVIEWING

MAIN IDEAS

Outdoor recreation is any activity people voluntarily do that involves using resources in the outdoors. Many kinds of activities are popular. Examples of outdoor recreation include water and winter recreation, birding, camping, hiking, horseback riding, fishing, and hunting.

The use of natural resources may be consumptive or nonconsumptive. Consumptive use is taking or using a resource so it is no longer available. Nonconsumptive use is using resources so they are not used up.

Good users of natural resources for outdoor recreation try to avoid an impact that affects the quality of the resources. They respect the rights of other people. Full and safe enjoyment begins with planning outdoor recreational activities. Outdoor areas are always left in good condition for the next user.

Nature study is an important part of outdoor recreation. It is observing and learning about nature. People who actively pursue nature study are known as naturalists.

Outdoor recreation may be in terrestrial or aquatic areas. Terrestrial areas are shaped by elevation, temperature, and precipitation. Aquatic areas are shaped by the amount of salt in the water, water temperature, and water movement.

Natural cycles are important in some kinds of outdoor recreation. Daily and seasonal cycles should be considered.

QUESTIONS

Answer the following questions using complete sentences and correct spelling:

1. What is outdoor recreation?

2. What are eight kinds of outdoor recreation?

3. What are the two major groups of outdoor recreational uses of natural resources based on consumption?

4. What is recreational impact?

5. Why are the rights of others important in outdoor recreation?

6. What should be considered in respecting the rights of others?

7. Why is preparation for outdoor recreation important?

8. What are three things to do when you leave an outdoor recreation area?

9. What is nature study?

10. Where is outdoor recreation found? What are the major land-based places for outdoor recreation?

11. Why are natural cycles important in outdoor recreation?

12. What circadian and seasonal cycles are important?

EVALUATING

Match the term with the correct definition. Write the letter by the term in the blank provided.

a. estivation   e. birding   i. recreational impact
b. circadian cycle f. hiking   j. naturalist
c. nocturnal species g. outdoor recreation
d. fishing   h. hunting

_____ 1. A person who studies nature.
_____ 2. The inactivity of animals during warm weather.
_____ 3. A species of animal that is active at night.
_____ 4. Killing animals for pleasure and/or food.
_____ 5. Capturing fish for sport or food.
_____ 6. The daily living cycle of animals.
_____ 7. The study of birds as a hobby.
_____ 8. The effect that using natural resources for recreation has on the resources and the surrounding area.
_____ 9. Any activity that people voluntarily do outdoors for enjoyment and satisfaction.
_____ 10. Walking in natural areas for fund and exercise.

EXPLORING

1. Make a tour to a park or wildlife refuge. Hike on trails in the area. Observe the plants and animals that are present. Note the geology and streams in the area. Classify the area as to the type of terrestrial area based on the vegetation that you observe. Prepare a report on your observations.

2. Organize your class into groups of three to five individuals. Plan an outdoor recreational activity. Identify and agree on an activity that your group would like to have. Explore the impact of your proposed activity. Identify how the rights of others could be involved. Prepare a plan for the activity. Identify the actions needed to leave the area in good order. Prepare a report on your recreational activity.

3. Invite a naturalist to serve as a resource person in class. Have the person discuss the plants, animals, and other natural features of the local area.

19

PROPERTY OWNERSHIP AND RESPONSIBILITIES

What material things do you have? You may name clothing, a bicycle, or a pet. Do you consider yourself as the owner of these things? You have some things that you consider to be yours. You will protect these things and try to prevent losing them. You are also want to use these things properly and keep them in good condition.

People have different opinions about ownership. Who owns natural resources? The answer is not easy. A good example is air. Does anyone own the air? Who owns the air in your bedroom at home or in your lungs? If you come up with an answer, share it with others.

Knowing a few basics about ownership and property will help you understand the complex issues that are involved. You will also develop an appreciation of ownership as we have it in the United States.

19-1. Putting up a posted sign to discourage trespassing on land.

OBJECTIVES

This chapter covers the basics of property ownership. It includes responsibilities that go along with ownership and how to protect property. The following objectives are included:

1. Explain the meaning of ownership and property

2. Distinguish between the kinds of ownership

3. Relate the history and basis of private property

4. Identify the rights and responsibilities of owners

5. Describe the protection of private property

T E R M S

amortization
buyer
deed
eminent domain
legal title
mineral rights
mortgage
ownership
personal property
posting
private property
property
public property
real property
rent
riparian right
seller
tax
trespassing
zoning

American Land Rights Association
http://www.landrights.org/

OWNERSHIP AND PROPERTY

Ownership is possessing something. What is owned belongs to an individual. Individuals may have the legal right of possession. A written document may give the title of ownership of property, such as the title to an automobile or land.

19-2. Land may have open areas for pasture and other uses. (This shows a flock of goats.) (Courtesy, Agricultural Research Service, USDA)

PROPERTY

"That belongs to me! It is my property. I worked hard and saved money to buy it."

People refer to what they own as their property. *Property* is what a person owns. It is the material resources that belong to a person. People obtain property in various ways. To buy or inherit property is legal. To steal or take another person's property without their consent is illegal.

Owners have certain rights to use property. They may buy

19-3. Land can be used for farming or other suitable purposes. (Courtesy, Deere & Company)

and sell property within the law. Things that are illegal are not bought and sold within the law. Having them is against the law, with a common example being illegal drugs.

BUYING AND SELLING

Property rights allow people to buy, own, and sell property. In most cases, the price for buying and selling property is agreed upon by the seller and buyer. A *seller* is the person who owns property and wishes to sell it. A *buyer* is a person who wishes to acquire property from a seller. Selling involves transferring the title of ownership to another individual. Buying is to acquire the possession of property.

Buying and selling involves exchanging something of value for the property. In most cases, money is paid for the property. In some cases, other property of value may be exchanged for it. For example, a buyer may exchange 50 acres of farm land with a seller who has a house on a lot in town. Money was not involved in the exchange.

In buying, the buyer may borrow money to pay for the property. The money is borrowed from a bank, mortgage company, individual, or other source. The lender provides the money in exchange for a mortgage. A *mortgage* is the conditional transfer of the title to the property to the lender as security for repayment of the loan. An amortization of the payments is made. *Amortization* is the scheduling of payments over a period of time (usually years) so the principal, interest, and other charges are gradually paid. Once

19-4. Land may have wildlife, such as turkeys.

the loan is fully repaid, the buyer is given clear title to the property by the lender.

KINDS OF PROPERTY

In general, there are two kinds of property: personal and real. Most individuals own personal property. Some individuals own real property.

Personal property is property that an individual owns and uses to satisfy needs and wants. It may be used in daily living and work. Examples of personal property include furniture, clothing, jewelry, and bicycles. Personal property also includes stocks, bonds, and other evidences of interest, such as ownership in a mutual fund. The notebook you may be using in class is personal property!

Personal property may be rented (leased) or lent. School textbooks are an example. School-issued textbooks are property of the school and not of the individuals who are using them. In some schools, students pay rental fees for books. In other schools, the books are issued without a fee to students. The

19-5. Harvest-size timber increases the value of land.

owner loaned you the property for your use. You are expected to return the property after use in good condition.

Real property is land, improvements to the land, and buildings permanently attached to the land. The land may vary widely. Some land may be quality land for growing crops. Other land may be hilly and covered with trees or in a swamp and covered with water most of the year. The buildings on land are of many kinds. They may be single-family houses, apartment buildings, businesses, factories, and recreation facilities. As real property, land also includes improvements, such as fences, ponds, and terraces. It includes the native trees as well as the tree farms that are growing on it. Wildlife that lives on the land goes with the land when it is bought or sold.

The natural resources on the land are typically sold with it. Trees, springs, minerals, soil, and other resources are considered in establishing a price. In some cases, sellers may hold a portion or all of the mineral rights. *Mineral rights* refer to ownership of minerals that may be on or under the surface. This means that the buyer profits only to the extent that ownership of the mineral rights has been transferred. Of course, minerals may never be located on the property. Oil and other fossil fuels are often treated as minerals.

TAXATION

Both real and personal property may be taxed. *Tax* is the payment of money people make to finance the cost of government. Property taxes are the taxes collected on real and personal property. States and local governments vary in the rate of tax charged and what is taxed. Most all local governments have real property taxes.

Individuals who own homes, farms, businesses, and other real property must pay the tax assessed on the property. The assessment is usually based in some way on the appraised market value of the property. Tax assessors determine the value of property for tax purposes. Most real property is valued for tax purposes below the market value of the property.

If the tax is not paid in a timely manner, the owner is penalized or the property can be seized over time. Seized property is sold by the government to recoup the taxes that were not paid. Laws on the sale of property for delinquent taxes vary among the states. It is typical for real property to be sold after a period of 5 to 10 years for unpaid taxes. The property is sold to the highest bidder and often at a public site, such as the "courthouse steps." Local newspapers publish a list of property with delinquent taxes each year.

KINDS OF PROPERTY OWNERSHIP

The two main kinds of property ownership are private and public. The property may be either real or personal items.

PRIVATE PROPERTY

Private property is owned by an individual or a business. Ownership of property may be shared by two or more individuals, such as a partnership.

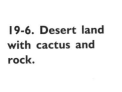
19-6. Desert land with cactus and rock.

Married individuals may also jointly own private property. Corporations, which are legal entities, may own property. How ownership occurs is based upon the laws of the state where the property is located or the owner lives.

A *legal title* is the right to property. It indicates who owns the property. The title is specified in a written document. Titles are most often used with real property, such as farm land or residential property. Titles may also be provided for motor vehicles, valuable gems, and other more expensive items.

A legal title should fully and accurately describe the property when ownership is transferred from one individual to another. The document for real property is often known as a deed. A *deed* is a prepared legal document that is filed with the appropriate offices of the local government.

A question that frequently arises is: What does a person have who owns property? Do they have the right to use the property as they wish? How far above the ground into the air and how deep below the ground does a landowner own? What is the relationship between the overall welfare of society and the rights of private owners? Some of the freedoms people have in the United States are related to private property and ownership.

Owners may delegate the use of their property to other people. This is known as renting or leasing. *Rent* is the payment made by a person to a property owner in return for use of the property. The person who rents the property is granted certain rights to use it. The owner retains responsibility for paying taxes and some liability associated with the property. Rental agreements should always be in writing and signed by the owner and the renter. The agreement should spell out the use to be made of the property, such as the renter's access to hunt game on the land.

PUBLIC PROPERTY

Public property is the land and other material items owned by government agencies. Local governments own city halls, jails, parks, and school facilities. State governments own office buildings, prisons, colleges, and highways. The federal government owns buildings, land, waterways, military bases, and other property.

How do people relate to public property? Overall, people are given access to most government property. Some restrictions apply. Access to offices dealing with national security may be restricted. National parks may have rules about use and charge user fees. In some cases, tracts of land may be rented to private citizens. An example is the rangeland of the western United States.

19-7. The Chattahoochee National Forest is public land.

Taxes are not assessed on public property. In some cases, the federal government may compensate counties for lost tax revenue where large amounts of land are in forests, military bases, and other uses. For example, millions of dollars are paid to county governments each year by the National Forest Service. It is based on the notion that the land would be taxed if it were privately owned. (An earlier chapter dealt with public rangelands.)

THE HISTORY AND BASIS FOR PROPERTY OWNERSHIP

Property ownership is granted by The Constitution of the United States. The Fifth Amendment to the Constitution guarantees Americans the right to own private property. The right to own property is a basic freedom. Our economic system is based on private ownership.

OWNERSHIP PROTECTION

Citizens are offered protection as property owners. This applies to actions by individuals and all levels of government.

Another individual cannot take away what a person owns. This includes both personal and real property. To do so would be theft, which is punishable by law.

Resource Connection

THE CONSTITUTION AND PRIVATE PROPERTY

The Fifth Amendment to The Constitution of the United States provides the right for people to own private property. This amendment states:

"No person shall be deprived of life, liberty, or property without due process of law...nor shall private property be taken for public use, without just compensation."

Many issues revolve around private ownership of land. Some people feel that actions by government agencies to protect wetlands, wildlife areas, and other properties may infringe upon private landowners. Other people feel that land use regulations infringe on the rights of landowners.

What do you think? This is a good issue for you to study. Involve your friends in a debate. Interview government and agricultural officials about the issues of private property.

The government cannot seize property without cause nor without paying for it. Exceptions to the seizure of property exist. Many states have laws that allow seizure of the private property of an individual who is illegally hunting. For example, the pickup truck an individual uses at night to shine in the eyes of game animals so they can be blinded and killed can be seized. This practice is sometimes called "headlighting." Guns and other property the individual has present at the time of the incident can also be taken. Many states have similar laws related to individuals who are involved in selling illegal drugs.

In order to build roads, military bases, water reservoirs, and other government facilities, the government needs land. Individuals who refuse to sell can be forced to do so by eminent domain.

EMINENT DOMAIN

Eminent domain is the right of the government to convert private property to the use of the public. Proper compensation is required by the Consti-

19-8. Land to build the Hollywood Freeway was obtained from private owners.

tution. Court action is usually involved to assure that the rights of individuals are being protected.

Here is an example where eminent domain would be used: Suppose a new highway is being planned. Land would be needed. The agency responsible for roads would survey and plan the route for the road. The land would be bought from private owners. If an owner refused, the land could be taken by eminent domain proceedings. The justification is that the overall benefit of the road to society is greater than the benefit of the property remaining in private ownership.

Private owners are compensated for land taken by eminent domain. Issues frequently arise over the amount of compensation. Landowners sometimes feel that they are not receiving adequate payment for the land.

19-9. A variance request sign on property that is not in compliance with zoning and building codes.

LAND USE REGULATIONS

19-10. Zoning usually restricts building a carnival next to your quiet home!

Land use regulations apply to how land may be used. It is sometimes known as zoning. Many issues exist today over restrictions on land use.

Zoning is a process for controlling the use of real property. The regulations restrict how land may be used as well as the kinds of structures that may be placed on it. The purpose of zoning is to provide quality environments for living and working.

Zoning promotes orderly growth and development. Cities have used zoning for many years to specify how land may be used. Some land is for single-family residential areas and other land is for apartments. Businesses, factories, and other uses may be designated to certain areas.

Zoning is increasingly being used with rural and agricultural lands. It may impact the extraction of minerals and other natural resources from the land. Land uses that interfere with the rights of other people are restricted. An example is regulating where animals can be raised. Odors and other pollutants from animal enterprises are often objectionable. Zoning is an attempt to keep animal production away from residential and commercial areas.

OWNER RESPONSIBILITIES

Property owners have responsibilities for what they own. This includes both personal and real property.

Here are a few common responsibilities.

■ Pay taxes—Owners are responsible for paying taxes on property.

19-11. The owner next to this home did not keep the lawn maintained and created an eyesore in the neighborhood.

■ Maintain property—Owners are responsible for keeping property in good condition. This may include cutting weeds and grass, keeping fences and buildings in good condition, and properly disposing of wastes. Property maintenance may include building fences to keep livestock from straying. Trash and junk cars are prohibited from being visible on property in many places. This helps keep our communities more attractive and appealing.

■ Use within the law—Property must be used for purposes that are legal. This includes uses that meet land use restrictions set by zoning ordinances. The hunting of game animals on private land by the owner or other individuals should be within the law. Property cannot be used to produce nor store illegal materials. An example is growing illegal plants. Drug enforcement agents can come onto property. A search warrant from a judge may be needed. They can seize and destroy illegal plants and materials used to grow them. The owner or producer can be arrested under provisions of the law.

■ Liability protection—Many landowners buy liability insurance to protect themselves against losses to other people. This insurance is especially important if other people are regularly on the property, as with a recreational sport fishing lake.

■ Nuisance control—Owners are to use land for purposes that do not pose nuisances in the surrounding area. A nuisance is any use that threatens the safety, health, or morals of a community. For example, waste disposal sites are sometimes viewed as undesirable in a community because they may harbor disease and pests.

■ Environmental damage—Owners should not carry out activities on their land that would threaten well being on other land. For example, improperly using pesticides poses a threat to neighboring land and can pollute air and water.

■ Follow codes—Most areas today have codes or standards for the construction of buildings and other property improvements. Construction may require a building permit. Landowners should always follow the codes and obtain the needed permits. Buildings should meet electrical, plumbing, and other appropriate standards.

19-12. Any structures built on land should comply with building codes.

■ Water rights—The use of water resources on land is often considered part of land ownership. Water rights are particularly important in dry land areas. In general, individuals can dig ponds and use the water from ponds as they wish. Individuals are restricted from using water from streams and natural lakes. Land ownership usually has riparian rights. A *riparian right* is the

19-13. The owner of land on both sides of this stream has the riparian right to use necessary water for livestock and the home. (Excessive water cannot be removed from the stream. The rate of stream flow leaving the property should be approximately the same as when the stream entered the property.)

right of an owner to use water from a body that is adjacent to the land. The amount is restricted to what is needed for domestic consumption and livestock. In dry areas, water rights are quite important in gaining access to irrigation water supplies.

TRESPASSING AND PROTECTING PROPERTY

Landowners protect their property and limit its use to authorized individuals. In the process, they are also attempting to reduce liability for losses that unauthorized individuals may have on the land.

TRESPASSING

Trespassing is entering the property of another person without permission to do so. The person who intrudes has violated the private rights of the owner.

People who trespass often damage property. In the first place, their presence on the property is illegal. They may cut wire fences, shoot livestock, and dump trash on the land. In some cases, trespassers start fires that burn valuable timber and pasture land. They may also take wildlife and living plants for their own use.

A general rule is to never go onto another person's property without written permission. Always contact the person well ahead of time to ask permission. Landowners have the right to say "no." In most cases, landowners need

19-14. A fence marks the location of property, confines animals, and protects from trespassing.

to say "no" and restrict access to their land from a legal perspective. Even though a person may be trespassing, the landowner still has certain liability in case of injury or harm to the trespasser. Who is responsible if a trespasser is injured in a fall or is attacked by a fighting bull? Remember, a trespasser has no more right to be on another person's farm or hunting land than the owner of the land has the right to trespass in your home!

PROTECTING PROPERTY

Several approaches can be used to protect property from trespassing. Some may work better than others. With any approach, no laws should be violated.

Posting

Posting is the practice of forbidding trespassing on land. State laws vary on the meaning of posting and the process that is to be followed.

In general, posting involves putting up "posted" signs on land where trespassing is forbidden. The signs should be placed on property boundaries and at regular distances apart. The wording should be large enough for easy reading from a distance.

A legal announcement may be published in the paper indicating that the land is posted. The number of times the announcement is run and the wording of the notice must meet state requirements.

Posting is used to discourage any form of trespassing. This includes hunting, wildflower picking, and wild seed and nut harvesting. It also includes damaging or taking vegetable and fruit crops. The landowner is protecting his or her rights as the owner.

Other Ways of Protecting Property

Many ways can be used in an attempt to protect private property from trespassing. Here are a few:

- ◼ Use fences—Fences with extra security features can be installed. Barbed wire or razor wire can be placed at the top. In some cases, electric fences may be used.

- ◼ Use locked gates—Gates can be placed at entrances to property. The gates can have locks or security codes that restrict passage into an area.

19-15. A locked gate helps prevent trespassing.

- Post warning signs—Warning signs can be posted. Signs may have information about guard dogs, attack animals, or protective devices that are on the property.

- Use guard dogs—Specially trained guard dogs can be used. These require fences and someone to control their behavior. Dogs that escape may create considerable liability if they attack innocent people.

- Hire security guards—Security officers can be placed at entrances or patrol areas to assure protection. This is rather expensive and limited to certain

19-16. Guard dogs and warning signs about such animals may be used to deter trespassing.

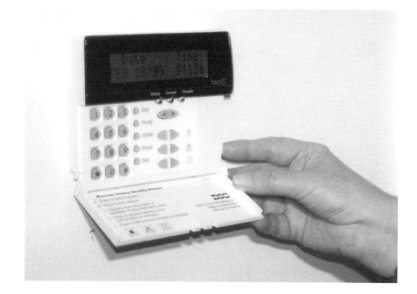

19-17. Control panel for a simple alarm system that uses motion sensors to alert the authorities.

residential and commercial areas. Private security services have increased considerably in recent years.

■ Install lights and sensors—Night lights that continuously burn or are instantly turned on by motion sensors may be used. These help keep trespassers away at night.

■ Install alarm systems—Alarm systems may detect motion or the opening of gates or doors. The systems may be connected to amplified sound systems or linked with the local police department.

REVIEWING

MAIN IDEAS

Ownership of property is a right guaranteed by the Constitution. Property is what a person owns. The individual may have a written title to the property. Personal property includes things a person uses in work and daily living. Real property is land and the improvements that have been made to it. Land includes some "ownership" of the space above and below the surface of the land.

Property rights allow people to buy, own, and sell property. They also allow property to be given to people, as with an inheritance. Property owners must usually pay taxes on real property and some personal property.

Private property may be owned by individuals, partnerships, and corporations. Married individuals may have joint title to property. Public property is land owned by the government at the federal, state, or local levels.

Land ownership is protected by the Constitution. Land can be taken by the government following eminent domain procedures. Land use is regulated, with most regulations based on the welfare of the overall society.

Landowners have certain responsibilities. These include paying taxes on the land and managing the land in a manner appropriate to the values of the local community. Anything on land that degrades the remainder of a community is typically not acceptable.

Landowners want to protect their property. Trespassing is sometimes a problem. Landowners may post their land or take other steps to prevent trespassing.

QUESTIONS

Answer the following questions using complete sentences and correct spelling.

1. What is ownership? What evidence does a person have indicating ownership?

2. Why are people interested in having property?

3. What is selling? What two parties are involved in selling property?

4. What are the two main kinds of property? Distinguish between the two.

5. Why is property taxed?

6. What happens if tax is not paid in a timely manner?

7. Who can own private property? Public property?

8. What is eminent domain? Why is it used?

9. What are the responsibilities of landowners?

10. What is trespassing? What steps can owners take to prevent trespassing?

EVALUATING

Match the term with the correct definition. Write the letter by the term in the blank provided.

a. ownership   e. legal title   i. posting
b. property   f. eminent domain   j. riparian right
c. real property   g. zoning
d. private property   h. trespassing

_____ 1. Land, improvements, and the buildings permanently attached to it.

_____ 2. What a person owns.

_____ 3. Possessing something, including, in some cases, a written legal title.

_____ 4. A written document that describes property and indicates who legally owns it.

_____ 5. Property owned by an individual or a business.

_____ 6. Entering the property of another person without permission to do so.

_____ 7. A process by which a local government controls the use of real property.

_____ 8. The right of government to convert private property to the use of the public.

_____ 9. The right of an owner to use certain amounts of water from bodies adjacent to real property.

_____ 10. The practice of forbidding trespassing on land.

EXPLORING

1. Visit the office of your local government where titles to real property are permanently recorded on public records. Have the person in charge explain the process, including the legal requirements and recording fees. Observe samples of recording titles. Prepare a report on your findings.

2. Determine the laws on posting land in your state. Contact a local attorney, the state commissioner of agriculture, or the attorney general of the state where you live for information on posting land. Prepare a report on your findings.

3. Investigate the issues surrounding private property ownership. Interview a local real estate agent, Farm Bureau official, or other person knowledgeable of property rights. Use the Internet to investigate property rights issues. Prepare a written report on your findings.

20

ENTREPRENEURSHIP AND CAREER SUCCESS

Are you creative? Think about it: Could you create a business in natural resources that serves the unmet needs of people? You are probably beginning to dream about what might be possible!

People who create new businesses can be quite successful. Some become wealthy. Others are not quite so successful and lose money. Success requires setting worthy goals and using the effort needed to reach the goals. Making good decisions is vital to your success. Not everyone is an entrepreneur. Many work for others.

You can begin success as an entrepreneur or by working in a natural resource job while in high school. You can likely be successful in your home community. Good information is essential!

20-1. Rainbow trout are being released into a stream to promote sport fishing. (Courtesy, U.S. Fish and Wildlife Service)

OBJECTIVES

This chapter provides basic information on entrepreneurship as related to natural resources. The following objectives are included:

1. Explain entrepreneurship as related to natural resources

2. Describe planning in natural resources enterprises

3. Assess the important business management practices in success

4. Identify important personal skills for job success

5. List examples of career opportunities in natural resources

TERMS

business plan
consumer
controlling
corporation
directing
economic system
entrepreneurship
free enterprise
management
manager
organizing
partnership
personal skills
planning
risk
sole proprietorship
staffing
work ethic

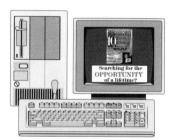

Entrepreneur
http://www.entrepreneurmag.com/

ENTREPRENEURSHIP AND ECONOMIC SYSTEM

Entrepreneurship is creating goods and services to meet the unique demands of consumers. The new "things" may be new ways of using natural resources to satisfy consumer needs and wants. You can probably think of new things that people will buy!

An entrepreneur is a person who practices entrepreneurship. The individual is most likely the owner of a business that provides goods or services. It is more than owning a business. Creativity is involved. Finding new areas of need and developing new products is the creative part. Entrepreneurs need to be good managers and organizers of resources. Regardless of their good intentions, they face risk.

Risk is the possibility of losing what has been invested. Various things create risk. Not enough demand can result in too few sales to cover the costs of providing the product or service. Good planning and decision making help reduce risk.

Many kinds of businesses involve natural resources and environmental technology. These range from mines to air testing services, hunting lodges, and waste disposal services. Just think about all of those in the area where you live! Opportunities for new businesses exist. Creativity is needed to identify them. Good management skills are needed to be successful with them.

20-2. Successful entrepreneurs get information from many people in making their plans.

ECONOMIC SYSTEM

The *economic system* is how people go about doing business. It is provided for by the form of government in a nation. The United States uses a form of capitalism known as free enterprise.

Free enterprise is an economic system that allows people to do business with a minimum of government interference. Some government regulations are needed. These are to assure smooth transaction of business and to protect consumers and entrepreneurs.

With free enterprise, people own the businesses. They make choices about how the businesses are operated and what will be produced. People are allowed to run their businesses as they choose. They cannot damage the environment, cheat consumers, or otherwise carry out illegal activity. People need to follow government regulations. The regulations are to protect people and assure ease of economic activity.

WAYS OF DOING BUSINESS

The economic system provides a way for people to do business. A way of doing business is how we organize and carry out free enterprise. Businesses are of three types.

■ Sole proprietorship—A *sole proprietorship* is a business owned by one person, known as a proprietor. For example, a fee fishing lake could be a sole proprietorship. The proprietor has responsibility for the success of the business. Some sole proprietorships are quite small; others are large. Most begin

20-3. A sole proprietorship country store that sells hunting and fishing supplies.

small and increase in size. Many are not designed to become large businesses. The proprietor assumes responsibility for success of the business. The individual must have the money and resources to start it. Records must be kept. Reports must be prepared.

■ Partnership—A *partnership* is a business owned by two or more individuals. For example, two people could open a fee fishing lake. Each would share in the business as a co-owner. In a partnership, the partners are usually bound by a written and legal contract. The role of partners often varies. What they provide to the business may vary. In some cases, partners have a silent role. They are not actively involved on a daily basis. A silent partner may provide resources, such as money. Partners share risks as well as income in the proportion to their investment in the business. Good understanding is essential.

■ Corporation—A *corporation* is a way for people to do business by creating an artificial entity. The name of the business is usually followed by the letters "inc." A corporation is viewed much as an individual in doing business but it is not an individual. The people who form a corporation must get a charter from the appropriate agency of state government. They elect officers and have a board of directors. People are hired to run the corporation. The corporation will issue stock. People buy stock as a way of sharing in the business. People who buy stock are known as stockholders. Individuals can have losses no greater than the amount they have invested in stock. Owners of stock can receive dividends. A dividend is part of the profit that is paid to stockholders for their investment in the business. A cooperative is a special type of corporation. Cooperatives are intended to provide services to the people who form them. Cooperatives are often used in agriculture.

CONSUMERS

Businesses must produce goods and services that will be consumed. This means that they are used to satisfy needs or wants. A *consumer* is a person who uses goods and services.

20-4. A sport hunter is a consumer of guns, ammunition, and special clothing.

Resource Connection

PROMOTING RESOURCES: SOME FIRE IS PLANNED

Forest resources may be promoted with fire and damaged by fire! Controlled burning is used to rid the ground of leaves and twigs before the accumulation is great enough to form a large fire that can damage trees. Wild fires, on the other hand, create huge losses and may entirely destroy a forest that has taken many years to grow.

Here is the caution: Only people who are trained in using controlled burns should do them. People who are not trained can create huge wildfires. Always get the assistance of trained fire fighters. Never take unnecessary risk.

This shows firefighters supervising a controlled burn. The ability to communicate and move quickly helps keep a burn under control. (Courtesy, U.S. Fish and Wildlife Service)

Every time you buy camping equipment, for example, you are a consumer. In some cases, consumers are viewed as businesses because they use goods and services in their operation.

Consumers make choices. This creates demand for what is needed. They can decide to go fishing or hunting. When they do so, they select and buy equipment and supplies. They choose a site for their activity. The same is true with most areas of life. What does a person use in water skiing, snow skiing, or camping? The economic system goes about providing these goods and services for consumers. Entrepreneurs use the system to create and deliver "things" that meet consumer demand.

OPERATING A BUSINESS ENTERPRISE

All business enterprises have managers. A *manager* is the person who is responsible for the operation of a business. Managers direct activities in the business. In a small business, the manager and owner may be the same person. Success or failure of a business is related to the skills of the manager.

20-5. An attractive sign promotes a business.

Managers are responsible for the operation of the business. They decide about the mix of inputs that will be used. This includes the amount of labor, raw materials, and money needed for the business. To make a profit, the mix must be such that costs are low and returns are as high as possible.

MANAGEMENT

Management is all of the activities needed to move a business enterprise toward its goals. A number of activities are included. These occur in all businesses–from the smallest to the largest. In small businesses, the owner may be the manager as well as the labor force.

Managers may need to get the help of trained professionals in the early stages. They may need an attorney and an accountant. An attorney prepares the necessary legal documents for a business. An accountant handles the details of financial status and taxes. Of course, a source of finances will be needed. This may involve using money that has been saved or getting a loan from an individual or a bank.

BUSINESS PLAN

A **business plan** is a written document that guides the operation of a business. A plan includes the goals and objectives, ways and means, deadline dates, and methods for assessing progress. New businesses will need plans to get them started. Continuing businesses also need good plans.

A new entrepreneur may need help in developing a business plan. Most communities have economic development offices that can provide the help. If not, a lending agency can likely provide information on where to get help with a business plan.

The book, *Agribusiness Management and Entrepreneurship* (3rd edition, Interstate Publishers, Inc.), lists ten steps in preparing a business plan. (These will likely be the areas in a written business plan.) The steps are:

20-6. Developing a good business plan takes time and attention to detail.

1. The idea—What is to be developed or done?

2. Competition—Is anyone else doing it or can it be done better or cheaper?

3. Market—Who will buy the product or service?

4. Resources—What material, human, capital, and technological resources are needed to operate the business?

5. Regulations—What are the federal, state, and local regulations that will affect this business?

6. Marketing plan—Will it be necessary to advertise? Will sales be seasonal or constant throughout the year?

7. Location—Where will the business be located? Is the location convenient for customers?

8. Employees—Are additional employees needed? What qualifications should they have? What will be the cost of wages and benefits?

9. Management—Who will manage the business?

10. Financial plan—What finances will be needed? What records will be kept?

BUSINESS MANAGEMENT PRACTICES

Management activities are in five main areas. These are often known as management duties or functions. Managers know these as the functions needed for a business to be successful.

■ Planning—***Planning*** is the process of deciding how an enterprise will operate. This includes what it will produce. Many possibilities are available. Individuals must choose the best from among the possibilities. Objectives are identified. Strategies for achieving the objectives are developed. Some plans are short-term; others are long-term. Plans should be regularly assessed to see if the business is making progress. If the business is not progressing, the plans need to be more realistic.

■ Organizing—***Organizing*** is the process of setting up a structure so the business can do what it is supposed to do. It deals with getting the work done. Organization makes it possible to produce products or services. Consumers buy what is produced to satisfy their needs.

■ Staffing—***Staffing*** is selecting, training, and rewarding employees. A small business may have only a few employees. Having good, productive people is essential for success. People who do not have the ability to be productive should not be hired. Records are kept on employees. Employees will need to be trained in their work. They will also need to be evaluated and receive suggestions on how to improve.

■ Directing—***Directing*** is the process of guiding employees to achieve the objectives for the business. Two major areas are involved. They are leadership and motivation. The manager will need to provide leadership so the employees perform well. Employees will also need to be motivated to do their work.

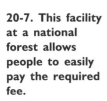

20-7. This facility at a national forest allows people to easily pay the required fee.

■ Controlling—**Controlling** is assessing goals and objectives to see if the business is making progress. It involves seeing if the performance of the business has measured up to what was expected. If not, changes should be made to improve the performance.

PERSONAL JOB SKILLS

People want to be successful. Success often depends on the personal skills of an individual. **Personal skills** are the abilities of an individual to relate to other people in a productive manner. People can develop personal skills. Once a person has a job, they need to go about work in a manner that shows that they can be productive.

GETTING A JOB

A person who is not an entrepreneur will likely work for another person or employer. Finding a job is not always easy. Knowing how to go about the job search process is important. Landing a job is part of gaining employment.

Career Profile

FOREST MANAGER

A forest manager supervises a small crew in establishing and caring for a forest. The work may involve hiring workers, supervising work, and demonstrating job tasks and equipment operation. This photo shows a forest manager reviewing aerial photographs of an area with a crew member. (Courtesy, U.S. Fish and Wildlife Service.)

Forest managers typically have a college degree in forestry or a related area. High school courses in agriculture, forestry, and biological science are helpful. Most have gained practical knowledge by working in forestry. Good communication skills are needed.

Jobs are in areas where forestry is important. Employment opportunities are with government agencies, private companies, and as consulting entrepreneurs.

Some suggestions for finding job openings are:

- Visit personnel offices of potential employers.

- Visit placement offices to identify job openings.

- Use job postings on the Internet or in the newspaper.

- Ask family and friends about possible job openings.

- Use contacts with teachers, counselors, and others at your school.

Once a job opening has been found, the next steps are to apply for the job and go through the employment process. The steps typically include the following:

20-8. The ability to meet and talk with people is important in job success.

- Fill out and submit a job application form.

- Prepare a personal data sheet if one is requested.

- Write a letter of application if a letter is needed.

- Go for an interview if selected to do so.

- Conduct yourself appropriately during the interview, including dressing properly, using good language skills, and demonstrating enthusiasm and work ethic.

GETTING ALONG ON THE JOB

Getting along on a job is essential. People who work for others must show that they will be productive. They need to have important personal skills. Here are a few of the essential personal skills:

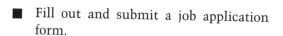

- Work ethic—***Work ethic*** is how a person views work. It reflects a person's attitude toward work. Successful people view work as a natural part of life. They strive to be productive as workers. Showing pride in work, taking care of tools and equipment, and doing extra work are indications of work ethic.

■ Getting along with people—The ability to get along with other people is important in a job. Entrepreneurs need to get along with those who work for them as well as the public. Getting along with customers is essential. Research indicates that more people lose their jobs because they cannot get along with other people than for any other reason!

■ Honesty—Honesty is the trait of individuals who have high principles. They do not steal, lie, or cheat. People who are honest are truthful. They do not speak or write inaccurate information. Honest people always do what they say they will do. Honesty includes paying debts and obeying laws and rules.

■ Life style—Life style is how a person goes about living. People need a life style that builds their well-being as well as that of the people around them. Keeping the human body in good condition is important. Getting adequate sleep, exercise, and nutrition promotes well-being. Substances that impair the body are to be avoided. A good life style helps a person to be productive when on the job.

■ Enthusiasm—Enthusiasm is indicated by the energy that a person demonstrates when talking or moving. They show enthusiasm and go about work in a way to get the job done.

■ Dedication—Dedication is probably best described as loyalty to work. The work has a high priority in a person's life. The individual goes about work to do what needs to be done as efficiently as possible.

■ Education and skill—Education and skill are important in most jobs. People gain education and skill through school and practical experience. Education includes the ability to read, write, and do the necessary mathematics. Computer skills are often needed for a job.

■ Dress, grooming, and personal hygiene—How people dress and present themselves create an image of the person. Being dressed appropriately is im-

20-9. Jobs often require specialized skill, such as operation of this equipment to clean out a water control structure at a fee lake. (Courtesy, U.S. Fish and Wildlife Service)

portant. Never dress in clothes that reflect fads nor groom your hair in a style that is a fad. Leave off inappropriate jewelry. Taking regular baths, using deodorant, and brushing teeth help make a good impression on others.

OPPORTUNITIES IN NATURAL RESOURCES

The opportunities in natural resources may be as an entrepreneur or as an employee. An individual can be successful in either type of employment.

Examples of natural resources areas with employment opportunities are described here.

RECREATION

Recreation is helping people use their leisure time. People want to have fun and feel good about themselves. Jobs are where recreation is found and at seasons of the year when recreation is carried out. These include:

- operating fee fishing lakes
- operating hunting preserves and clubs
- operating supplies stores for hunting and fishing
- providing guide services for hunting and fishing
- providing supplies for water sports, such as skiing and boating
- providing supplies for winter sports, such as skating, sledding and skiing
- riding stables and trails

20-10. Making recreational facilities attractive and comfortable helps promote business. (These facilities are at a trout fee lake facility in Virginia.)

MINING

Mining includes working in mines or, in some cases, establishing mines. Examples of mining opportunities include those in extracting sand and gravel, metals, minerals, and coal. Jobs may include operating equipment, exploring new areas, and preventing environmental damage. Opportunities are in locations where mining occurs.

WASTE DISPOSAL

Waste disposal jobs vary from driving trucks to operating landfills and managing wastewater treatment facilities. The work may involve designing facilities, constructing facilities, and using testing procedures to assure proper operation. All communities have jobs in these areas.

WILDLIFE

Opportunities with wildlife include a wide range of jobs in locations where wildlife is found. These may involve protecting wildlife, studying various habitats, and developing ways to protect endangered species. The work may be outside in remote areas where wildlife is found. Some of the jobs are associated with recreation, preserves, and refuges.

20-11. Wildlife specialists are involved in many areas, such as establishing educational trails.

RECYCLING

Recycling jobs are found in many towns and cities. They may be associated with waste handling and management. The work may involve cans, glass, plastic, paper, and other materials. Some jobs involve managing recycling centers and dealing with the public to assure their cooperation.

SOIL AND WATER CONSERVATION

Soil and water conservation deals with preventing the degrading of soil and water. The work may include planning and installing erosion control devices, installing silt fences, and testing water for sediment. Some may involve using survey equipment to design structures. Other jobs involve operating heavy equipment to build terraces and ponds. Opportunities are found in most all parts of the nation.

ENERGY PRODUCTION AND CONSERVATION

People are in jobs that produce and conserve energy. This includes the fossil fuels as well as solar, wind, and nuclear energy. The work may involve designing and building plants, operating facilities that use energy, and developing ways to conserve energy.

FORESTS AND WOOD PRODUCTS

Opportunities for people to work in forestry are found nationwide. This includes setting and caring for trees as well as harvesting timber and manufac-

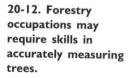

20-12. Forestry occupations may require skills in accurately measuring trees.

turing products. The work may involve operating equipment, hiking through woodland, using measuring devices, and grading timber and wood. In some cases, individuals may be involved in fighting fires and controlling other pests.

WEATHER AND CLIMATE

Some jobs are found in weather forecasting, weather broadcasting, and related areas. Other jobs are in meteorology and climatology. People in this area also provide education on how to prepare for and deal with weather disasters, such as hurricanes, floods, and tornadoes. Some jobs involve emergency vehicle operation.

LAND

Opportunities are available in land management, classification, and use planning. Some people are involved with zoning, taxation, and assessing property values. Real estate agents and brokers sell land and the improvements made to it. Attorneys prepare legal documents and see that transactions are properly recorded.

SUSTAINABLE AGRICULTURE

The jobs in sustainable agriculture often involve skills in land, soil, water, crops, and related areas. The work is to plan and implement practices that sustain agricultural production.

OTHERS

Areas of opportunity in natural resources and environmental technology are broad and diverse. Many others exist. Creative entrepreneurs can often make opportunities in any local community.

REVIEWING

MAIN IDEAS

Entrepreneurship is creating goods and services to meet the demands of consumers. People who do so create and operate businesses. They are often thought of as business owners.

Free enterprise is the economic system used in the United States. This system allows people to start and own businesses. The businesses are operated with a minimum of government control. There are three ways of doing business: sole proprietorship, partnership, and corporation. The cooperative is a special type of corporation to serve its members.

Initiating and operating a business requires management. One of the first tasks in management is to prepare a business plan. Such a plan describes what is to be produced and how it is to be done to achieve success. Many factors are involved in a business plan.

Business management involves five major functions: planning, organizing, staffing, directing, and controlling. In all cases, the functions are to contribute to the success of the business.

Individuals are successful in working for others when they have the needed personal and job skills. An individual must first get a job. Success is based on job performance. Getting along on the job includes a number of important personal skills. An individual's attitude toward work is definitely important!

QUESTIONS

Answer the following questions using complete sentences and correct spelling.

1. What is entrepreneurship? An entrepreneur?

2. What is an economic system?

3. What is the economic system used in the United States? What are the major characteristics of this system?

4. What are the three ways of doing business? Briefly describe each.

5. Why are consumers important?

6. What is management?

7. What is a business plan? What are the major parts of a plan?

8. What are the five functions of management? Briefly explain each.

9. What are personal skills? How do these relate to being successful with jobs?

10. Name at least four personal skills for getting along on a job. Select the one that you feel is most important and explain why.

EVALUATING

Match the term with the correct definition. Write the letter by the term in the blank provided.

a. risk   e. consumer   i. personal skills
b. economic system   f. manager   j. work ethic
c. free enterprise   g. business plan
d. partnership   h. planning

_____ 1. The abilities of an individual in relating to other people in the work setting.
_____ 2. The possibility of losing all that has been invested.
_____ 3. How a person views work.
_____ 4. An economic system that allows people to go about business with a minimum of government interference.
_____ 5. A person who uses goods and services.
_____ 6. How government provides for people to go about doing business.
_____ 7. The person responsible for the operation of a business.
_____ 8. A type of business owned by two or more people.
_____ 9. A written document that guides the operation of a business.
_____ 10. The process of deciding how to operate a business.

EXPLORING

1. Investigate job opportunities in areas of natural resources in your community. Use a variety of sources, including the newspaper, employment offices, Internet postings, interviews with counselors, and visits to personnel offices. Assess which opportunities may match best with your interests and skills. Prepare a report on your findings.

2. Organize a group of three to five students to plan an entrepreneurship to meet a local need. Begin by assessing possible niche opportunities and the potential for being successful. Use resources from the school library, Internet, and other sources. Present an oral report on your findings to the class.

3. Interview the manager of a business about the nature of the work. Determine the greatest problems in management and how these problems are solved. Investigate trends in the area and how these trends will impact the business on a long-term basis. Prepare a written report on your findings.

GLOSSARY

Acid rain—any precipitation that has a lower pH (more acidic) than normal; precipitation with a pH below 7.0

Aerial photograph—a photograph taken from an airplane to show important features of land.

Aesthetic benefit—any feature that adds beauty and creates psychological benefits for people.

Agricultural industry—all of the processes in producing food, clothing, and forest products and getting them to the consumer in the desired forms.

Air—the mixture of gases that surrounds the planet Earth.

Air pollutant—a material or substance that pollutes the air.

Air pollution—the entry of materials and substances into air that damage its quality.

Air pollution sampling pump—a device used to collect air samples for analysis to determine contents of the air.

Air quality—the suitability of air for a particular use.

Air quality standard—the maximum level of pollution allowed at one time in a geographical area.

Airshed—the geographic area of land and the factories, homes, highways, forests, and other features that contribute to the air, especially air pollution.

Altitude—the distance above or below sea level of a point on Earth.

Ambient air—outside air.

Amortization—a schedule for repayment of borrowed money plus interest over time.

Amphibious habitat—a habitat for animal species that require both land and water.

Anadromous—animal species that live in saltwater and spawn in freshwater.

Animal—an organism that gets its food by consuming other materials and can usually move about.

Animal unit month—the amount of forage needed to keep a 1,000 pound (454 kg) animal well fed for a month.

Aquatic community—a community comprised of a water-based environment.

Aquatic habitat—a water-based habitat for animals that live in water or depend on it for their food and reproduction.

Aquifer—an area below the earth's surface comprised of porous sand, gravel, and limestone that is saturated with water in spaces between particles and cracks.

Area measurement—determining the amount of land within given boundaries.

Ash—the residue from combustion; remains of burned wood, paper, and other carbon materials.

Atmosphere—the area of air that surrounds the planet Earth; contains gases, particulate, and water vapor.

Atmospheric pressure—the pressure exerted by the weight of the atmosphere on the surface of the earth.

Atmospheric temperature—the measure of temperature taken in the atmosphere in describing the weather.

Bag limit—legal restriction on the number of animals that can be taken in one day or hunting season.

Bait—live organisms or dead material used to attract fish.

Base line—in surveying, an east-west line perpendicular to a meridian.

Basic human needs—the three requirements for humans to live: food, clothing, and shelter.

Belief—the conviction or opinion of a person about an issue; beliefs form a person's value system.

Bennett, Hugh H.—a strong leader for soil conservation and the first head of the federal agency that dealt with soil conservation; 1881-1960.

Best land use—using land to produce the most benefits for society.

Biofuel—any plant or animal material that burns to release heat or produces methane or other gases during decomposition.

Biome—a community of living organisms.

Biosolids—the dried remains of wastewater treatment processes.

Biosphere—the part of the ecosphere that supports life.

Birding—the identification and study of birds as a hobby.

Botany—the study of plant organisms.

Boundary—the limit or line of a tract of land.

Brackish water—a mixture of saltwater and freshwater.

Brush—plants, such as shrubs, scrub trees, vines, and herbaceous plants, that provide habitat for some species of animals.

Bulky solid waste—large, discarded items, such as refrigerators and TV sets.

Business plan—a written document that guides the operation of a business.

Buyer—a person who wishes to acquire property from a seller.

Canopy—dense growth of limbs and leaves formed by the upper part of trees.

Capability factors—the characteristics that determine the best use of land for crops.

Capillary water—water held between soil particles.

Carbon monoxide—a poisonous gas produced when certain materials burn; CO.

Carrying capacity—the number of animals that an area of rangeland will grow sufficient forage for food.

Carson, Rachel—an acclaimed writer for efforts in informing the public about the risks of pesticides; 1907-1964.

Catadromous—freshwater species that spawn in saltwater.

Chemistry—the study of the makeup of matter; study of anything that takes up space and has weight or quantity.

Circadian cycle—the daily living cycle that is repeated every 24 hours.

Clay—the soil component with the smallest size.

Cleavage—smooth, flat surfaces formed when gems split.

Climate—the weather that is generally found in a location.

Cloud—a mass of tiny water droplets or ice crystals in the atmosphere.

Common name—the name used by people in their everyday work for plants and animals.

Community—the assortment of plants, animals, and other organisms that live together in a kind of harmony.

Compass—the instrument used to make direction measurements; determines true north.

Conifer—a group of tree species that have needles and produce cones.

Conservation—wise use of resources.

Conservation practice—a structure, vegetative measure, or other approach that protects, enhances, or manages soil and other resources, especially water.

Conservation tillage—using tillage practices that disturb the surface of the soil very little.

Consumer—a person who uses goods and services; includes businesses that use goods and services.

Consumptive use—using a natural resource so the amount used no longer exists.

Continuous grazing—keeping animals on an area year-round.

Contouring—performing all field operations on the contour of the land elevation.

Controlling—one of the management functions that deals with assessing accomplishments to determine if the business has lived up to expectations.

Corporation—a way to do business by creating an artificial entity.

Course—in surveying, directional lines at an angle to the point of reference.

Cover crop—a crop planted to protect the soil and increase fertility.

Crepuscular species—animals active at dusk and dawn.

Cropland—land used for corps.

Crop rotation—alternating the use of land in producing crops; rotation cycles of two or three years may be used.

Crown—the top part of a tree including limbs, leaves, and flowers and fruit, if present.

Crust—the outer portion of Earth's surface.

Cultural practices—the procedures followed in growing a crop.

Decreaser—a plant species that is easily damaged by grazing.

Deed—an executed and delivered contract about land; usually prepared in association with the sale of land.

Demography—the study of human population.

Desalination—the process of removing salt from saltwater.

Desertification—the formation of desert on land that was once productive.

Dew point—the temperature of air when dew begins to form.

Diadromous—species that migrate between freshwater and saltwater.

Diameter breast high (dbh)—the standard distance above the ground where the trunk of a tree is measured; 54 inches (1.37 m).

Directing—one of the management functions that deals with providing leadership and motivation for employees.

Direction measurement—the process in surveying of determining the location of a reference line in terms of true north.

Distillation—the process of making water pure; collecting water vapor from steam in a controlled environment that prevents contamination.

Diurnal species—species of animals active during the day.

Domestication—bringing plants and animals under the control of humans.

Dominant species—the trees that grow the largest and shade the other trees in a forest.

Dust bowl—an area of the Great Plains where large wind erosion occurred in the 1930s.

Earth science—the area of physical science that deals with the environment in which organisms live and grow.

Ecology—the study of how living organisms exist in their natural environment.

Economic system—how a nation provides for people to go about doing business or engage in commerce.

Economic threshold—a term used in integrated pest management that speaks to the use of control measures based on monetary returns to the producer.

Ecosphere—where living things are found on Earth.

Ecosystem—the part of the environment where an organism lives.

Edge—the area where two habitats meet.

Effluent—water released by a factory or wastewater treatment plant; used or treated wastewater.

Elevation measurement—determining the altitude of a point on land in reference to sea level.

Eminent domain—the right of the government to convert private property to the use of the public.

Emission—a gas-borne pollutant that is released into the air.

Endangered species—a species that is threatened with becoming extinct.

Endangerment—a condition in the ecosystem that threatens the continued existence of a species.

Energy—the ability to do work.

Entrepreneurship—creating goods and services to meet the unique demands of consumers.

Environment—surroundings of living or nonliving things.

Environmental technology—using science and inventions to understand and improve the environment.

Estivation—a time of inactivity by members of some species to escape hot weather.

Ethanol—a colorless, liquid kind of alcohol that can be made from corn and other grains; sometimes used as an alternative fuel.

Evaporation—the process of water going from liquid to gas by exposure to air or heat.

Exhaustible energy—energy that is used up by human activity.

Exhaustible natural resources—kinds of resources that are available in limited quantity that can be used up; resources that are not replenished after use.

Exploitation—using natural resource for profit and without regard to other people and future needs.

Extinct species—a species that no longer lives on Earth.

Fertilizer—soil amendments that contain nutrients.

Fishing—capturing fish with hooks, nets, seines, traps, and other means.

Fishing tackle—the equipment used in sport fishing.

Flood plain—the area along a stream that may be covered with overflow.

Fog—a kind of cloud at or very near the surface of the earth.

Food chain—the sequence in which organisms obtain their food.

Food web—a graphic representation of feeding behavior by the organisms in a community.

Foot-pound—the amount of work done in lifting one pound a distance of one foot.

Forage—leaves and stems of plants that are eaten by animals.

Forb—a small broad-leaved plant that does not develop a woody stem.

Forest—an area where trees and other plants grow.

Forest region—a geographical area characterized by trees of a particular species or group of species.

Fossil fuel—materials used for energy; formed thousands of years ago by the decomposition of plants and animals.

Free enterprise—the economic system that allows people to go about doing business with a minimum of government interference.

Freshwater—water that has little or no salt.

Fuel—a substance that is burned to make a fire.

Fuel energy—a source of energy using a substance that is burned to make a fire.

Garbage—solid material discarded from a kitchen; includes cooked and uncooked food scraps.

Gem—a mineral valued for beauty and rarity.

Geodetic surveying—a method of land surveying that considers the curvature of Earth's surface.

Geographic information system (GIS)—a method using a computer to integrate information with geographical data.

Global climate—the general or average climate of Earth.

Global positioning system (GPS)—a method of locating geographical positions using ground units that receive information from satellites.

Grass—a plant with flat leaves that have parallel veins.

Grassed waterway—a shallow ditch planted with a perennial grass that removes runoff from cropland with a minimum of erosion.

Grassland—an area that grows grasses and forbs.

Gravitational water—water that drains downward through the soil.

Grazing program—the schedule and sequence of allowing animals to graze an area.

Greenhouse effect—a condition caused by the buildup of gases and solid particles in the atmosphere that traps infrared radiation near the earth.

Groundwater—water stored below the surface of the earth.

Gully erosion—severe erosion that develops on land following rill erosion in which large washed areas destroy use of the land.

Habitat—the characteristics of a community that allow a particular species to live there.

Hail—large lumps or balls of ice precipitation formed in clouds during storms in warm weather.

Hardness—a condition in water caused by the presence of calcium and magnesium ions.

Hardpan—a compacted layer of soil beneath the topsoil.

Hardwood—a group of trees that have broadleaves and wood that is hard and has a fine grain.

Hazardous waste—waste that is potentially dangerous to the environment and/or human health.

Haz-Mat—the term applied to hazardous materials; part of a national system to communicate about hazardous materials and how they are handled should a spill or accident occur.

Hibernation—a time of seclusion and inactivity in a safe environment.

Hiking—walking in natural areas for pleasure and exercise.

Home range—the area over which an animal travels.

Household waste—garbage and rubbish that originate in the home.

Humus—organic matter that is well decomposed in soil.

Hunger—a condition that exists when an organism does not have sufficient food.

Hunter safety—using hunting practices and safety equipment to prevent accidents and injury.

Hunting—killing game for food or sport.

Hurricane—a large, whirling storm that develops over water in the region.

Hydropower—a method of using the energy in falling water to operate turbines to produce electricity.

Hydrosphere—the sphere formed by all of the water on Earth.

Hygroscopic water—water that adheres to soil particles and is not readily available for plant use.

Ice—solid form of water.

Incineration—disposing of dead animals and tissues by burning in intense heat.

Increaser—a plant species that tends to do well in areas where animals are grazing; species have a lower palatability to animals than most forage plants.

Inexhaustible energy—a form of energy that occurs repeatedly even after it is used.

Inexhaustible natural resources—kinds of resources that are continuously being replenished.

Injury threshold—a term in integrated pest management that deals with determining if sufficient damage has been caused by a pest to merit the use of a control measure.

Inorganic substance—a substance that does not have the structure of living things; substance that does not contain carbon.

Insulation—material that restricts the exchange of heat.

Integrated pest management (IPM)—using a number of techniques in a unified program of pest control.

Interdependent relationship—a way of life in which organisms depend on each other; organisms assume different beneficial roles.

Invader—a plant species that is not appealing as food to animals.

Invertebrate—an animal that does not have a backbone; the exterior is covered with a hard material known as an exoskeleton.

Irrigation—the artificial application of water to crops.

Issue—a problem or question to be solved that has more than one side or solution.

Land—all of the natural and artificial characteristics of a geographical area on the surface of the earth.

Land capability—the suitability of land for agricultural uses.

Land capability classification—a system for classifying land based on its highest potential use.

Land description—a written statement that describes the boundaries and location of a tract of land.

Landfill—a large excavation in the ground for the permanent disposal of wastes.

Landscape alteration—changing the natural features of the earth's surface.

Landscape degradation—doing things that make the natural features of the earth less appealing.

Land surveying—the process of measuring and marking real property.

Land-use planning—a process of making decisions about how land will be used.

Latitude—an imaginary line that runs east and west that gives the distance north or south a point is from the equator.

Leachate—liquid that is produced by a landfill and contains suspended or dissolved materials from solid wastes.

Legal title—the right to property.

Legume—a plant that has the ability to convert nitrogen from the air into nitrogen in the soil.

Leopold, Aldo—a pioneer in using ecology to study wildlife and developing training in wildlife management; 1886-1948.

Lichen—an organism made of a fungus and an alga that live together as a single unit.

Life science—the study of living things.

Life span—the period of life of an organism.

Linear measurement—determining the distance between two points using an appropriate scale of measurement.

Lithosphere—the solid portion of the planet Earth.

Log—a segment of tree stem or trunk that is suitable for sawing into lumber or manufacturing into other materials.

Longitude—the east-west distance between any location on Earth.

Malnourishment—a condition that exists when an organism lacks proper nutrients.

Management—all of the activities needed to move a business enterprise toward its goals.

Manager—the person who is responsible for the operation of a business.

Mantle—the solid part of Earth located between the crust and the core.

Mathematics—the science of numbers.

Meridian—a true north-south line used in surveying land.

Metes and bounds—a system of describing land in which a known starting point is used to establish and describe lines forming the boundaries of property.

Methane—a colorless, odorless, and combustible gas produced by the decomposition of organic matter.

Migration—the movement of individuals from one region or continent to another to have a suitable environment for life processes.

Mine—an excavation for removing minerals from the earth.

Mineral—a natural inorganic substance on or in the earth.

Mineral rights—ownership of minerals on or under the surface of land.

Mineral soil—soils that are high in minerals.

Minimum tillage—a method of plowing so the surface of the land is disturbed as little as possible.

Monument—in surveying, a known and permanent marker on land.

Mortgage—the conditional transfer of the title to property to a lender as security for repayment of a loan.

Muir, John—an explorer and naturalist who traveled and studied forest and other natural resources in the United States; 1838-1914.

Mulch—a layer of straw, burlap, or other material placed on soil to protect it from erosion and conserve moisture.

Native forest—a forest in which the species are voluntarily growing and are naturally present in the area.

Naturalist—a person who studies nature.

Natural resource conservation—the wise use of natural resources; protecting and using resources so they last a long time.

Natural resources—resources found in nature; materials or substances that naturally occur.

Nature study—learning about things in nature.

Niche—the unique way a species lives in a community.

Nocturnal species—species of animals active at night or when it is dark.

Nonconsumptive use—using a natural resource so the supply available is not reduced.

Nonfuel energy—a source of energy that is not consumed when it is used, such as solar energy and wind energy.

Nonpoint source pollution—pollution from sources that cannot be readily identified.

Nonrenewable natural resource—a resource that cannot be restored when it is used.

No-till—producing crops without plowing.

Nuclear energy—energy produced by the fission of atomic nuclei of uranium or a similar heavy chemical element.

Nutrient analysis—a chemical process for determining the nutrients present in soil.

Old-growth forest—an uncut forest.

Ore—rock that contains desired minerals.

Organic matter—decaying plant and animal remains that forms soil.

Organic soil—a soil that is high in organic matter.

Organizing—in business, one of the five management functions that deals with establishing a operating structure for a business.

Outdoor recreation—any activity people voluntarily do in the outdoors for enjoyment and personal satisfaction.

Ownership—the act of possessing something; legal title to property.

Ozone layer—a layer in Earth's atmosphere that filters out harmful radiation from the Sun.

Parent material—the mineral and organic matter from which soil is formed.

Partnership—a business owned by two or more individuals.

Pathogen—a living or nonliving thing that causes disease.

Permeability—the ability of soil to move water.

Personal property—property that an individual owns and uses to satisfy needs and wants.

Personal skills—abilities of an individual to relate to other people in a positive manner.

Pest—anything that harms plants, animals, or other living and nonliving things.

Physical science—study of the non-living things on Earth.

Physics—the area of physical science that deals with the nature of objects, including mechanics, heat, light, and electricity.

Pinchot, Gifford—promoted the conservation of forests; headed federal agency that became the U.S. Forest Service; 1865-1946.

Plane surveying—making flat measurements of land that do not consider the curvature of the earth's surface.

Planning—in business, the process of deciding how an enterprise will operate.

Planting date—the period in the year that is best for planting a crop.

Plant population—the density of the plants in a field.

Plat—a map that shows land boundaries; prepared by a land surveyor.

Plate tectonics—a theory used to explain the internal structure and movement of Earth.

Point of reference—the known starting point in surveying land.

Point source pollution—pollution from sources that can be readily identified.

Pollutant—substances that cause pollution.

Pollution—releasing hazardous or poisonous substances into the biosphere.

Population—the number of people living in a geographic area, such as a city, state, or nation.

Posting—the practice of forbidding trespassing on land.

Potable water—water that is safe to use for drinking, cooking, and washing.

Precipitation—the moisture that is deposited on Earth from the atmosphere.

Precision farming—combining information and technology to manage crop production.

Predation—the capture and consumption of one animal, known as prey, by another, known as predator.

Prescriptive agriculture—application of materials in crop production based on testing and mapping fields and using equipment that varies the rate of application based on needs.

Preservation—maintaining a resource without using it; the resource is protected and set aside.

Private property—property owned by an individual or business; not owned by the government.

Property—what a person owns.

Protoplasm—the liquid-like substance in cells that carries out chemical processes for life to exist.

Public property—land and other material items owned by government agencies.

Pulpwood—the wood materials used to make paper and similar products.

Quarry—a large pit made in mining.

Radon—an invisible, tasteless, and odorless radioactive gas produced by the natural decay of uranium in the soil.

Rain—liquid precipitation.

Rangeland—land that grows native forage plants; used for animal grazing.

Rare species—a species that exists in small numbers and could become threatened.

Real property—land and improvements that have been made to it; land and buildings.

Recreational impact—the effect using resources for recreation has upon the resources and the surrounding area.

Rectangular survey system—a method of describing land based on two fixed lines that are at right angles to each other.

Recycling—using a product or the materials used to make a product more than one time.

Refraction—the bending of light waves as they pass through a gem.

Refuse—anything that is discarded because it is useless or worthless.

Regrowth forest—areas of forest that have been cut and have regrown.

Relative humidity— a comparison of the amount of moisture in the air with the ability of the air to hold moisture.

Remote sensing—collecting information about something from a distance.

Renewability—the ability or lack of ability to restore a resource after it has been used.

Renewable natural resource—a natural resource that can be replaced when it is used.

Rent—payment made by a person to a property owner in return for use of the property.

Resource depletion—using resources faster than they can be renewed.

Reusing—using a product repeatedly without remanufacturing.

Revolution—the circling of the plant Earth around the Sun.

Rights of others—a concept that deals with assuring the opportunity for other people to enjoy a natural resource in a responsible manner.

Rill erosion—loss of soil on sloping land where small channels are formed by running water.

Riparian right—the right of a landowner to use water from a body that is adjacent to the land for domestic consumption and use by livestock.

Risk—the possibility of losing what has been invested.

Rock—the hard, solid, and natural part of Earth's crust.

Roosevelt, Franklin D.—lead the establishment of many programs to protect soil, water, and other natural resources as U.S. President; 1882-1945.

Roosevelt, Theodore—a leader in early natural resource conservation efforts; served as President of the United States; 1858-1919.

Root zone—the area of the soil where roots grow.

Rotation—the turning of Earth on an axis.

Rotation grazing—restricting animals to one area for a period and moving them to another area.

Rubbish—also known as trash; includes wastes, such as paper, plastic, bottles, and yard materials.

Saline water—water that contains salt.

Saltwater—water with more than 16.5 ppt salt content.

Sand—the soil component with the largest particle size.

Science—knowledge of the world in which we live; knowledge based on experiments and research.

Scientific name—the name of a species based on its scientific classification.

Scrubbing—the processes of removing particulate from exhaust materials; often used at factories on smokestacks.

Section—a block of land that contains 640 acres.

Seedling—a young tree; typically a tree that is 15 to 18 inches (38 to 46 cm) tall.

Seller—a person who owns property and wishes to sell it.

Septic tank—a steel or concrete container buried in the ground that receives wastewater for action by microbes.

Sewage—liquid waste containing water and solid materials.

Sheet erosion—loss of thin layers of soil; may go unnoticed for a while.

Shelterbreak—a row or cluster of shrubs, trees, or combination of plants to protect soil or animal areas from the wind.

Shrub—a perennial plant that grows only a few feet tall—no more than 15 feet (4.5 m) tall.

Silt—the soil component with a size smaller than sand but larger than clay.

Silt fence—a structure placed at the bottom of a slope, which allows water to flow through but holds back soil particles.

Silviculture—managing tree stands and using practices to improve the quality and quantity of timber production.

Sleet—precipitation as raindrops that have frozen as they fall through the air.

Slope—the rise and fall in the elevation of land.

Smelting—heating ore so the metal separates from the undesirable materials.

Smog—a mixture of dense radiation fog and gaseous pollutants in the atmosphere.

Snow—precipitation as frozen hexagonal-shaped crystals.

Social science—the study of human behavior.

Soil—the outer layer of Earth's surface that supports plant life.

Soil amendment—a material added to soil to improve its ability to support plant growth.

Soil conservation—using and managing soil so damage or loss is very little.

Soil degradation—any action or event that lowers the quality of the soil.

Soil depth—the thickness of the soil layers that are important in crop production; includes topsoil and subsoil.

Soil erosion—loss of soil by water, wind, or other forces.

Soil pH—the acidity or alkalinity of soil; measured on a 14-point scale with 7.0 being neutral; above 7.0 is alkaline (basic) and below 7.0 is acidic.

Soil profile—a vertical section of soil that shows layers or horizons at a site.

Soil structure—the arrangement of soil particles into shapes and pieces.

Soil texture—the proportion of sand, silt, and clay in soil.

Soil triangle—a graphic representation of soils by proportion of sand, silt, and clay.

Solar cell—a collector that converts energy from the Sun into electrical energy.

Solar energy—energy from the Sun.

Solar system—a group of objects in space held together by a sun.

Sole proprietorship—a business owned by one person who is known as the proprietor.

Solid waste—garbage, refuse, and other nonliquid discarded materials.

Sphere— the environment in which something exists.

Staffing—one of the management functions; deals with selecting, training, and rewarding employees.

Stand—the number of plants distributed over the ground.

Storm—violent weather; may be thunderstorms or winter storms.

Stormwater—excess precipitation that collects on streets, parking lots, and other places.

Story—the horizontal layers of growth in forests.

Stream—a flowing body of water.

Stream channel—the sides and bottom of a stream.

Streamflow—the volume and velocity of water movement in a stream.

Strip cropping—planting crops of different types in alternating strips on the contour across a hillside.

Subsurface mine—an excavation made deep inside Earth to retrieve minerals, gems, and solid fossil fuels.

Succession—the replacement of one community by another in a fairly definite sequence.

Surface mine—an excavation to get minerals that are on or near the surface of the earth.

Surface water—water that is on the surface of the earth.

Survey—the exact dimensions and location of land.

Sustainability—using resources so they are available for future generations.

Sustainable agriculture—using practices that indefinitely maintain the ability to produce food, fiber, and forestry products.

Sustainable agriculture system—using multiple practices to assure long-term agricultural productivity; one single practice does not stand alone.

Sustainable resource use—using resources so they last a long time.

Symbiotic bacteria—bacteria that form nodules containing nitrogen on the roots of legume plants.

Symbiotic relationship—species of organisms living together and benefitting from each other.

Tailing—the solid waste material that remains from ore.

Tax—the money people pay to finance the cost of government.

Temperate climate—the climate between the tropic of Cancer and the Arctic Circle and the tropic of Capricorn and the Antarctic Circle.

Temperature—the measure of the warmness or coldness of the weather.

Terrace—a long ridge of soil that follows the contour of land to slow or stop runoff and conserve soil and water.

Terrestrial community—a land-based community.

Terrestrial habitat—a habitat for animals that live on land.

Thermometer—a device for measuring temperature.

Threatened species—a species that is facing serious dangers and likely to become endangered.

Thunderstorm—a weather condition often characterized as having gusty wind, hail, lightning and thunder, and rain.

Tillage—plowing the soil.

Tilth—the physical condition of soil that makes it suitable for crops.

Timberline—the altitude above sea level at which trees will no longer grow.

Topography—the study of the detailed landform features of an area of the earth's surface.

Topsoil—the first few inches of soil with the greatest fertility.

Tornado—a powerful and violent storm with wind that moves in a circular direction.

Township—a six-mile square area of land; a block of land containing 36 square miles.

Transpiration—the release of water from the leaves of plants.

Tree—a perennial plant more than 15 feet (4.5 m) tall.

Tree farm—an area that has been planted to selected and improved tree species for the production of wood products.

Trespassing—entering the property of another person without permission to do so.

Tropical climate—the climate between latitude 23½° north and 23½° south.

Trunk—the main stem of a tree connecting the crown with the roots.

Tundra—geographical areas with permafrost subsoil.

Turbidity—a condition in water caused by suspended particles of solid material, usually suspended soil particles.

Undernourishment—a condition in an organism when it lacks proper food to provide the calories needed for energy.

Urban forestry—establishing and caring for trees in urban areas.

Variable rate technology—using crop production practices that vary based on the conditions that are present within a field.

Vegetative cover—protective crop that is grown between rows of tilled crops to prevent soil erosion.

Vertebrate—an animal that has a backbone.

Vine—a plant that creeps or climbs on other plants, rocks, or the ground.

Volatile organic compounds (VOC)—any compounds containing carbon that is a part of the photochemical reactions in the air; reactions in the atmosphere initiated by the Sun.

Warranty deed—the type of deed used when land is sold, which conveys the title to the land from the seller to the buyer.

Waste—unused materials or discarded products.

Wastewater—used water that contains suspended or dissolved matter.

Water—a tasteless and colorless liquid natural resource; a liquid with the chemical formula of H_2O.

Water cycle—the circulation of water through the hydrosphere; the movement of water from the earth's surface to the atmosphere and back to the surface; also known as the hydrologic cycle.

Water distribution—moving water from its source to where it is needed.

Water erosion—loss of soil due to water movement.

Waterfowl—swimming birds that live in water habitats.

Water quality—the condition of water for a particular use.

Water requirement—the amount of moisture needed by plants.

Watershed—an area that provides runoff for a stream or reservoir.

Water table—the elevation of the surface where groundwater is detected.

Weather—the condition of the atmosphere at a specific time.

Weather front—a condition in the atmosphere resulting from the meeting of a warm air mass with a cold air mass.

Weathering—the process of materials becoming soil.

Wetland—an area where the soil is often saturated with water; water may stand on the surface part or all of the year.

Wildlife—any plant, animal, or other living thing that lives in the wild; any living organism that is not domesticated; may refer only to animal wildlife.

Wildlife animal—animal species that have not been domesticated.

Wind—the large scale movement of air.

Windbreak—a row of trees or shrubs planted to slow the movement of surface wind and reduce wind erosion.

Wind erosion—loss of soil due to wind.

Winter storm—a cold weather storm that typically involves snow, freezing rain, and sleet.

Woodland—an area of trees, shrubs, vines, mosses, and fallen limbs and tree trunks; preferred habitat for some species.

Work—in physical science, moving objects vertical distances; measured in foot-pounds.

Work ethic—how a person views work.

Zoning—the process for controlling the use of real property by restricting how it may be used.

Zoology—the study of animal organisms.

BIBLIOGRAPHY

Allaby, M. *Ecology*. New York: Oxford University Press, 1994.

Arms, K. *Environmental Science*. Austin, Texas: Holt, Rinehart and Winston, 1996.

Benyus, J. M. *The Field Guide to Wildlife Habitats*. New York: Simon & Schuster, 1989.

Bitton, G. *Wastewater Microbiology*. New York: Wiley-Liss, 1994.

Brady, N. C. and R. R. Weil. *The Nature and Properties of Soils*, 12th Edition. Upper Saddle River, New Jersey: Prentice-Hall, Inc., 1999.

Brinker, R. C. and R. Minnick, ed. *The Surveying Handbook*, 2nd Edition. New York: Chapman & Hall, 1995.

Brown, C. M.; W. G. Robillard; and D. A. Wilson. *Boundary Control and Legal Principles*, 4th Edition. New York: John Wiley & Sons, Inc., 1995.

Burton, D. *Ecology of Fish and Wildlife*. Albany, New York: Delmar Publishers, 1996.

Camp, W. G. and R. L. Donahue. *Environmental Science*. Albany, New York: Delmar Publishers, 1994.

Camp, W. G. and T. B. Daugherty. *Managing Our Natural Resources*, 2nd Edition. Albany, New York: Delmar Publishers, 1991.

Cribbet, J. E. and C. W. Johnson. *Principles of the Law of Property*, 3rd Edition. Westbury, New York: The Foundation Press, Inc., 1989.

Deal, K. H. *Wildlife and Natural Resource Management*. Albany, New York: Delmar Publishers, 1998.

Francis, B. M. *Toxic Substances in the Environment*. New York: John Wiley & Sons, Inc., 1994.

Gordon, N. D.; T. A. McMahon; and B. L. Finlayson. *Stream Hydrology*. New York: John Wiley & Sons, Inc., 1992.

Gralla, P. *How the Environment Works*. Emeryville, California: Ziff-Davis Press, 1994.

Hehn, D. and B. Newport. *Introduction to Natural Resources.* Stillwater, Oklahoma: Mid-America Vocational Curriculum Consortium, Inc.

Holland, I. I. and G. L. Rolfe. *Forests and Forestry*, 5th Edition. Danville, Illinois: Interstate Publishers, Inc., 1997.

Kircher, H. B.; W. L. Wallace; and D. J. Gore. *Our Natural Resources and Their Conservation*, 7th Edition. Danville, Illinois: Interstate Publishers, Inc., 1992.

LaTourette, J. *Wildlife Watcher's Handbook.* New York: Henry Holt and Company, 1997.

Lee, J. S. and M. E. Newman. *Aquaculture: An Introduction*, 2nd Edition. Danville, Illinois: Interstate Publishers, Inc., 1997.

Lee, J. S. and D. L. Turner. *Introduction to World AgriScience and Technology*, 2nd Edition. Danville, Illinois: Interstate Publishers, Inc., 1997.

Leick, A. *GPS Satellite Surveying*, 2nd Edition. New York: John Wiley & Sons, Inc., 1995.

Morgan, E. M.; R. E. Chelewski; J. S. Lee; and E. Wilson. *AgriScience Explorations*, 2nd Edition. Danville, Illinois: Interstate Publishers, Inc., 2000.

Office of Hazardous Materials Transportation. *Emergency Response Guidebook.* Washington: Department of Transportation, 1990.

Owen, O. S.; D. D. Chiras; and J. P. Reganold. *Natural Resource Conservation*, 7th Edition. Upper Saddle River, New Jersey: Prentice-Hall, Inc., 1998.

Porter, L.; J. S. Lee; D. L. Turner; and M. Hillan. *Environmental Science and Technology.* Danville, Illinois: Interstate Publishers, Inc., 1997.

Smith, R. L. *Elements of Ecology*, 3rd Edition. New York: HarperCollins Publishers, Inc., 1992.

Stutzenbaker, C. D.; B. J. Scheil; M. K. Swan; J. S. Lee; and J. D. Mattics. *Wildlife Management.* Danville, Illinois: Interstate Publishers, Inc., 1999.

Swan, M. D., ed. *Tips and Tricks in Outdoor Education*, 5th Edition. Danville, Illinois: Interstate Publishers, Inc., 1995.

Symons, J. M. *Plain Talk About Drinking Water*, 2nd Edition. Washington: American Water Works Association, 1990.

Waldon, J. *The Right to Private Property.* New York: Oxford University Press, 1990.

Wight, G. D. *Fundamentals of Air Sampling.* Boca Raton, Florida: Louis Publishers, 1994.

INDEX